JESUS

A SHORT BIOGRAPHY

JESUS

A SHORT BIOGRAPHY

Martin Forward

ONEWORLD
OXFORD

JESUS: A SHORT BIOGRAPHY

Oneworld Publications
(Sales and Editorial)
185 Banbury Road
Oxford OX2 7AR
England
http://www.oneworld-publications.com

Oneworld Publications
(US Marketing Office)
160 N. Washington St.
4th floor, Boston
USA

ISBN 1–85168–172–8

Cover design by Peter Maguire
Printed and bound in England by Clays Ltd, St Ives plc

CONTENTS

ACKNOWLEDGEMENTS

I am thankful to many friends and colleagues for helping me formulate the views recorded in this book. My present colleague and Principal of Wesley House, Ivor Jones, helped develop my creative imagination in supervisions he gave me long years ago, when I was a student and he a tutor at Hartley Victoria Methodist Theological College, Manchester. A number of my students have offered insightful comments, which I have not hesitated to purloin. In particular, I am grateful to Chris Chivers, Samuel McBratney and Philip Turner. I also wish to thank Anders Bergquist and Eric Lott for conversations about Jesus. Mark Goodacre offered wise and helpful comments on the first draft of this book, from which it has greatly benefited and for which I am most grateful. I would not wish any of these friends and colleagues to be blamed for how I have appropriated their insights.

I have often remembered many wise words of the late Paulos Mar Gregorios, Metropolitan of Delhi and the North in the Malankara Orthodox Church. A wonderful teacher, he helped me visualize Jesus through the eyes of a Christian from the one of the ancient Orthodox Churches of the East. May he rest in peace and rise in glory. I am glad to record my thanks to friends of former Christian churches where I was once priest and pastor, in Secunderabad (India), London and Leicester; and to members of the church in Carterton, Oxfordshire, which I joined in my teenage years. I learned much from them and hope it was mutual.

My reflections upon the meaning of Jesus have taken me away from standard Christian interpretation into the wide world of religious pluralism. I am especially indebted to David Craig. When he was Executive Producer of Religious Broadcasting for the BBC World Service, he and I travelled the world together and made radio programmes which have helped form much of the material in chapters 4, 5 and 6. He encouraged me to strive after factual accuracy in programme making, and to bear in mind the need to communicate simply and clearly yet without condescension to an intelligent though uninformed audience. I hope I have not fallen far short of these aims in this book.

Friends of different faiths in India, Pakistan, South Africa and elsewhere have often made me ask myself: why has Jesus of Nazareth continued to fascinate all sorts of women, men, and children in many ages, religions and cultures? This book has enabled me to draw together some of the tangled threads of this question that for years have woven through my mind.

I am once again indebted to Novin Doostdar and Juliet Mabey of Oneworld Publications. On a previous occasion they encouraged me to write an account of Islam's central figure, and have now allowed me to reflect on the central focus of Christianity's faith. Helen Coward, Judith Wilson, Meg Davies and other colleagues at Oneworld will no doubt bring this book to birth with their usual speed, good humour and eagle-eye for detail. Happy is the writer who places his creations in such hands. I am duly grateful.

My wife Udho and daughter Naomi have helped me to accomplish this book: Udho, by quiet and steadfast support; Naomi by staying out of my study long enough to let me finish it. My thanks are also owed to David Primrose. He encouraged me to write this book, and helped sort out my life so that I could do.

Three Jewish friends have been very helpful to me. Jocelyn Hellig is Professor in the Department of Religious Studies at the University of the Witwatersrand, Johannesburg, South Africa. A few years ago, a throwaway line in a conversation with her made me realize how much work still needs to be done to construct a picture of Jesus, free from the taint of anti-Semitism yet convincing, honest and authentic. I am also greatly indebted to Jocelyn and her husband Mike for their wonderful hospitality. Edward Kessler, Executive Director of the Centre for Jewish–Christian Relations in Cambridge, has cheered me up with meals and countless conversations. I am particularly grateful to him for offering many points of view which helped to shape chapter 4. He will not agree with everything in that chapter or in the work as a whole (who will?!), but it is to Edward that I dedicate this book, a small token of love and admiration.

INTRODUCTION

PERSPECTIVES

Of the making of books about Jesus, there is no end. In order to justify another such publication, I need to explain my own perspective and my intention in writing.

I am a Christian, ordained a deacon of the Church of South India and a presbyter of the British Methodist Church. Although I occasionally went to Sunday School and even to church, for much of my childhood and adolescence I had little or no attachment to any church. Yet from the age of five I had a strong emotional and even spiritual commitment to the person of Jesus. At that young age, I read a book by the author Enid Blyton, more famous for stories about Noddy and the Famous Five than devotional subjects, called *The Children's Life of Christ* (London, Methuen & Co., 1943). I found myself captivated by the figure of Jesus, and I still am.

I read that book in Singapore. Indeed, I spent my childhood in many different parts of the world, because my late father was a member of the Royal Air Force. My earliest memories are of Chinese religious festivals, rather than Christian rites. Later, in Aden, at the heel of the Arabian peninsula, I met Muslims before I had ever heard of Methodists. Therefore, my earliest memories inclined me to interpret the meaning of Jesus within the wide world of religious pluralism, rather than in the narrower though no doubt necessary parochialism of Christian ecumenism that has dominated much of my life. I have long valued the inspired if rather free rendering of Psalm 31, verse 8 in the King James Bible: 'Thou hast set my feet in a large room.'

My education has been Western, imbued with the values (or, some would claim, lack of them) of the European Enlightenment. These values have come under recent attack from within the same tradition; specifically, from postmodernism, its bastard child, inheritor of its least engaging qualities of parochialism and rampant individualism. More searching criticisms of the Enlightenment heritage have been made by other cultures and traditions, though often they have not acknowledged what they have learned as well as what they scorn. I have tried to learn from some of these criticisms, not least those from within Islam which, at its best, comments out of a profound, moving, subtle and majestic vision of a single human community in which political, social and economic matters are held together as the will of the one God for humankind.

Truth to tell, many aspects of Western modernism have been arrogant and presumptuous. Modernism has often reduced the world to an object of technological research; it has habitually been unreasonably proud of its own narrow perspective in the face of mysteries that the human mind alone cannot fathom. Even so, its pursuit of truth and knowledge rather than superstition and vested interest seems to me to be both honourable and valuable. Its willingness to apply the historical-critical method even to sacred books need not be an act of impiety, but rather a means of unlocking meaning from them, appropriate to people on the verge of the third millennium. Fundamentalists may be on the move in many religions, but they are as much the product of modernism, though in reaction to it, as are those who gratefully accept and use its tools to uncover truth and significance.

So this investigation into Jesus of Nazareth comes from within the household of Christian faith, yet is aware of religious and even secular diversity, and draws appreciatively, but not uncritically, upon modern Western historical scholarship.

INTENTION

Any modern-style biography of Jesus, in the sense of an account giving important factual information about him, can be written in rather a short compass, as I show in Chapter 2. This is not as surprising or as disconcerting as it may seem. All the world's religious leaders have become the focus of myth and legend. It is understandable and (as I shall argue in Chapter 1) even desirable that the impact of Jesus (as of the Buddha, Muhammad and other such figures of widespread veneration) has been refracted through the creative imagination, and hence been subjected to pardonable exaggeration. It has never been possible to separate historical interpretation from historical facts. In the ancient world, history was a branch of rhetoric, which is to say that it was spoken as much as written. Herodotus (485–424 BCE), the father of history, did not hesitate to put speeches into the mouths of his characters. His are not accurate reproductions but rather interpretative evaluations of what his heroes and villains said and did. Yet he was a true historian, not a mere chronicler, since he sought meaning in his stories, and was not interested in narrative as an end in itself.

Similarly, Jesus is filtered to us through many minds and from many perspectives, but that does not remove him from the discourse of history, precisely because what his living and dying means for the story of humankind is crucially important. So, not only would a book offering a straightforward chronicle of the life of Jesus be very brief, it would miss the point of his influence upon many human beings and upon much human civilization. His life has changed many individual lives and, indeed, the life of the world itself. This book is chiefly concerned with this area. Thus, as with my *Muhammad: A Short Biography*, I have freely interpreted the title of this book to describe not only the importance of its subject's life in its historical context, but also what aspects of that life have meant and continue to mean for succeeding generations, particularly our own.

I write from the point of view of a student of religious studies, at the verge of the third millennium when, in certain respects, the world has become closer than ever before, yet is divided by many things, not least by intolerant religious diversity. The aims of religious studies include reflection on: what should be the relationship between different religious systems? What should be the role of women in religions in the contemporary world? How does transcendent reality impinge itself upon this world of sensory perception and rational discourse, and what does it require of us? And what is the place not just of history but also of the creative imagination in understanding the truths religions aspire to articulate and structure? Such issues will be raised in the course of this book.

The significance of Jesus is more than the product of 'historical Jesus research'. Exegesis by itself (that is, the process of bringing out the meaning or meanings of the New Testament texts) is only the preliminary task of the student of theology and religious studies. Jesus speaks to us equivocally, not univocally, through the Christian scriptures. He is reached through the various convictions and interpretations of his earliest followers. As we shall see, those meanings are often diverse and multi-valent. Although the first four chapters of this book are rooted in historical Jesus research, this very enterprise implicitly raises questions such as are outlined in the preceding paragraph. For example: what do Jesus's rare encounters with people other than Jews portend about Christianity's claim to be a universal religion? What do his remarkably open and sympathetic relationships with women offer for Christians and others to ponder in the light of late-twentieth-century concerns about relationships between the sexes?

Any tolerably credible and coherent historical portrait of Jesus draws much material from the first three Gospels, often called the Synoptic Gospels. Although there has recently been a reaction against the so-called 'tyranny of the Synoptic Gospels', it is difficult to maintain convincingly that a more adequate stream of knowledge about Jesus is to be found elsewhere. This issue of sources for his life and meaning is raised in Chapter 1. Chapter 2 offers an outline of Jesus's life, and reflects on Christological issues: that is, who other people thought he was and what he came to do; indeed, his own views on the tasks God had called him to do, and the person God had created him to be. Chapter 3 looks at Jesus's teaching about the kingdom of God, and how it might be interpreted relevantly for us today, as well as how it seemed to him and his contemporaries. Chapter 4 attempts an understanding of Jesus the Jew, and what that might portend and imply for Jewish–Christian relations at the end of a century in which Christian teaching was exploited to destroy six million Jews under Nazi rule. Therefore, this chapter overtly raises questions about the significance of Gospel (and some later) assessments of Jesus for living faithfully and harmoniously in the contemporary world, in which technology has been harnessed to wicked and destructive ends, often in the name of religion, even in the name of Jesus himself.

The last two chapters disengage themselves further from straightforward New Testament exegesis and theology, in order to ask questions about the importance of Jesus in the wider world. Material here seems endless. I have concentrated on two areas of particular importance for people in today's world. Chapter 5 depicts Jesus in the world of religions beyond Christianity and even Judaism: particularly in Islam, where he has always been at home; but also in Hinduism and Buddhism. It asks how compatible these portraits are with Christian estimates of his importance. The last chapter asks whether contemporary Western theological reflections on the importance of Jesus are appropriate for the diverse world in which we live, and if other Christian appraisals of him may have more to say to wider groups of people.

CONVENTIONS

Throughout, dates in the text that are simply given as numbers indicate events from the Common Era, except in very rare cases when otherwise the reader might be misled. Dates followed by BCE mean before the Common Era (CE). So Jesus was born about 4 BCE, but died about 30. But I have written, for example, 200 BCE–100 CE. The designation 'Common Era' is recent, created very properly to reflect sensitivities in our religiously plural world. Otherwise, this system of dating is known as BC (Before Christ) and AD (*Anno Domini*, the year of the Lord). The fact that the most widely understood system of dating divides the world between the period before Jesus and after him is an indication of his enormous impact on world history.

Where appropriate I have preferred to write Jesus's rather than Jesus', so, for example, Jesus's mother, not Jesus' mother. It is quite difficult to choose a precise word to describe adequately Jesus's career of preaching, healing, suffering and death, so in the text I have offered a number of more or less equivalent terms. Occasionally, I have resorted to the word 'ministry'. This has the demerit of making Jesus seem like a rather traditional Protestant pastor, which is not an analogy that fits him comfortably. It would therefore be wise to dismiss that connotation of the word, and focus instead on its useful purport of vocation, craft, prayer and dedication.

I have occasionally written of the evangelists' readers or readership. Although this is convenient shorthand, many more people would have heard the Gospels, part or entire, read to them than would themselves have read them.

Quotations from scripture are nearly always from the New Revised Standard Version (Oxford, OUP, 1989), though very occasionally I offer my own renderings. Translations from the Quran in Chapter 5 are my own. I have usually given scriptural references where appropriate, perhaps to the point of pedantry. My intention is not to encourage readers to mistake this introductory, though I hope innovative, work for a technical book, but to invite them to read the scriptures to check my views and to formulate their own. I have used upper case – Gospel(s) – to refer to the works of the four evangelists, and lower case – gospel – when I have meant to denote the 'good news' they and others have believed Jesus brought.

I have tried to keep notes to a minimum, and have used the Harvard method of referring to a book by author's surname, date of publication and page number(s). I have not been as successful in economizing on notes as I was in *Muhammad: A Short Biography*. Mainly this has been due to the fact that, because of the application of the historical-critical method by biblical scholars to the Gospels in the last two hundred years, there is no received version of the life of Jesus as there is of the life of Muhammad.[1] The implications of this issue will be addressed in Chapter 5. I have not used diacritical marks on foreign words, or even for letters that are signified by apostrophes in English, except in the Bibliography, since scholars know these, and others often only find them confusing.

The Bibliography records books that have been particularly useful to me in writing this book, and also other works that will prove helpful for further reading. Arbitrarily, but I hope usefully, I have occasionally recorded the subtitle of a book in the Bibliography, if I think it illuminates its content and so may encourage readers to ponder it. I am no longer sure of the origin of many of the views I now have of Jesus. I apologize if I have failed to acknowledge influences, or conformed others' perspectives to my own.

NOTE
1. Forward 1997, 98–102.

1

SOURCES FOR A LIFE OF JESUS

I n the reign of the Roman emperor Tiberius, about the year 29, a young
wandering Galilean teacher and healer named Yehoshua (colloquially
shortened to Yeshua or even Yeshu) began a short ministry that ended in
his violent death by execution. We call him Jesus, based on the Latinized
version of the Greek form of his name recorded in the pages of the New
Testament. What can we know about his life? This chapter will briefly
look at early works that mention him and his followers, starting with
material outside the New Testament.

ROMAN SOURCES

Jesus lived and died in the eastern Mediterranean land of Palestine, a
region then controlled by the Roman Empire. Emperor Augustus, who
died in the year 14, had brought to an end a period of civil war in the
empire. During Jesus's ministry, Pontius Pilate was prefect of Judaea
(from about 26 to 36), which included Samaria and Idumaea. Yet there is
hardly any evidence about Jesus's life and career from Roman sources.

That the Roman historian Publius Cornelius Tacitus (c.56–c.120)
knew something of events in Palestine is certain, since he recorded the
Jewish rebellion against Rome of 66 to 73 in his *Histories*. In another
work, his *Annals*, he wrote about the burning of Rome in 64 and made
this reference to the Christians and their master:

> Nero fabricated scapegoats – and punished with every refinement the
> notoriously depraved Christians (as they were popularly called). Their

originator, Christ, had been executed in Tiberius's reign by the governor of Judaea, Pontius Pilatus. But in spite of this temporary setback the deadly superstition had broken out afresh, not only in Judaea (where the mischief had started) but even in Rome. All degraded and shameful practices flourish in the capital.[1]

Tacitus saw the Christians as belonging an anti-social Jewish sect, emerging from within a religion which, although it had received special consideration from Roman political authorities, had encouraged its adherents to rebel. He records that they were convicted more because they hated the human race than for starting the fire. This could indicate that they held world-denying views, but may mean no more than that they refused to participate in Roman pagan rites. There is confirmation of the unpopularity of Christians in Rome at the end of the book of Acts (written about 100 but referring to events around 60). Paul, imprisoned there, summoned local Jewish leaders to him. They said that 'with regard to this sect [Christianity] we know that everywhere it is spoken against' (28:22).

Tacitus had no reason to sympathize with the Jews or with variant forms of their religious faith: hence one reason for his short and dismissive reference to the Christians and their founder. Even so, the passage goes on to record that people began to feel compassion for the Christians, because Nero had them killed by animals or burned alive on crosses. Tacitus was ignorant of any details of their beliefs or of the life and teaching of Jesus. All he knows is that 'Christus' was a Jew from a far-flung part of the Empire, who was executed by Pontius Pilate as the instigator of a new religious movement whose followers were named after him. His source for this information is not known to us.

Also in his *Annals*, Tacitus tells of a woman of noble birth named Pomponia Graecina, who was arraigned before the Roman senate in 57, perhaps as a Christian. She lived on until his own day. He records that she 'had a long life, spent in unbroken gloom'.[2]

Another historian, Gaius Suetonius Tranquillus (70–c.130), was equally uninformed of significant facts about Jesus or the early Christians. He referred in his *The Twelve Caesars* to the expulsion of Jews from Rome in c.49 (as did Luke in Acts of the Apostles chapter 18, verse 2) by the Emperor Claudius (who reigned from 41 to 54). This punishment was inflicted because they 'caused continuous disturbances at the instigation of Chrestus';[3] it did not last long, since Jews were soon back in Rome again. Although Suetonius assumed that Chrestus was an individual, this is more likely a reference to trouble caused by Christian preaching among Jews that Jesus was the Messiah. Again, the source of his information is not known to us, but its disapproving tone suggests that it cannot have been a Christian one.

Suetonius also confirms Tacitus's account of Nero's punishment of the Christians after the fire of Rome. He wrote of 'the Christians, a kind of men given to a new and mischievous superstition, [whom] he tortured and put to death'.[4]

The most interesting relatively early reference to Jesus by a Roman was not by a historian but by a politician. It concerns events that occurred between c.110 and 112, when Gaius Caecilius Pliny (c.61–112), a friend of Tacitus, was legate in Bithynia and Pontus at the southern end of the Black Sea. He wrote letters to Trajan, emperor from 98 to 116, which make it clear that he punished Christians for their faith. If they still insisted that they were Christians after three warnings that the penalty for being such was death, he executed them or, if they were Roman citizens, sent them to Rome for chastisement. After his first investigation he received an anonymous accusation against many people, accusing them of being Christians. Those defendants who denied that they were Christians were required to pass a test to prove the truth of their denials. Pliny led them in an invocation of the gods and the offering of incense and wine to an image of Trajan. They were also required to anathematize Christ. (Such a test was not universally applied to Christians as an act of loyalty to the emperor until over a century later, under Decius in 250.) Pliny dubbed their religion 'a crude and exaggerated superstition'. He discovered that Christians

> were accustomed to meet on a fixed day before dawn, to say an antiphonal hymn to Christ as to a god, and to bind themselves with an oath – not for performing any crime but for abstaining from theft, robbery, adultery, and the violation of oaths, and the refusal to repay a deposit on demand. After this they were accustomed to depart and then meet again for a meal which was ordinary and harmless.[5]

None of these Roman writers tell us anything at all detailed about the life of Jesus, and they offer only a limited amount of information about the growing influence of his followers. All three described Christianity in negative terms, as a superstition and as anti-social. None seem to have known that 'Christ' was a Messianic designation rather than a name. None called the founder of Christianity by his correct name. If we relied upon them for understanding Jesus, we should know absolutely nothing at all of importance about him.

The major reason why Jesus merited no particular attention from any Roman writer of his day was his political, social and economic insignificance. Men like Julius Caesar and the Emperor Augustus were important figures, so people wrote quite a lot about them. (Julius Caesar, an inveterate self-publicist, wrote about himself.) In the case of Jesus, no secular writer from or of the master race would trouble to write much about an obscure figure from a far-flung and troublesome part of the empire.

JEWISH SOURCES

Jesus was a Jew. It could therefore be assumed that his ministry would have attracted widespread attention among Jewish politicians and historians of the period. In fact, this is not the case. During Jesus's ministry, Herod Antipas was the tetrarch of Galilee and Peraea; he ruled as a vassal of Rome from 4 BCE to 39. Herod killed John the Baptist (Josephus, of whom more below, mentions this event); Matthew and Mark even claim that Herod thought of Jesus as John, risen from the dead (Mark 6:14; Matthew 14:2; in Luke 9:7, Herod was perplexed because others reported that John was risen). Luke records that he took part in the trial of Jesus (23:6–12).

There is no evidence that Jesus ever had dealings with Philip, who from 4 BCE to 34 was tetrarch over territories to the north and east of Galilee. Luke mentions Philip when he locates the ministry of Jesus in a historical context, but was probably mistaken to claim that he ruled Iturea (3:1).

The theologian and philosopher, Philo, who lived in Alexandria from about 15 BCE to 50, did not mention Jesus. The Qumran writings (scrolls found by the Dead Sea, probably written by the pietistic Essene community) do not mention Jesus. Too much must not be made of this silence: for example, Philo does not mention John the Baptist, and the Dead Sea Scrolls do not refer to Herod Antipas, although both these figures undoubtedly existed and were modestly important figures.

The Jewish historian and polemicist, Joseph ben Matthias, who styled himself Flavius Josephus, does mention Jesus. The son of a priest and a

Pharisee, he was born in Jerusalem in 37/38. He was a commander in Galilee during the Jewish War. After he was captured in 67, he saved his life by prophesying correctly that Vespasian, whose son Titus led the Roman army, would become emperor. When this happened in 69, he was freed. Thereafter, he lived in Rome until his death some time after 100.

Josephus did not mention Jesus and the Christians in his account of *The Jewish War*, published in 73. A later work, dating from the 90s, *Jewish Antiquities*, mentions 'James, the brother of Jesus, who is called the Christ', who was executed in 62 (XX, 200). This seems a credibly authentic though tantalizingly brief reference. What, however, about an earlier section on Jesus, the so-called *Testimonium Flavianum*?

> About this time there lived Jesus, a wise man, *if indeed one ought to call him a man*. For he was one who wrought surprising feats and was a teacher of such people as accept the truth gladly. He won over many Jews and many of the Greeks. *He was the Messiah*. When Pilate, upon hearing him accused by men of the highest standing amongst us, had condemned him to be crucified, those who had in the first place come to love him did not give up their affection for him. *On the third day he appeared to them restored to life, for the Prophets of God had prophesied these and countless other marvellous things about him.* And the tribe of Christians, so called after him, has still to this day not disappeared. (XVIII, 63; my italics)[6]

Since the sixteenth century, scholars have rightly questioned the authenticity of this passage. Josephus was not a Christian and would not have written any pietistic statement of faith. Nor was he an impressed outsider, recording what he did not believe; the paucity of information about Jesus and Christians elsewhere in his writings illustrates their lack of importance to him. It may be that this whole section was inserted by a Christian apologist. More likely, it has been 'improved'. One suggestion is that only the sentence 'He was the Messiah' was added to the original text. On this view, the reference to 'if indeed one ought to call him a man' could reflect Josephus's belief that Satan inspired Jesus, rather than that he was divine,[7] but this seems unlikely. More probable is that the parts that I have italicized are interpolations into the original text. Even if there is an original core to this passage, it does not amount to very much information.

Other Jewish references to Jesus are abusive and malevolent and found in collections that are much later than the first century. References to

Jesus in the Talmud (compiled after c.400, though containing earlier material that is hard to date) are few and depreciative. The *Toledot Yeshu* (History of Jesus) is a scurrilous account of Jesus's life, which circulated from about the thirteenth century onwards, though it may have been based on an earlier Aramaic work. It describes him as the illegitimate son of Mary and a Roman soldier called Panthera (a claim that goes back to the pagan Celsus's denunciation of Christians in the late second century). It claims that his powers derived from black magic and that he suffered a shameful death. In all likelihood, this was a polemical response to the disgraceful slanders Christians spread about Jews, their actions and beliefs.

A STOIC SOURCE

A pagan philosopher called Mara bar Sarapion tantalizingly referred to Jesus (though not by name) in a letter, probably composed soon after 73. He wrote to his son from a Roman prison, commending wisdom as life's only prize. He used Jesus as an illustration of how unjust executions bring no good to their perpetrators. He commented, 'What did it avail the Jews to kill their wise king, since their kingdom was taken away from them from that time on?' and observed that the wise king is not dead 'because of the new law he has given'.[8]

This Syrian Stoic from Samatosa was certainly not a Christian, since he referred to 'our gods'. His is a positive reference, with echoes of Matthew's view of Jesus. Many scholars believe that that Gospel originated in Syria, so perhaps Mara was aware of the traditions which, a little later or even about the same time, were incorporated by the evangelist in his work. However, Mara's positive assessment was necessary for his portrayal of himself as being in a similar situation to the wise king, imprisoned and perhaps waiting a death that could not destroy the fundamental wisdom of his life's work.

All these non-Christian writings, whether Roman, Jewish or Stoic, offer tantalizingly brief glimpses of the founder of Christianity. Their limited significance for a student of the life of Jesus is twofold. First, they do not doubt that Jesus existed and had a certain impact upon his contemporaries that had spread well beyond the boundaries of Judaea. Second, they offer a few points of information that confirm a few of the earliest Christian traditions about Jesus. For example, Josephus tells us that Jesus had a brother named James; and he, Tacitus and Mara affirm that Jesus's death was violent. Both Josephus and Mara refer to Jesus as 'wise'. These are interesting and useful comments. But if they were all we had, they would not suffice to conjure up the import over the last two millennia of the man from Nazareth.

THE EARLIEST EXTANT CHRISTIAN WRITINGS

Unsurprisingly, it is the early Christian writings that reveal most about Jesus. Our earliest witness is Paul. The first letter he wrote that has survived as part of the New Testament is probably 1 Thessalonians, which dates from about 50. His last dates from only a few years later. Probably Paul was executed during the reign of Nero (54–68), at some time in the early 60s. Thus the facts he gives are from only one generation after the death of Jesus.

Yet Paul gives only a small amount of information about Jesus. From his letters, we glean that Jesus was a Jew, a real human being 'born of a woman' (Galatians 4:4), that he died and was raised from the dead, after which he appeared to over five hundred of his followers, his brother James and all the apostles, and to Paul himself (1 Corinthians 15:3–8). We know that Jesus prohibited divorce (1 Corinthians 7:10); and we have an account of Jesus's last supper with his disciples (1 Corinthians 11:23–5). Yet that is all that Paul's letters tell us about Jesus. Indeed, if 1 Corinthians had not survived, Paul would not tell us anything substantial at all about the life and teaching of Jesus.

Paul's letters are more important for their information about who Jesus was (in a word, for their Christology) than about the course of Jesus's life. Paul believed Jesus to be God's representative who would bring in the Messianic age (indeed, he had already done so), in which God's promises of salvation would be extended to the Gentiles. As a result, some scholars have argued that Paul was too interested in the Christ of faith to be much concerned with the Jesus of history, but that is a questionable judgement. After all, we have only a few surviving letters by which to judge the teaching and major concerns of Paul. He could have assumed knowledge of Jesus's life on the part of his correspondents, or else (though this is much less likely) written about Jesus more extensively in works that have been lost. Probably Paul's post-Easter conversion experience inclined him to emphasize Jesus's death and resurrection, rather than his earthly life. In a moving passage, Paul wrote that 'even though we once knew Christ from a human point of view, we know him no longer in that way' (2 Corinthians 5:16). Elsewhere he affirms that 'I want to know Christ and the power of his resurrection and the sharing of his sufferings by becoming like him in his death, if somehow I may attain the resurrection from the dead' (Philippians 3:10f.).

This hardly means that Paul had no interest in the historical Jesus. He knew about the existence of collections of sayings and deeds of Jesus. In Acts, Paul tells Ephesian church leaders to remember the words of Jesus, that it is more blessed to give than to receive (20:35). These words are found nowhere else in the New Testament. (How far the authentic Paul is found in the book of Acts is, however, a matter of much debate.)

Elsewhere in the letters of the New Testament, there are a few references to the life of Jesus. His transfiguration is mentioned in a late work, 2 Peter chapter 1, verses 17–18. (Probably, neither letter associated with Peter was written by the apostle. This association of anonymous works with important authors was followed by many writers in the ancient world. We might regard this as dishonest; they did not.) The author of 1 Peter gives an account of an event that is found nowhere in the Gospels: having been put to death in the flesh but alive in the Spirit, Jesus 'went to preach to the spirits in prison' (3:19). It is uncertain what this means, though the passage seems to have a baptismal context.

APOCRYPHAL GOSPELS AND SIMILAR MATERIAL

Such a difficult text as 1 Peter chapter 3, verse 19 prepares the ground for the proliferation of strange material that was created and circulated in early times, mostly after the period in which we are interested. Even though the canonical Gospels (i.e. those that were accepted into the canon of the New Testament, which was fixed in the Greek churches in 367 and a little later in the other churches) do contain the secret, the miraculous and the magical, material elsewhere greatly develops this perspective.

Such material often turns the miracles of Jesus into magic tricks that do no particular credit to him. For example, the Infancy Gospel of Thomas records the five-year-old Jesus creating birds from clay. Much of this genre reflects the variant forms of Christian faith that proliferated in the second and ensuing centuries. Some apocryphal Gospels reflect the philosophy of the Gnostics, who believed they had a special knowledge (Greek: *gnosis*) of God that enlightened them and guaranteed their salvation. They were spiritual snobs who depreciated the fleshly and physical. A possible example of their attribution of sayings to Jesus can be found in Logion 42 of the Gospel of Thomas (not the same work as the Infancy Gospel; both were attributed to the same apostle, though he wrote neither of them). It records that 'Jesus said, "Become passers-by."' Interestingly, there is a fuller account of this saying by a medieval Muslim scholar and mystic who taught in Baghdad, al-Ghazali (1058–1111): 'Therefore live your life in it [i.e. the world] as men who are passing through, and not as men who have taken up their abode in it, and know that the root of all sins is the love of the world' (quoted in Jeremias 1964, 113). Al-Ghazali ascribed the saying to Jesus, though other Muslim authors attributed it to the Prophet Muhammad. In 1559, the Emperor Akbar, who ruled much of north India, began building the city of Fatehpur Sikri, near to Agra. On a visit there in 1601, he had made an inscription in Arabic on the main portal at the south side of the mosque. Part of it read: 'Jesus, on whom be peace, has said: "This world is a bridge. Pass over it. But build not your dwelling there."'[9] Thus, this saying has had a long and varied history. It could be based on an original saying from Jesus. Just as likely it is not, but is instead indebted to world-denying views somewhat alien to the man from Nazareth. It is, of course, equally possible that there is no link at all between the Logion in the Gospel of Thomas and the inscription in Akbar's city, since it is a rather commonplace spiritual admonition, even platitude. But it is fascinating to suppose that there might be.

As it happens, in recent years there has been much debate about whether the Gospel of Thomas records the beliefs of the Gnostics, as used to be widely believed. If there is a majority view, it is moving away from this position.[10] The Jesus Seminar, set up in 1985 by a radical group of North American scholars, has made much of the importance of the Gospel of Thomas as a fifth Gospel source alongside the canonical Gospels for understanding Jesus.[11] They and some other scholars believe it to be very early indeed. Dominic Crossan supposes that it is a document from the 50s, contemporary with Paul's letters and the Q source (about which, more shortly).[12] However, unlike other colleagues in the Seminar, Crossan does not attach much value to Thomas in constructing his account of Jesus as a Jewish peasant cynic.[13]

However, Thomas may not be an early work, but derivative from other Gospel material. Its independent value may have been overstated by those who think that the first three Gospels have had too great an influence on most people's perception of who Jesus was and what he did. Even if there is a measure of truth in their view (we shall shortly see that the first three Gospels are far from being straightforward histories or biographies), it is unwise to hope for too much reliable information about Jesus from extra-biblical sources.

Even so, members of the Jesus Seminar and other scholars have helpfully drawn attention to what some Americans would call pro-canonical bias in historical Jesus research. For example, Dominic Crossan and Helmut Koester have drawn attention to other works than the four Gospels that they believe to be early and to impart important information about the impact of Jesus's life and ministry.[14]

Yet, as we shall see in Chapter 2, even members of the Jesus Seminar agree that Thomas tells us almost nothing about Jesus that we do not know from the other Gospels. Rather, they maintain that it is important in providing independent attestation of about thirty otherwise singly-attested Gospel sayings. For example, the sixth saying of the Oxyrhynchus Papyrus 1, a Greek fragment of the Gospel of Thomas discovered by two British archaeologists in central Egypt in 1897 and dating to about 200, contains an expansion of Luke chapter 2, verse 24: 'Jesus says: A prophet is not acceptable in his own country, neither does a physician work cures upon those who know him.' The second half of the saying, an addition to Luke's account, could be a more original form, shortened by Luke. More likely, it is an inauthentic gloss, based on the reference to a physician in the previous verse in the Gospel.[15]

It may be that, in the course of the next few years, material from Thomas and other early works will gain credence among scholars and filter down into wider public consciousness. For the moment, the four Gospels of the New Testament still inform most Christian perceptions of Jesus.

THE FIRST THREE GOSPELS

The earliest Gospel is very probably Mark's, and references in it to the destruction of the Jerusalem Temple (13:1–4; see also Matthew 24:1–3 and Luke 21:5–7), which occurred in 70, suggest that it was written very soon after that event. It is likely that the other three Gospels emerged before 100. The last Gospel to be written, John's, was probably finally edited in the last decade of the first century. The four Gospels slowly disseminated widely and gained authoritative status in the churches.

About 170, Tatian composed his *Diatesseron,* or compilation of the four Gospels. It is most likely that all were widely known and used by the end of the second century.

Often, when someone wants to emphasize that she is not lying but communicating the literal reality, she says that she is telling the gospel (or maybe Gospel) truth. But what sort of truth are the Gospels conveying? Although Jesus is central to their message, they are not biographies of him in the modern sense, interested in giving precise information about his life and career, usually in chronological order. For example, we have no idea whether Jesus was married or a widower; it would have been unusual, though not impossible, for a Jewish man to be single.

Even so, the first three Gospels are much alike in some ways. In some places they are verbally very similar. For example, the story of the healing of the leper in Mark chapter 1, verses 40–5, Matthew chapter 8, verses 1–4 and Luke chapter 5, verses 12–16, has parts that are word-for-word alike. Some accounts that are found only in two Gospels are also similarly told: for example, the healing of the man with the unclean spirit recorded in Mark chapter 1, verses 21–5 and Luke chapter 4, verses 31–5; and Jesus's lament over Jerusalem in Matthew chapter 23, verses 37–9 and Luke chapter 13, verses 34–5. Yet elsewhere, the first three Gospels are quite different. For example, Matthew and Luke record stories of Jesus's birth from very different perspectives which are not easily harmonized, whereas Mark is completely silent about the young Jesus. Again, the genealogies of Matthew and Luke about the origins of Jesus (respectively, 1:1–17 and 3:23–38) are utterly different in content, and irreconcilable as historical accounts.

The similarities and dissimilarities between the first three Gospels cause the so-called Synoptic Problem (*synopsis*: Greek, 'to view at the same time'). How is this problem of likeness and unlikeness to be explained? What is fairly certain is that there is a prehistory to the Gospels, and that some of this earlier material is shared by all three or at least two of the Synoptic Gospels. In other words, each Gospel depended on earlier sources, some of which they share. If each Gospel is written out in parallel columns, so that material common to two or all three of them is placed side by side, the point already made about similarities and dissimilarities between them is confirmed.[16] Yet all we have by which to locate the earlier material are the Gospels themselves. What these sources were and how they were arranged and transmitted has been the subject of abundant fascinating and creative speculation. Much ink has been spilled in finding answers to this problem, and many authors have turned their hypothetical solutions, sometimes very dubious ones, about the component parts of these earlier sources into assured convictions. There is a fine irony here, since some such scholars, though very sceptical about the possibility of locating any contact with the historical Jesus, are not equivocal at all about the validity of their often extravagant presuppositions masquerading as certainties.

Broadly speaking, the most widely accepted solution to the Synoptic Problem assumes (1) that Mark was the first Gospel to be written; (2) that there was another source or sources called Q by modern scholars (from *Quelle*, German for 'source') which was used by both Matthew and Luke; (3) that Matthew and Luke had access to material (often called M and L, respectively) which the other Synoptic writers did not know, or at least did not use.

The reason for assuming Mark to be the first Gospel is that Matthew and Luke appear to amend Mark, usually expressing what he writes more grammatically and concisely. Only about 30 out of 609 verses are found in Mark but not in either Matthew, Luke or both. Further, wherever Matthew and Luke agree with Mark, they tend to agree with the arrangement of his account of Jesus's ministry, but where they do not, they go their own way. It simply makes better sense of the evidence to assume that Matthew and Luke depended upon Mark and refined and extended it to speak to the communities for which they wrote, than to postulate that Mark abbreviated, sometimes rather unskilfully, the two other Gospels. Interestingly, Luke omits two significant sections of Mark: chapter 6, verses 17–29 and, even more extensively, chapter 6, verse 45 to chapter 8, verse 26. This may indicate that Matthew and Luke used different versions of Mark. However, it may simply be that Luke was a more creative or at least a more ruthless editor than Matthew.

Matthew and Luke also share other material in common, which Mark does not include in his Gospel. It is possible to derive this data, Q, from the two Gospels. Some scholars suppose that it was originally a written document. Certainly, some passages are so close in verbal agreement as to suggest a written origin. For example, the passage referring to the lilies of the field that are arrayed in more glory than Solomon is textually very similar in both Gospels (Matthew 6:28–30, Luke 12:27–8). Yet it is certainly true that if some shared passages are, word-for-word, very close, others are not. A number of scholars believe that Luke edited Q less than Matthew, and so follow Luke's version when they wish to trace their way to its original form. However, it has to be borne in mind that not all material common to Matthew and Luke necessarily came from Q, if it was a written source. In default of possessing that document, we cannot know what was in it.

Some writers have suggested that Q is a quite unnecessary hypothesis. For example, John Spong, building upon the work of Michael Goulder, believes that Matthew created what we call Q as he expanded Mark to fit the Jewish liturgical year. He also suggests that Luke used both Matthew and Mark; his use of Matthew explains the presence of so-called Q material in his book.[17]

It is undoubtedly true that much scholarship about the sources behind the Gospels builds speculation upon hypothesis; it is fascinating yet, one suspects, also fantasy. Yet, in my judgement, by trying to simplify the sources, Spong and other radical writers offer even more implausible solutions. Probably R. M. Grant was right to suggest that Q is not a specific book or similar document; rather 'it is no less and no more than a convenient symbol to designate non-Markan materials common to Matthew and Luke'.[18] If so, then these common materials were almost certainly a mixture of oral and written sources. The possibility that Matthew and Luke had access to some similar or even identical written traditions would explain the close agreements between them. The disagreements would come where they freely and differently adapted this common written material; they would also arise from the diverse form of oral material they received about comparable events.

What is equally fascinating about these varied sources is not what was in them, but what was not. There is no story in them of Jesus's birth, nor of his trial and execution, nor of the resurrection. These missing events have provided Christian thinkers throughout the following centuries with much material from which they have constructed answers to the questions of who Jesus was and what he accomplished. Yet this lack of such material in Q does not mean that it consisted of important early traditions reaching back to a credible portrait of the historical Jesus that is free from theological accretions. It is a remarkable fact that such early material, dating from the early years after Jesus's crucifixion, does not come value-free. Q offers important theological reflection as well as historical information. In it, Jesus appears as a teacher and as the agent of God's rule and his calling of human beings to discipleship. Just like the Gospels themselves, this evidence witnesses to Jesus's role in God's will for humankind.

Other than Mark and Q, there is also material used only by Matthew or by Luke. Again, many scholars have analysed this material very carefully. The fact that much of Matthew's special source or sources is interested both in Jewish religion and the church, in eschatology and judgement, alerts the reader to his major concerns, around which he fashions material he shares with Mark, Luke or both. Equally, Luke's own mine of information picks out and stresses certain themes, including, as we shall discuss below, the universality of God's love. It seems more likely that Matthew and Luke inherited yet shaped this tradition, rather than that they invented most of it (though some scholars believe that they did invent some or even all of it). Certainly, Luke claimed to have written an orderly account delivered to him by eyewitnesses and ministers of the word (Luke 1:1–4).

Still, the Synoptic Gospels, and the sources on which they draw, are not literal accounts of the life of Jesus. They seek to tell his importance as the climactic messenger of God. This is very clear from the beginning of Mark's Gospel: 'The beginning of the good news of Jesus Christ, the Son of God'. Mark wishes to tell good news (which is what 'gospel' – in Greek, *euangelion* – means). Jesus is the bearer of God's latest revelation. Thus, the evangelists have a theological agenda. This does not mean that they were not interested in what actually happened, so that nothing of importance can be discerned from them about the historical Jesus. Rather, theology and history are in a symbiotic relationship in the Gospel accounts. Actually, if Jesus was the Son of God (we shall explore what that title meant in Chapter 2), then no doubt the people for whom Mark and the other evangelists wrote would have wanted to know something about his life, death and resurrection.

THE AIMS AND INTENTIONS OF THE GOSPELS

The enormous changes that have recently taken place in tracing the prehistory of the Gospel material have had profound effects on understanding the aims and intentions of the Gospels. This can be illustrated from three commentaries on Mark's Gospel written in the second half of the twentieth century. Vincent Taylor's *The Gospel According to St Mark* (London, Macmillan, 1952) is written from the viewpoint of the source critics. Source criticism is the study of the antecedents from which the New Testament writers drew their material: these include eye-witnesses as important sources of the events. As a result of employing this tool, Taylor believed that Mark was able to provide answers to such questions as what Jesus had said and done, and what the order of events was in his ministry. Mark could do so, because (in Taylor's view, though there is reason to doubt this) he had been a friend of the apostle Peter.

Eleven years later, Dennis Nineham, in his commentary *The Gospel of St Mark* (Harmondsworth, Penguin, 1963), took the very different position of a form critic. He did not deny that early tradition contained some historical memories, but chiefly he asked questions about how Jesus was interpreted by the early communities who gathered and interpreted the various literary forms in which the tradition was transmitted. Form critics, who arose in Germany after World War I but whose findings took time to find widespread acceptance in Britain, usually interpreted the evangelists more as collectors of material than as creative theologians. Thus Nineham's commentary sees Mark as describing the views of the church of his day, which was probably located in Rome or Antioch c.75.

After World War II, the tool of redaction criticism was forged in Germany (but again not put to use in England until some years later). Redaction criticism is concerned with how the early material was handled and changed by the evangelists; with what was put in and what was left out of their Gospels, and why. If Matthew and Luke are indeed later than Mark, then it is easier to employ redaction criticism upon their works than Mark's, because their use of his Gospel illustrates their omissions and additions, and causes the reader to ask what they hoped to achieve thereby. There is no previous document by which to measure Mark. Even so, Eduard Schweizer's commentary, *The Good News of Mark* (German edition 1967; English edition Atlanta, John Knox Press, 1975), concentrated on how Mark portrayed the good news of Jesus to his community. This not only affirms Mark as a creative interpreter, but also as a pastor who tailored his account to the needs of his community.

Professor Morna Hooker refers to

> The many different ways in which, in the course of a few years, a commentary can be written: the focus of concern has shifted from the historical Jesus, through the early history of the traditions, through Mark the evangelist, through the community for which he wrote, to what modern readers can make of the text.[19]

In fact there are many more 'criticisms' that have grown up in recent years than the three just mentioned: structuralism and its offspring deconstructionism or poststructuralism, narrative and rhetorical criticism might be added, and others too. But my purpose is to point out, not exhaustively to name and describe, the bewildering variety of tools employed to locate meaning within the Gospels.

At any rate, by whatever route or routes (whether by assiduous interviewers of early Christians, or from the work of interpreters of their communities, or by imaginative reflective practitioners of faith in Jesus, or by some other way or ways): about the year 70, a new genre of literature appeared, the Gospel.[20] It takes the form of an account of the ministry and meaning of Jesus; however, it is selective and reflective rather than a precisely chronological history.

The rise of this genre of Gospel writing may seem to undermine any possibility of locating the historical Jesus, dependent as it is upon a creative and interpretative process of different sources, editors and authors. Yet it is precisely through this symbiosis of community memory, combining history and theology, that the real meaning of Jesus was revealed. So, at least, the evangelists believed. For example, the author or editor of John's Gospel stated his aims at the (original) end of his work: 'These things are written so that you may come to believe that Jesus is the Messiah, the Son of God, and that through believing you may have life in his name' (20:31).

It is significant that the Gospel genre appears about the year 70. The previous decade had seen the death of many of the first generation leaders of the Christian church, who had either known Jesus at first hand or else knew others who had. Also by 70, the Jewish rebellion against Rome climaxed with the trauma of the destruction of the Temple that year. This encouraged Christians to produce portraits of Jesus that were not only compatible with memories of a passing generation of Christians, but could persuade Roman authorities that the universalizing Christian interpretation of Jewish faith was not fundamentally anti-social and revolutionary.

MATTHEW, MARK, LUKE AND JOHN: THE ART OF GOSPEL WRITING

There are New Testament scholars (we have mentioned Vincent Taylor) who wish to emphasize the historical value of the Gospels. Some of them insist that the Gospel writers had important access to eyewitnesses of

Jesus's ministry. Did they? In fact, none of the Gospels mentions an author's name. The present names became attached to the Gospels in the second century. It is by no means certain, or even probable, that the apostles Matthew and John wrote the Gospels associated with their names. So it cannot easily be claimed that they preserve the memories of two of Jesus's closest followers. Nor are the traditions that Mark knew Peter and Luke know Paul watertight. The earliest reference to Mark is by Papias, Bishop of Hierapolis, in c.130, which is preserved by the fourth-century writer Eusebius of Caesarea in his *Ecclesiastical History*. Papias claimed that Mark 'having been the interpreter of Peter, wrote down accurately but not in order, all that he remembered of the Lord's sayings and doings'.[21] Maybe so. Yet this could be a mistaken tradition. Certainly, an association of Peter with the Gospel raises at least as many problems as it solves: for example, why is the Gospel so vague about geographical knowledge of Palestine? It has also been seriously questioned whether Luke's Gospel was written by a companion of Paul, as the Muratorian canon and afterwards a number of other church authorities, claim. The canon probably reflects the views of the church in Rome about 170, though a few scholars see it as a much later document from the fourth century.

The Gospel of John, referring to the beloved disciple whom it mentions on a number of occasions, affirms at its close that 'This is the disciple who is bearing witness to these things, and who has written these things; and we know that his testimony is true' (21:24). It does not name that disciple. Tradition has associated him with John, son of Zebedee. It is widely held that chapter 21 is a later addition to the Gospel. It is also widely held that John's Gospel is the work of a school of writers, who may have had a link with the disciple John. So it is by no means clear how much store can be given to any claim that the Gospel preserves the memory of one of Jesus's first followers.

Its very different style indicates that if the beloved disciple was in fact the apostle John, his memories were filtered through a highly interpretative theology. Even so, there have been many attempts to stress the historical reliability of John's sources, but it is clear that, even if he taps into traditions other than those of the Synoptics, some of which are equally reliable, he uses them in a very different way. Anyone who reads John's Gospel can tell that it is very unlike the others. In it, Jesus uses universal symbols about himself and others, such as light and life. He tends to speak reflectively, majestically and at length, rather than in the pithy and earthy style of the Synoptic Gospels. Some have called John the 'spiritual Gospel'; this was first suggested by Clement of Alexandria (c.150–c.215).

Even if (which seems unlikely) Mark preserves Peter's recollections and John retains those of that eponymous disciple, they are filtered through very different interpretative memories. Among those who doubt such a hypothesis, there has been much debate about whether John knew one or more of the other canonical Gospels or else some of the traditions that they record. Actually, there are clear echoes of common, or at least closely linked, tradition between John's Gospel and Mark's. For example, compare John chapter, 12, verses 25f. and Mark chapter 8, verses 34f. The first reads:

> Those who love their life lose it, and those who hate their life in this world will keep it for eternal life. Whoever serves me must follow me, and where I am, there will my servant be also. Whoever serves me, the Father will honour.

The second reads:

> If any want to become my followers, let them deny themselves and take up their cross and follow me. For those who want to save their life will lose it, and those who lose their life for my sake, and for the sake of the Gospel, will save it.

A link between John's and Mark's Gospels would explain why to some extent the same events, and the order of their happening, are found in each. However, sometimes the same event is differently located; most famously, the cleansing of the Temple is found at the beginning of John's Gospel (2:13–22), but at the beginning of the last week of Jesus's life in the Synoptic Gospels (Mark 11:15–19 and parallels). The important point here is not, as some scholars assert, that John puts it there because he is making a theological point about Jesus's relationship to the Jewish religion of his day. More significant is that Mark, Matthew and Luke are also making theological points. It seems most likely that the historical moment for this event is where the Synoptic Gospels place it, since such an event would have aroused Roman suspicions that Jesus was a trouble-maker and hastened his arrest and execution. However, the symbiosis between historical and theological reflection is true for all four Gospels, not just John's. (There are also passages in John and Luke which share common sentiments, which has led some scholars to think that John had Luke's Gospel before him when he wrote.)

It is most helpful to think of the creation of the various Gospels as an art, rather than a science. By this, I mean that the Gospel writers were artful, in the positive sense of being imaginative, aesthetic and adroit arrangers of the information they possessed and edited. They performed, as many artists do (whether of the plastic arts, music, drama or other such pursuits), not simply or even mainly to please and entertain, but to unveil the truth. Like most artists, they sought an audience to dazzle and instruct. It seems most likely that the first audience for each Gospel writer, or evangelist, was the several communities in which they lived and witnessed.

What and where were these communities? Here again, evidence is slight and we are best employed looking at the internal evidence of the Gospels rather than relying on pious 'memories' of fathers of the church in the second and later centuries, though that internal evidence may occasionally confirm or at least cohere with such memories. Still more, we should be not wholly sceptical but certainly wary of the findings of twentieth-century scholars who attempt to reconstruct the sociological, anthropological, psychological or liturgical settings within which they suppose the Gospels to have been written. Some such insights are brilliant exercises of the imagination, but as historical reconstructions, they can seem more plausible than credible.

Thus the evangelists creatively used the various traditions that they inherited about Jesus. They chose, ordered, edited, elaborated and maybe even created material in order to evoke faith in God, as revealed in Jesus of Nazareth. They exercised a creative imagination. Mark wrote his Gospel to commend 'the good news of Jesus Christ, the Son of God' (1:1), who was also 'the Son of Man [who] came not to be served but to serve, and to give his life as a ransom for many' (10:45). Matthew depicted Jesus as a teacher who fulfilled the Law and the prophets (5:17). Discipleship is an important theme for Matthew. At the end of his Gospel, the risen Lord gives his original eleven disciples (minus Judas, who betrayed him) the authority to disciple the nations (28:16–20). The Gospel of John was the product of a community that believed that 'the whole world lies under the power of the evil one' (1 John 5:19). Even so, the world remains the object of God's abiding love (John 3:16). He sent his Son to it, so that all who believe might become children of God (John 1:12f., 3:16–21).

LUKE: THE PILGRIM CHURCH

In order to illustrate the 'artistic' aims and achievements of the Gospels, I shall examine one of them in rather more detail: Luke's Gospel and also the second volume of his work, Acts of the Apostles. What were Luke's aims and achievements?

It is important not to be sidetracked by questions of authorship. Whether or not he was a companion of Paul, a doctor and an artist are of secondary importance. It cannot even be known with any confidence from his own writings whether he was a Jewish or a Gentile Christian. He has no knowledge of the geography of Palestine, which could lead one to assume that he was a Gentile. On the other hand, his writing reveals considerable knowledge of the Septuagint, the ancient Greek translation, first of the Pentateuch and later of the whole Hebrew Bible. One possible solution is that Luke was a Jew of the Diaspora, who had no detailed knowledge of Palestinian terrain. An even more agreeable solution would be that he was a God-fearer. These were Gentiles who admired much of Jewish religion and ethics. Luke relates stories about some of them: the centurion whose servant Jesus heals in the Gospel (7:1–10), and the Ethiopian eunuch and Cornelius in Acts (8:26–40, 10–11:18). The last two of these became followers of Jesus. It is pleasant to speculate, though that is all one can do, that Luke invested much of his own experience in recounting these stories.

His Gospel was probably written during the 90s. By that period, mainstream Judaism was redefining itself after the traumatic event of the destruction of the Jerusalem Temple by the Romans in 70. That redefinition led to antagonism between Jews and Christians, which is strongly expressed in Luke's Gospel. Further, if we accept, as do the vast majority of scholars, that Luke and Acts of the Apostles were both written by the same hand, then the theme of the spreading gospel in that two-volume work betokens a date not only by which the Christian message had reached Rome and taken firm root there, but also a period of reflection upon the meaning of the momentous fact that belief in Jesus as the Messiah had reached the heart of the civilized world.

Many scholars have pointed out that Luke is interested in 'redemption history' or 'salvation history'.[22] Within this secular world of taxation, rulers and religious leaders (Luke 2:1), God sends his angels to human beings, his spirit descends, and his son comes to fight the forces of evil. So secular history is shot through with salvation history; it is a time when human beings can respond faithfully to God's grace. Luke traces Jesus's descent back to Adam, the first man (Luke 3:38). There is a period of time up until and including John the Baptist, the period of the law and the prophets. Then there is the time of Jesus's proclamation of God's kingdom (Luke 16:16). A third period, of the apostolic preaching of the church, will end with the parousia, the return of Jesus, at some undisclosed date in the future (Luke 21:9; Acts 1:7).

From another perspective, Luke's reading of history can be seen as a journey of faith, a pilgrimage. This interpretation of the meaning of the religious quest has had a long tradition in Christianity. For example, until recent generations in Britain, the other important book than the Bible read by devout and educated people was the seventeenth-century Puritan John Bunyan's *Pilgrim's Progress*. In it, the hero Pilgrim journeys through this troublous life until he crosses over to the other side. That theme of pilgrimage is based on Luke's Gospel and its sequel, Acts of the Apostles.

Luke and Acts record many journeys. Apart from the birth stories, the only other story told of Jesus's childhood in any of the canonical Gospels records that, at the age of twelve, he stayed behind in Jerusalem when he and his parents journeyed there for the feast of Passover. They found him sitting among the teachers in the Temple (2:41–51). Only Luke's Gospel contains the two best-known and most loved of Jesus's parables: that of the good Samaritan (10: 25–37) and that of the prodigal son (15: 11–32). In the first of these, a man is waylaid by thieves on a journey from Jerusalem to Jericho, in the course of which he, and Jesus's listeners, discover who truly acts as a neighbour to him, rather than who might be expected to. In the second parable, the younger son journeys to a far land, away from and then back to his father's love, whereas his elder brother makes no journey at all, and so learns nothing of faith, hope, and love. Both stories hint that travelling holds within it the possibility of radical change in the understanding of self, other and God. Another transforming story is told towards the end of the Gospel (24:13–35). On the evening of the day Jesus rose from the dead, two disciples, Cleopas and an unnamed companion, all unknowing of that event, walked from Jerusalem to Emmaus, a distance of about seven miles. Jesus joined them, but they did not recognize him. Jesus told them of the need for the Messiah to suffer and then enter into his glory. At their urging, he shared a meal with them, and they knew him as he broke bread. There is an obvious allusion to the Eucharist here. Perhaps the evangelist deliberately failed to name one traveller so that the reader could imagine herself as the unnamed pilgrim, part of the continuing story of the church, surrounded by the presence of Jesus who travels with every believer and, in word and sacrament, makes God's will and presence plain. Finally, Jesus's followers (these are faithful pilgrims with no doubters among them, unlike Matthew's record in chapter 28, verse 17) travelled to Bethany, where he was carried up into heaven. Then they returned rejoicing to Jerusalem and to the Temple.

The emphasis upon Jerusalem is a particularly crucial theme in the Gospel. Chapter 9, verse 51 tells that 'he set his face to go to Jerusalem', a journey that takes up much of the Gospel, for he does not arrive there until the end of chapter 19! This is significant. The story begins in the small, insignificant village of Nazareth (not even in the nearby thriving town of Sepphoris, which this Gospel, like the others, does not mention at all), yet ends up in the Temple in Jerusalem, the centre of Jewish religion.

From there, Acts continues the saga. The gospel quickly moves out from Jerusalem. Indeed, just before he was lifted up into the heavens, Jesus tells his apostles that 'you will be my witnesses in Jerusalem, in all Judaea and Samaria, and to the ends of the earth' (1:8). The persecutor Saul becomes the apostle Paul by a vision on the road to Damascus, where he was going to root out followers of 'the way' (9:2); that designation by Luke of the earliest Christians has the feeling of movement and journeying about it. Meanwhile, Philip had converted an Ethiopian eunuch who was returning home from Jerusalem, where he had gone to worship (8:25–40). Also, Peter set out for Caesarea to baptize another God-fearer, the Roman centurion Cornelius, and all his household (10–11:18). That story ends with Peter telling other Jewish Christians in Jerusalem of the descent of God's spirit upon Cornelius' entire household. These Christians responded: 'Then God has given even to Gentiles the repentance that leads to life.' However, God's chief instrument to take the gospel to the Gentiles was to be Paul rather than Peter (15:7). The Council of Jerusalem ratified this mission, insisting only that Gentiles abstained from food that had been sacrificed to idols and that was not kosher, and from fornication (15:1–29). (Luke probably simplified and sanitized a much more complicated and contentious debate or series of debates in the early church about whether the Gentiles should be admitted to God's covenant mercies and, if so, on what terms.)

So, in a series of missionary journeys (again, probably somewhat schematized and simplified by Luke), Paul took the good news of Jesus the Messiah to various places in the Mediterranean world. At Antioch, the followers of the way of Jesus were first called Christians (11:26). Towards the end of Acts, Paul returns to the city of Jerusalem, but his provocative act of taking Gentile believers into the Temple led to his arrest. As a Roman citizen, he appealed to Rome. Acts leaves him in Rome, the political centre of the world (Acts 28:16).

Luke's Gospel had begun with an obscure and pietistic setting in a country far from the political centre of things, yet with hints of its setting within the concerns of the wider world: for example, Jesus is born on a journey undertaken by Mary and Joseph during a general registration of the Roman world (2:1ff.). By the end of Acts, the good news has moved from humble and obscure origins to the religious centre of Jerusalem, and thereafter, within about thirty years to the imperial, secular capital of Rome.

So Luke's Gospel and Acts are about journeys. Of course, there is a historical dimension to this emphasis. The news of Jesus did spread with amazing rapidity in the first century, helped by the unified Roman Empire which, by and large, maintained peace within its borders, and built good roads on which to travel. Sea journeys were more perilous, but still possible. Yet Luke's emphasis upon the theme of journeying was not simply an attempt to be historically accurate; indeed, we have seen that, although he paints a reasonably coherent and credible picture of what happened, it is somewhat schematized and simplified. This is understandable, since he tells his story concisely and fairly briefly.

It is also true, however, that Luke had points to make other than those that were historical. He wanted to emphasize that individual believers must be personally involved in the tales he tells, since each is a pilgrim in the way of Jesus. Each must take up her cross daily and follow him (Luke 9:23). The word 'daily' is Luke's addition to the saying. It does not water down a difficult, specific reference to Jesus's cruel death on the cross, by generalizing it. Rather, it is an integral part of Luke's conviction that the Christlike life (the believer's imitation of Christ is important to him) is a daily journey of the heart, soul, strength and mind. If he himself was a Gentile 'God-fearer' who became a follower of the way of Jesus, then his own personal pilgrimage had been long and complex, from paganism through an admiration for and some sort of commitment to Jewish faith, and finally to belief in Jesus as the Messiah. Yet even this final commitment was not simply a matter of coming to rest content and safe in faith in Jesus, so that 'Journeys end in lovers meeting, Every wise man's son doth know'. Rather, pilgrims in the way of Jesus have to live out their faith, and the Gospel and Acts offer allusions to difficulties that believers face and resources upon which they can rely.

A major difficulty believers face is a false attitude towards wealth. Luke would have agreed with the author of the first epistle to Timothy that 'the love of money is a root of all kinds of evil' (6:10). It was, however, the use of money that Luke analysed, not necessarily its possession. There are many well-to-do characters in his works, some of whom are commended for their support of the work of Jesus or members of the early church. Perhaps Theophilus, for whom both of Luke's works were written, was one such person, if he was not simply a literary construct. (His name in Greek means 'lover of God', so the two books could be for anyone who loved God and wanted to know more of him. Maybe Luke was in the happy position of being able to offer his readers a pun, since, although his works were dedicated to a real man, he realized the name's potential for a wider reference.) Other prosperous people like Ananias and Sapphira, who kept part of their wealth for themselves, suffered violent and supernatural death for their greed and dishonesty (Acts 5:1–11), or, like Simon the magician, were severely rebuked for thinking that money could buy God's grace (Acts 8:9–24).

The chief resource upon which believers can rely is the Spirit. Jesus was anointed with and filled with the power of the Spirit (e.g. Luke 3:22, 4:1, 14). The disciples become pilgrim witnesses to Jesus when the Spirit comes upon them (Acts 1:8, 2:1–4). There are other hints in the Gospel and Acts of further resources upon which to draw. The remembered deeds and character of the earliest followers of Jesus were a source upon which others could draw: the Council of Jerusalem, consisting of the apostles and the elders, and with the consent of the whole church, approved the Gentile mission, including the words 'it has seemed good to the Holy Spirit and to us' (Acts 15:28). Luke hardly ever calls Paul an apostle (Acts 14:4 and 14 are rare exceptions), though he admired him greatly and plays down divisions between him and other church leaders. There is not much of a hint of the tensions that Paul recalls about the meeting at Jerusalem, and the divisions between him and Peter, James and John about the terms upon which Gentiles could become heirs to God's covenant promises to the Jews (Galatians 2:1–14). Also, although Luke records some tensions in the early church (such as the condemnation of Ananias, Sapphira and Simon the magician), the squabbles and immoralities that Paul candidly admits and condemns in the church at Corinth are barely hinted at in Luke's assessment of Christian character and behaviour. Further, in his Gospel's account of Peter's confession of faith in Jesus as the Messiah, Luke omits the subsequent reference to Peter's denial that Jesus must suffer and his designation by Jesus as Satan (9:18–27, cf. Mark 8:27–33; Matthew 16:13–28). For Luke, the Spirit unites Christians with Christ in their life and mission.

Another resource upon which believers can draw, in addition to the Christian character of the apostles, are the two sacraments of baptism and the Lord's Supper. Although their deepest meaning has been the fruit of later and more detailed reflection by theologians of the church, both are important markers of the Christian life for Luke. Acts records many baptisms, associated with the gift of the Spirit. Christians can therefore point to their baptism as identifying them with that of Jesus (Luke 3:21–2). The eucharistic overtones of the story of the journey to Emmaus have already been noted, when Jesus was recognized in the breaking of the bread.

It is a truism, but one worth emphasizing, that Luke's concerns (like those of all the other evangelists) are primarily Christological. So the resources upon which the believer draws for her Christian pilgrimage are all intensely related to Jesus: the baptism he shared, the Spirit that empowered him, the meal he ate with his earliest followers, the life of the kingdom he lived and taught and which was emulated by his earliest followers.

According to Luke, anybody can become a follower of the way of Jesus who repents and is thereby forgiven. To Jesus's words in Mark's Gospel 'I have come to call not the righteous but sinners' (2:17), he adds the words 'to repentance' (5:32). The root meaning of 'repentance' is to change one's mind or way of looking at things. For Luke, it is a gift of God that enables, for example, the tax collector Zacchaeus to strike out on a new way of life (19:1–10). Indeed, Peter preaches that 'God exalted him [Jesus] as Leader and Saviour that he might give repentance to Israel and forgiveness of sins' (Acts 5:31). Yet, as we shall see when discussing the parable of the prodigal son (chapter 3), Luke's Jesus also sometimes teaches the much more subversive notion that God's grace can forgive even the impenitent sinner who is at the end of his tether. Repentance remains an ideal of, not a precondition for, the life of the kingdom.

Luke sees Jesus as the Saviour filled with the Spirit, who proclaims salvation to the poor, the powerless and the outcast. The so-called

Nazareth manifesto, placed at the beginning of Jesus's ministry, quotes Isaiah chapter 61, verses 1f. and chapter 58, verse 6. It illustrates Luke's picture of Jesus as one who is concerned for the poor (e.g. 14:12–14, 16:19–31), sinners (e.g. 5:1–11, 7:36–50), tax collectors (e.g. 18:9–14), women (e.g. 7:11–17, 10:38–42) and Samaritans (e.g. 9:52–6, 10:25–37). (Samaritans were descendants of the people settled in Samaria, in the Northern Kingdom, after the king of Assyria deported the ten tribes in 722 BCE. They developed separate religious practices from mainstream Jews, many of whom treated them as if they were idolaters.) It was natural for Luke to stress a universalist tendency in Jesus's message, since he chose to develop the story of the church's spread among the Gentiles. Quite probably his picture of Jesus was constructed out of real historical memories, but it was also Luke's creative artistry that has preserved a picture of Jesus as compassionate, the champion of the underdog, the spinner of marvellous tales that 'lifted up the lowly' (Luke 1:52).

THE CREATIVE IMAGINATION

Luke's portrait of Jesus and the early church was his creative interpretation of sources, to depict the spread of the gospel during the first two generations of its life. The themes he chose were intended to encourage, to warn and to inspire pilgrims who trod the way of faith in Jesus as the Messiah.

The creative imagination of all the evangelists can be illustrated by examining how differently each of them handles a story common to them all. Let us take the account of Jesus's triumphal entry into Jerusalem, focusing on a few of the interesting similarities and differences (Mark 11:1–10; Matthew 21:1–11; Luke 19:29–40; John 12:12–19). The Synoptic Gospels all begin with Jesus sending two disciples to a nearby village to collect a colt (Matthew includes a donkey with the colt). Jesus tells them to respond to any queries that the Lord had need of him (them, in Matthew). A modern, rationalistic interpretation would be that Jesus had made arrangements for this. More likely, the original readers of the Gospels were impressed by Jesus's prescience in knowing that a colt (or a donkey and a colt) would be there, and that passers-by would (as happens in Mark and Luke) question what the disciples were doing.

The reason for Matthew's curious reference to two animals becomes clear when he (unlike Mark and Luke) quotes from the Hebrew scripture

(Zechariah chapter 9, verse 9, in a slightly different form from the Septuagint that we have, linked with phrases from Isaiah chapter 62, verse 1). This refers to a king riding upon a donkey, and a colt, the foal of a donkey. In employing this example of Hebrew parallelism, the prophet referred only to one animal. Matthew misunderstood his source, and its use of that literary convention. His somewhat literalist inclusion and interpretation of the text is all of a piece with his emphasis upon Jesus as the one who fulfils the Law and the Prophets. Possibly it rather implausibly and comically leads him to sit Jesus on both the colt and the donkey! However, maybe when the text says 'he sat on them' (21.7), it refers to the cloaks upon which Jesus sat, rather than the two animals.

John does not include the Synoptic story of Jesus's foreknowledge but, like Matthew, includes Zechariah chapter 9, verse 9, in a shortened form. However, unlike Matthew, John characteristically makes the point that the disciples did not understand the import of the words, or indeed the event itself, until after Jesus was glorified.

The words of the bystanders are rather different in each Synoptic Gospel (and, for that matter, also in John). In Matthew (which is close to but not identical with Mark's account, where the Old Testament background to the story is implicit) the crowds explicitly say, 'Hosanna to the Son of David! Blessed is the one who comes in the name of the Lord! Hosanna in the highest heaven.' The reference to King David, characteristically for Matthew, links Jesus to Israel's past. Luke's account has the whole multitude of disciples (not the crowds, as in Mark and Matthew) saying 'Blessed is the king who comes in the name of the Lord! Peace in heaven, and glory in the highest heaven.' There is resonance here with the words of the angels to the shepherds in Luke's account of the birth of Jesus (2:14). Among other changes from Mark and Matthew, Luke does not include the expression 'Hosanna', probably because Hebrew would be meaningless to the largely Gentile audience he had in mind.

The context within which the story is told in the Gospels is also instructively different, even though each includes it towards the end of Jesus's life. Let us take Mark's and Matthew's position of the material as an example. Mark has the triumphal entry, followed by the return to Bethany, the cursing of the fig tree, the cleansing of the Temple and the message of the fig tree. Matthew has the entry into Jerusalem, the cleansing of the Temple and the Messianic healings there, and the return to Bethany. This difference in order may seem of trifling importance, but, arguably, it shows Matthew as a more consoling and positive editor of his material than Mark:

> In Mark the impression is given that a prophetic proclamation of punishment on Jerusalem has begun. The fig tree has been cursed and has already begun to wither. In Matthew the addition of the messianic healings after the cleansing of the temple introduces a new factor: it adds to the prophecy of destruction a prophecy of hope.[23]

So the account of Jesus's entry into Jerusalem and its positioning within each evangelist's narrative shows the creative imagination of Matthew, Mark, Luke and John. To re-emphasize: they chose, ordered, edited, elaborated and maybe even created material in order to evoke faith in God, as revealed in Jesus of Nazareth. In this sense, they can be described as creative theologians. Even so, this does not necessarily mean that they were wholly uninterested in matters of historical accuracy. Certain common features can be traced in this story, not least its context towards the close of Jesus's life. It is, of course, possible to be sceptical about this, since the other evangelists may simply have followed Mark's lead. Another common thread is the implicit assumption of the story (explicit in Matthew) that Jesus is the Messiah, even though Luke and John in particular are anxious to emphasize that he came in peace, not as an agent of war. Whether Jesus himself thought that he was the Messiah is another matter, to be raised in Chapter 2.

Contemporary readers of the Gospels also have to exercise their creative imagination and measure it against the balance of historical probability. So, this reader intuits that the evangelists' location of the story at the end of Jesus's life is a real historical memory. Other readers may be more sceptical. At any rate, the narrative will have served the evangelists' purpose if it has drawn the reader into the story and made her confront claims for Jesus that, in him, God worked his purpose for human beings and, indeed, his whole world.

JESUS: A LIFE OUTSIDE CHRISTIANITY

The fact is that Jesus has captured the imagination of many people, not just Christians. He captured the imagination of Islam's prophet, Muhammad (c.570–632), and of many Muslim mystics in the centuries that followed.[24] His picture is found on the walls of the houses of many contemporary pious Hindus, next to other deities from their pantheon.

Many Sikhs, Bahais, Buddhists and members of other faiths identify him as a man of charismatic grace and power, quite unlike ordinary, run-of-the-mill people, though there are contrary voices raised by Ahmadiyya Muslims and some other religious and secular people.[25] Their perceptions have refracted him through the prism of their very different views of the world, and they have interpreted him so as to impose meaning on or draw it out of the extraordinarily diverse contexts in which they live.

Some members of other faiths have even claimed a direct revelation of or about Jesus. The great medieval Muslim mystic Ibn al-Arabi (1165–1240) named Jesus among his teachers. They communicated in visions which shaped his life and teaching about the 'Unity of Being'. He wrote that Jesus 'was my first teacher, the master through whom I returned to God'.[26] Some Indian spiritual leaders claim to have had revelatory access to Jesus. One contemporary example is Baba Virsa Singh, by origin a Sikh. At a place in Gobind Sadan, one of a number of farms he and his followers have reclaimed from barren land in north India, he had a vision of Jesus. Nowadays, a cross and a statue of Jesus mark the spot where Jesus appeared to Baba Virsa Singh. Babaji, as his followers call him, intuits and interprets words from Jesus, appropriate to his present context.[27]

In this process, Ibn al-Arabi, Baba Virsa Singh and others are quite close to the process by which the evangelists compiled the Gospels. There are New Testament scholars who hold that some of the sayings attributed to Jesus were originally the ecstatic utterances of early Christian prophets.[28] These prophets and their listeners believed them to be authentic utterances of the risen Christ, though they were placed by the evangelists in the context of the earthly ministry of Jesus. At any rate, all those who respond to Jesus have needed to exercise their creative imagination to appraise and encounter him. This is so, whether they inhabited first-century Syria or Rome, or reside in India or North America at the brink of the third millennium since he, an obscure Galilean artisan, lived and died.

NOTES

1. Tacitus 1971, 365.
2. See further, Whittaker 1984, 146–9.
3. Suetonius 1957, 197.
4. Whittaker 1984, 149.
5. Grant R. M. 1971, 100–2.

6. Josephus 1965, 49f.
7. Kee 1990, 7f.
8. Theissen and Merz 1998, 76–9.
9. Jeremias 1964, 111–18.
10. Davies 1983, *passim*.
11. See, for example, Funk et al. 1993, 15f.
12. Crossan 1991, 230.
13. Altizer 1997, 37.
14. Crossan 1991, 427–50. Koester 1990, xxx.
15. Jeremias 1964, 7, 36.
16. Such a work is Sparks 1964.
17. Spong 1996, xiv.
18. Grant R. M. 1963, 116.
19. Hooker 1991, 3. I am indebted to Professor Hooker's work for my summary in the previous paragraph.
20. I am inclined to think that the Gospels are a new literary genre. There has been widespread debate about this. A good, brief summary is found in R. E. Brown 1997, 102–7.
21. For a detailed account of Peter's possible association with Mark's Gospel, see Hooker 1991, 5–8.
22. See, for example, Perrin 1974, 200–5.
23. Jones 1994, 127.
24. Muslims would not put my sentence in quite the way I have written it. For them, God, not Muhammad, is the author of the Islamic scripture, the Quran, which contains fascinating information about Jesus. See further, Chapter 5.
25. See further, Chapter 5.
26. Addas 1993, 39.
27. Forward 1998c, 18–21.
28. Perrin 1974, 46f.

2

WHO DO YOU SAY THAT I AM?

O n one occasion, Jesus asked his closest followers, 'Who do people
say that I am?' They offered a variety of answers: John the
Baptizer;[1] Elijah; one of the prophets. But Jesus pressed them for a
personal response: 'But who do *you* say that I am?' (Mark 8:27–30;
Matthew 16:13–20; Luke 9:18–20). This story underlines the point that
theology and history are intertwined in the Gospels. Yet some scholars
have retained the hope that a history of Jesus can be disentangled from
theology.

This chapter briefly examines the quest for the historical Jesus. It
attempts a reconstruction of what can be known of his life, then it
examines what theological claims for him the evangelists are making. In
the process, it explores whether Jesus made any claims for himself, or
characteristically pointed, not inwards, but outwards to God's character
and will for humankind.

THE QUEST FOR THE HISTORICAL JESUS

The European Enlightenment encouraged some scholars to treat the Bible
as they would any other book, and to subject it to historical criticism and
other tools of learning that were then being created or refined. In its early
phase, the quest for the historical Jesus assumed that one could reach
through the maze of myth and legend to locate a figure free from
theological and miraculous accretions. This was hardly the objective
search that many of its practitioners claimed it to be. It reflected
Enlightenment convictions. One such is that the miraculous cannot

happen within an orderly, mechanistic universe. Another is that, whilst it is reasonable to portray Jesus as a heroic figure of extraordinary integrity, it is hardly rational to associate him with God in the way that the Gospels do, or to ascribe miraculous deeds to him. Many lives of Jesus written in the nineteenth and the early twentieth centuries merely reflect the liberal, Enlightenment values of their authors. The colleague of one Cambridge academic who wrote such a work, tartly observed that he had written his autobiography, yet for some unaccountable reason called it *The Jesus of History*. The major criticism of this whole genre was brilliantly made by Albert Schweitzer (1875–1965) in his *The Quest of the Historical Jesus* (1906; first English translation from the German in 1910). He wrote that 'each successive epoch of theology found its own thoughts in Jesus; . . . each individual created Him in accordance with his own character'.[2]

Then came a phase of Jesus research in Germany that emphasized the Christ of faith rather than the Jesus of history. This is associated with the work of Rudolph Bultmann. For him, faith was a post-Easter phenomenon, and it coloured the evangelists' accounts to the point where it is almost impossible to glean any substantial information about Jesus. There is certainly not enough on which to base faith. So faith should be based on the *kerygma* or proclamation about Jesus made by Paul and other early witnesses. Although there are scholars who have bravely attempted to describe and affirm Bultmann's credentials as a historian, in effect his position seems to suggest that history does not matter very much. It recalls the statement of Mohandas Karamchand Gandhi (1869–1948), the *mahatma* or 'great soul' of modern India, that the Sermon on the Mount would be true whether or not Jesus spoke it, or indeed whether Jesus existed at all.[3] Christians have not usually felt able to treat history with that level of indifference.

Precisely because most Christians cannot evade history, either for academic or for pietistic reasons, since Bultmann's heyday there have been many cautious attempts to embark on new quests for the historical Jesus. One of his most distinguished pupils, Ernst Käsemann, began the new quest when he gave a lecture in 1953 to other 'Bultmannians' on 'The Problem of the Historical Jesus'. He and others concentrated largely on attempting to rediscover the teaching of Jesus and its coherence with the early proclamation of the church.[4]

Since then, what may be deemed a third quest, beginning in the 1970s with the works of, especially, Geza Vermes and Ed Sanders, has concentrated on recovering the Jewishness of Jesus. Sanders, in particular, has asked what Jesus did; he and Vermes, what sort of Jew he was. Recent works by other authors have made much of anthropological and sociological tools. There are now significant tributaries to the river of Life of Jesus research.

One interesting recent way of examining the historical truth of the Gospels has been that of the Jesus Seminar. Its members decide on the historical value of sayings of Jesus or incidents in his life by voting with plastic beads: in effect, red means 'I believe this piece of the Gospel story is authentic'; pink indicates 'maybe'; grey, 'probably not'; black is 'definitely not'.[5] This method is based not on the principles of American democracy, but is taken from the practice of translation committees, such as the United Bible Society committees that vote on the critical edition of the Greek text of the New Testament.[6] No doubt, criticisms can be made of this method. Certainly, it seems odd to think that truth is proved or falsified by a majority vote, even of experts in the field. Yet it does draw attention to the fact that committed Christians are willing to take historical criticism very seriously as a tool with which to interpret the Gospels.

Members of the Jesus Seminar thoroughly doubt the historical value of John's Gospel. None of Jesus's words in the fourth Gospel merits a red bead and only one a pink bead (4:44).[7] In contrast, a number of sayings from the Gospel of Thomas merit red or pink beads, though only one supposedly more authentic form of a saying of Jesus is found in Thomas rather than in the canonical Gospels. Specifically, the form of Jesus's story of the mustard seed in Thomas (Logion 20:2–4) is considered worthy of a red bead whereas all the Synoptics' accounts are deemed pink (Mark 4:30–2; Matthew 13:31f.; Luke 13:18f.).[8]

Perhaps many New Testament scholars, not just those of the Jesus Seminar, are too willing to adopt a sceptical attitude towards the New Testament. It is an interesting fact that many scholars of the ancient world are far more generous about the historical worth of their sources than are New Testament academics. One such distinguished scholar, Michael Grant, a former Cambridge don and Vice-Chancellor of the Queen's University, Belfast, has written a recent book about Simon Peter, the disciple, that few reputable New Testament scholars would feel able to write. (He has previously written books on Jesus, Paul and other more secular themes within Roman history.) He accepts the accuracy of many of the New Testament accounts of Peter more readily than most New

Testament scholars. Of course, it may be argued that he mistakes the aims and concerns of his sources. Yet he has a section entitled 'How do we obtain information?', looking at the problems of research and the sources; his is by no means an uncritical survey of these areas.[9] Indeed, many New Testament scholars might be faulted by intelligent outsiders for mistaking detailed textual analysis for historical research, a classic example of mistaking the means for the end. Some can even be fairly reproached for retrojecting Enlightenment philosophical conceptions onto the first-century evidence they sift and evaluate. Many biblical exegetes do not always seem to have a feel for the customs, practices, or 'spirit' of the world they have entered as honest enquirers. (In Chapter 4, we shall illustrate this with reference to the Jewish background of Jesus's life. Moreover, Chapter 5 discusses the reservations Muslims have about the supposed impiety of many engaged in historical criticism of the scriptures.)

There are some books whose disciplined yet imaginative scholarship enables the reader to exercise her creative imagination. One of the best recent books on Jesus is Gerd Theissen's *The Shadow of the Galilean* (1986; English translation, 1987). It reads as a novel. Its narrator is a young first-century Jew called Andreas, who gets drawn into the lives of people whose own lives have been touched by Jesus. Jesus never appears in the book, but his shadow is everywhere. Although written as a narrative novel, it is meticulously researched and footnoted. By the device of corresponding with the fictional Dr Kratzinger at the end of every chapter, Theissen is enabled to justify how he uses contemporary sources to construct his tale.

Theissen's book is a remarkable illustration of the fact that it is possible to locate certain historical facts about Jesus's life and times, even if they are garbed in theology, propaganda or some other raiment. Moreover, in locating these facts, it is possible to be challenged by theological, especially Christological statements: what, if anything, was God working out in the life, death and resurrection of Jesus? This leaves each reader with the demand, who do *you* say that I am?

JESUS'S LIFE: AN OUTLINE

What, then, with confidence can be written of Jesus's life? This section will offer an outline of Jesus's life, aspects of which will be developed later in this book.

Matthew (2:1) and Luke (1:5) tell us that he was born during the reign of Herod the Great. If so, which seems likely, it must have been shortly before that king's death in 4 BCE.[10] Jesus was brought up in the village of Nazareth in Galilee (Mark 1:9; Matthew 2:23; Luke 1:26; John 19:19). His father's name was Joseph (Matthew 1:16; Luke 3:23; John 1:45). His mother was called Mary (Mark 6:3; Matthew 13:55; Luke 1:27). He had brothers: James, Judas and Simon; and a number of sisters (Mark 6:3; Matthew 13:55). He was the first-born (Luke 2:7), and may have been a carpenter or 'worker with materials' by trade (Mark 6:3 describes him as such), like his father Joseph (Matthew 13:55 calls Jesus the son of a carpenter or 'worker with materials', and may deliberately have been correcting Mark on this point). Although the Gospels (like the rest of the New Testament) are written in Greek, Jesus spoke Aramaic, like other Galileans of his day. Whether he ever married is unknown to us. It cannot seriously be argued that he chose not to because of his itinerant life-style. That vocation probably came suddenly to him, perhaps in his late twenties, before which he could easily have been wed. Certainly, his most famous disciple, Peter, was married, since his mother-in-law is mentioned early in Mark's Gospel (1:30; cf. 1 Corinthians 9:5). It is likely that the call of Jesus overrode all other commitments, including family ties (Mark 4:31–5; Matthew 8:22; Luke 9:60).

Probably, Jesus was first of all a disciple of John the Baptizer, but left him because of certain fundamental disagreements about the demands God made of human beings. John emphasized impending, cataclysmic judgement, remedied only by a baptism of repentance. Jesus came to believe in God's willing forgiveness, even of the wicked. Thereafter, Jesus went his own way.

Luke dates John's appearance in the wilderness to 'the fifteenth year of the reign of Emperor Tiberias, when Pontius Pilate was governor of Judaea' (3:1). Tiberias became sole ruler in September, 14 CE, when Augustus died. This would date the emergence of John and, soon after, of Jesus, to the year between August, 28 CE and August, 29 CE. However, Tiberias had been co-ruler in the east of the Empire for three years before he assumed full power. Given that fact, and taking various calendars into account, Luke could have meant any time between January, 26 CE and April, 30 CE. Luke also says that Jesus was about thirty years old when he began his work (3:23), but this is clearly a round figure, and must be treated with some caution. In John's Gospel, the Jews say that Jesus is not yet fifty years old (8:57), another round figure. Given the view that Jesus was born towards the end of Herod the Great's reign, Luke's seems a reasonable estimate.

The length of Jesus's ministry is also uncertain. John mentions at least three Passovers (2:13; 6:4; 11:55), with perhaps a fourth implied (5:1). This would mean that Jesus was itinerant for about three years. The Synoptic Gospels mention only one Passover, and readers would probably infer a shorter period from them of only some months or a year.

Maybe some help can be obtained from the date of Jesus's death. All four Gospels locate it around the Passover festival, and on a Friday (Mark 15:42; Matthew 27:62; Luke 23:54; John 19:31, 42). John (who does not record a Last Supper) presupposes that it was 14 Nisan in the Jewish calendar, the day of preparation for Passover before it began with the hour of darkness (18:28; 19:31). The Synoptic Gospels suggest that Jesus died on 15 Nisan, since the Last Supper of Jesus and his disciples was a Passover meal, which must have been held on the night of 14/15 Nisan (Mark 14:16; Matthew 26:19; Luke 22:13). John could be making the theological point that Jesus is the true Passover lamb, dying at the hour Passover lambs were being slaughtered in the Temple. In his account, the soldiers do not break Jesus's legs, as a fulfilment of the Old Testament saying about the Passover lamb: 'None of his bones shall be broken' (John 19:36; Exodus 12:46). However, the Synoptic accounts are also theologically motivated. Their timing enables the Last Supper, the memorial meal of the new covenant, to be depicted as a replacement of the old covenant's Passover meal, or at least modelled on it. It is therefore difficult to choose between the two accounts.

If John is right, then in the years when Jesus's ministry could have taken place, 14 Nisan would probably have fallen on a Friday in 30 CE and 33 CE. If the Synoptic accounts are correct, then 15 Nisan was probably a Friday in the years 27 CE and 34 CE (and possibly, though less likely, in 31 CE). All in all, the most likely date of Jesus's death is 7 April 30 CE, since 27 CE would be rather early, and 33 CE and 34 CE somewhat late.[11] If this date is correct, then the Synoptic authors were correct that Jesus's ministry is likely to have been shorter rather than longer in length, yet John's would be the correct timing of his death. But this is only a reasonable hypothesis.

The Synoptic and Johannine frameworks of Jesus's career clearly reflect theological concerns more than they offer historical data. It is therefore impossible to construct a credible itinerary of Jesus's ministry, an orderly account of what he did and where he went, except, as we shall see, for the last week of his life. However, it is possible to infer certain likely occurrences, and even the probable order in which they happened. Early on, Jesus called twelve apostles, though the names vary in the different Gospels, and cannot credibly be harmonized (Mark 3:13–19; Matthew 10:1–4; Luke 6:12–16); many others followed him as well. He taught in parables. Although some of these reflect urban situations, many more arise from rural ones. Nazareth was only six kilometres from Sepphoris, which was rebuilt as a major urban centre by Herod Antipas after its destruction in 4 CE. Yet the absence of Sepphoris and of Herod's new capital of Tiberias (there are three indirect references to Tiberias in John chapter 6, verses 1 and 23 and chapter 21, verse 1) from the pages of the Gospels indicates that his audience was mainly people in the countryside. Although Jesus's home province was called 'Galilee of the Gentiles' (Isaiah 8:23, quoted in Matthew 4:14), the majority of the population was Jewish, who based their lives on the Torah. Despite the fact that it was ruled by a Jewish client king of Rome, it was no more free from political, religious and social tension than any other part of Palestine.

Roman rule was not accepted with equanimity by Jews. There had been a number of revolts, or potential revolts, during Jesus's lifetime, in areas under direct and indirect Roman rule. For example, the Romans deposed the client king Archelaus in 6 and imposed direct rule over Judaea and Samaria. A tax assessment at the time when Quirinius was legate of Syria (probably the one recorded in Luke's account of the birth of Jesus – chapter 2, verse 2 – but wrongly located by him a few years earlier), formed the basis for a taxation system there, to be paid directly to Rome. Judas the Galilean inveighed against it on two grounds: only God ruled, so no other ruler could be recognized; and human beings must work to establish God's sole rule. In Roman eyes, this looked like rebellion. Certainly, in practice Judas's words meant that no taxes should be paid. It is not clear whether Judas created any active resistance movement against Rome, but his ideology helped later rebels justify their insurrection. Acts chapter 5, verse 37 maintains that he died violently. Judas's protest illustrates how politics and religion were mixed up in first-century Judaism. No wonder Jesus, with his teaching about the kingly rule of God, was the object both of suspicion and hope. It was in such a potentially explosive context that he taught and healed.

The Synoptic accounts of the last week of Jesus's life, climaxing with his death and its aftermath, seem relatively orderly and coherent. It would be natural that so important a time should be remembered and retold in a connected way in the early church. Towards the end of his career, Jesus went to Jerusalem for the Passover meal. He entered the city on a donkey, probably thereby making a claim, however implicitly, to be the Messiah. He went to the Temple where he overturned the tables of moneylenders and those who sold sacrificial animals. Later in the week, just before his arrest, he shared a meal with his disciples. This meal was probably intended as a symbolic action, forming a new centre of religious life to replace the compromised Temple cult.

These events have the whiff of death about them, even with the benefit of hindsight. Jesus must have known that his actions courted Roman disapproval and would probably end in his arrest and execution. He may have interpreted his Messianic role in the light of his self-understanding as the Son of Man, who suffers to bring in the fullness of the kingdom of God. He may even have thought of himself as the Suffering Servant of Isaiah chapter 52, verse 13 – chapter 53, verse 12. There are echoes of this in Mark chapter 10, verse 45, where like the servant of old, Jesus reflects on giving his life for many. Further, his silence before Pilate (John 19:9) picks up the dumbness of the servant, like a sheep before the shearer (Isaiah 53:7). Probably, however, Jesus as the Suffering Servant was created by the very early church (e.g. Acts 8:32f.), whose Jewish as well as Gentile audience understood its import rather more than Jesus's preferred designation of Son of Man.

No doubt the evangelists exaggerated the impact of the last week of Jesus's life. According to Luke, Cleopas and his companion on the road to Emmaus berate the unrecognized Jesus with the words: 'Are you the only stranger in Jerusalem who does not know the things that have taken place there in these days?' (24:18). But it is possible to underestimate the impact of Jesus's actions, too. His actions certainly brought down the wrath of the Roman authorities upon his head. They would have seen him as a troublemaker, exactly at a time when many people were in Jerusalem for the festival and any disturbance based on religious sensibilities was least welcome. He was arrested at night, when only a few of his supporters were with him. They fled. He was quickly interrogated by some religious leaders, then taken to Pilate, who may have tried unsuccessfully to persuade Herod to deal with the matter. He was condemned, executed, then buried.

This section has summarized what, with some confidence, can be known of the historical Jesus. It ends, tantalizingly, with his followers' belief that God had raised him from death; another example of the symbiosis of history and theology even from the earliest days of the church. What light, then, do the evangelists' accounts of the story of Jesus cast upon who they believed him to be and what they supposed him to have accomplished? And is there any way of assessing Jesus's own perception of these matters?

THE BIRTH STORIES

Only Matthew (1–2) and Luke (1–2) record birth stories about Jesus. Mark begins his Gospel with the story of Jesus and John the Baptizer. John opens with his statement about the divine Word of God becoming flesh in Jesus. It is just possible, though extremely unlikely, that John chapter 1, verse 13 has an allusion to the virgin birth; it refers to children of God, born 'not of blood, or of the will of the flesh or of the will of man, but of God', which to some extent corresponds with the church's traditional teaching about the birth of Jesus. Even if this is an echo of the story of Jesus's virgin birth, John is not sufficiently interested in it to develop it further.

Matthew's and Luke's accounts differ more than they agree. Matthew has the story of a star leading wise men to Jesus. Jesus is born in Bethlehem (which Matthew implies is his home town), then his family flees to Egypt from the wrath of King Herod. They leave just in time to escape the slaughter of male babies in the neighbourhood. The central figure of the story is Joseph; Mary does not speak at all. Matthew traces Jesus's lineage back to Abraham and David. This highlights Jesus's significance as 'King of the Jews' for the Jewish people, as the fulfilment of God's promises to them. The family return from Egypt after the death of Herod, but to Nazareth rather than Bethlehem.

In Luke's Gospel, Mary and Joseph live in Nazareth, and Jesus is born in the courtyard of an inn (so the Gospel infers) at Bethlehem where his parents went during the census held when Quirinius was governor of Syria. Instead of a star leading wise men to Jesus, an angel directs shepherds to him. There is no mention of the slaughter of male infants. The central figure of the story is Mary, and Joseph does not speak at all. Luke's story emphasizes Jesus's status as a marginalized victim of society, echoing the Gospel's theme of Jesus's compassion towards the poor and the vulnerable. Jesus's parents take him to the Temple, nearby in Jerusalem, where Simeon blesses him and declares him to be 'a light for revelation to the Gentiles, and for the glory of your people Israel' (2:32).

It is possible to seek a historical basis for some of the material in the birth stories. For example, the star of Bethlehem may have been one of two events. It has been claimed that there was a conjunction of Jupiter and Saturn in the sign of Pisces observed three times in 7 BCE.[12] Alternatively, Chinese astrologers reported a comet, visible in March, 5 BCE and April, 4 BCE. Luke's misunderstanding about the date and nature of the census under Quirinius has already been mentioned (it was certainly not a registration for the whole world, as chapter 2, verse 1 affirms). Yet Luke and Matthew give very different accounts that cannot easily be reconciled, so seeking agreement where none is intended or really exists may be a pointless exercise. Maybe Matthew's reference to an astrological phenomenon and Luke's mention of a census betray memories of real events that happened near enough to Jesus's birth to be associated with them in the popular imagination. After all, it is a common phenomenon in the history of religions to impute miracles to events surrounding the birth of a religious leader. For example, stories about a supra-natural involvement in the conception of Muhammad were told relatively early on in the history of Islam.[13]

Members of the Jesus Seminar would regard these stories as black material, entirely the creation of the early community, and are probably right to do. It is fair enough to suggest that:

> The virginal conception, the journey to Bethlehem, the birth in a manger, the shepherds, the star and the wise men, and Herod's slaughter of the infants are not facts of history but images and metaphors used by early Christians to speak of the significance of Jesus.[14]

That passage goes on to propound that 'the images and metaphors of the birth stories are ... powerfully true, even though not historically factual'. Indeed, the balance of probability is fairly evenly divided as to whether Jesus was born in Nazareth or Bethlehem, though the former seems more likely. It is likely that Matthew and Luke stressed that Jesus was born in Bethlehem to conform his origins to claims that he was a descendant of David, the foreshadowed Messiah, as they saw it (cf. Micah 4:2–5a). John's Gospel does not mention the tradition that Jesus was born in Bethlehem. Indeed, it seems to assume that he hailed from Nazareth (1:46). John chapter 7, verse 42 indicates a knowledge among a doubtful part of a crowd listening to Jesus that the Messiah should come from Nazareth, rather than Galilee where Jesus in fact originated. This may confirm that John did not know or was not persuaded by the tradition that Jesus was born in Bethlehem. Or it may be a nice example of Johannine irony: little do the doubters know that Jesus was actually born in Bethlehem, yet how important it is for them to believe in him on other, more important grounds!

Some readers may feel short-changed by this method of creative writing, on the grounds that facts are facts and alone are to be trusted as valuable and authentic. This point of view is a modern Western overstatement. Literature and the arts provide examples of truth that are often greater than mere factual exactitude. For example, Charles Dickens's novels about the social and economic depravations of early and mid-Victorian England reveal truths about human behaviour. To ask whether Oliver Twist or Ebenezer Scrooge really existed is to miss the point. It could be retorted that everyone knows how a novel works and does not expect factual accuracy from it, even though a novel may wring the human heart and mightily reveal the human condition. The response to that criticism would then be that readers should recognize that the Gospels were, to some extent, a new and special kind of literature. They are a mixture of factual accuracy, imaginative development and interpretative reflection, undertaken to evoke and sustain faith in Jesus as God's messenger.

Art, poetry, music and many other forms of human expression have interpreted themes from the birth narratives: the Madonna and Child (such as Leonardo da Vinci's *Madonna Litta* on the front cover of this book); the visit of the shepherds or wise men and the flight into Egypt, and other themes. Even a sceptic like the French musician Hector Berlioz (1803–69) found a particular musical language for his *L'enfance du Christ*, far removed from his more public and grandiose styles, that movingly captures its wonder, simplicity and profundity. Here, the creative imagination may plumb truths that mere facts never could.

One of the most powerful images in the birth narratives is, ironically, that of death. In Matthew, the old king, close to his own death, seeks the death of the young child whom he sees as a rival, and wreaks destruction on defenceless children. In Luke, Simeon, who knows from God that he will die once he has seen the Messiah, tells Mary that her child will cause many to fall and rise in Israel: 'and a sword will pierce your own soul too' (2:26, 35).

Some imaginative writers have intuited, in the stories of the birth of the Messiah, the death of old ways of life, and even real death. Two

brilliant examples, one drawn from Matthew, one from Luke, occur in
T. S. Eliot's poetry. In *Journey of the Magi*, one of the Magi reflects, long
years later:

> Were we led all that way for
> Birth or Death? There was a Birth, certainly,
> We had evidence and no doubt. I had seen birth and death,
> But had thought they were different; this Birth was
> Hard and bitter agony for us, like Death, our death.
> We returned to our places, these Kingdoms,
> But no longer at ease here, in the old dispensation,
> With an alien people clutching their gods.
> I should be glad of another death.

And in *A Song for Simeon*, Simeon reflects:

> Before the time of cords and scourges and lamentation
> Grant us thy peace.
> Before the stations of the mountain of desolation,
> Before the certain hour of maternal sorrow,
> Now at this birth season of decease,
> Let the Infant, the still unspeaking and unspoken Word,
> Grant Israel's consolation
> To one who has eighty years and no to-morrow.[15]

Eliot has located a powerful theme within the birth stories themselves.
From the very beginning of Jesus's life, the birth stories tell us, life and
death are inextricably linked. This is a theological point, also cogently
and equally movingly made by Paul, though in a rather different way
(e.g. 2 Corinthians 4:7–12).

Another theological point that Matthew and Luke make in their
accounts of the birth stories is the marvellous creative and re-creative
power of God. The story of the virgin birth has offended modern liberals
because it seems to depreciate human sexual love. That was not the point
of the original story, though it is easy to understand how New Testament
scholars in a post-Victorian and post-permissive society like Britain could
read it back into the original text. Rather, the two evangelists, and no
doubt the traditions from which they drew their separate accounts, were
mindful of the story of God's original creation of the world by his word
of power, recorded in Genesis chapter 1. Just as God worked a great deed
of creation then, so, in Jesus, he creates a new and powerful possibility

for humans to respond, repent and live in his fatherly, kingly presence. Paul makes this point in a straightforward theological way in, for example, Colossians chapter 1, verses 15–20. John, similarly, makes his point in a highly cultivated and theological fashion at the opening of his Gospel, affirming that the divine word of creation, which enlightens all human beings, became flesh in Jesus, in whom is revealed grace and truth (John 1:1–18). John wonderfully weaves together narrative and theology here and elsewhere, whereas Paul is a pastoral theologian, writing letters of instruction, exhortation and encouragement to Christian congregations. However, it is the Synoptic Gospels' genius to make forceful, life-changing theological points through the medium of stories, just as Jesus himself did, stories that are understood only by people of discernment, those 'who have ears to hear' (Mark 4:9; Matthew 11:15; Luke 8:8).

BAPTISM AND THE CALL OF THE DISCIPLES

John the Baptizer appears towards the beginning of all the Gospels. There is no need to doubt that he existed, that he baptized followers in the River Jordan, and that he was arrested and executed by Herod Antipas. Josephus refers to John in his *Antiquities* (18:116–19), though characteristically, and improbably, he turns him into a Hellenistic teacher of virtue. He had the habit of forcing individuals and movements into moulds suitable for his largely Gentile, Roman audience.

The Gospel writers are rather embarrassed by John. All of them, especially the fourth evangelist, emphasize how much greater Jesus was than the Baptizer. He disappears from the scene soon after Jesus's ministry begins. Mark's and Matthew's accounts (Mark 6:14–29; Matthew 14:1–12; cf. Luke 3:19f; 9:7–9) record that John's death was ordered by the wife of King Herod Antipas. John had condemned Herod for marrying Herodias, because she had previously been married to his brother Philip (Mark 6:17; Matthew 14:3). So when the opportunity arose, she took her revenge by having him executed. This does not concur with Josephus's account, which records that Herodias was married to one Herod and that their daughter, Salome, was married to Philip the Tetrarch.[16] The complicated family affairs of Herod the Great's descendants do not figure in Josephus's account of John's death. Rather, he was arrested and put to death on the orders of Herod, lest his eloquence led to some form of sedition.[17]

At any rate, John's and Jesus's careers were not a seamless transition from the one's ministry to the other's, from a lesser to a greater figure, from forerunner to Messiah, as the Gospels might seem to indicate. Luke makes John and Jesus relatives (1:36), but this is highly unlikely. His purpose seems to have been to harmonize the two figures, with Jesus's career taking off and fulfilling John's after John was arrested (Luke 3:20; cf. Mark 1:14; Matthew 4:12). Yet the fourth evangelist records that John's and Jesus's careers coincided to some extent (3:22–4), which is probably true. This suggests that Jesus withdrew from John's circle, and began a career that had, in crucial respects, different emphases. Not all John's disciples left with him; many, indeed most, may have stayed loyal to the memory of the Baptizer for years thereafter. There is evidence in Acts (18:24–19:7) that John had followers even many years after his own death and the death of Jesus.

Why would Jesus have come to differ with the Baptizer, and parted company with him? The Synoptic Gospels (Mark 1:1–6; Matthew 3:1–10; Luke 3:1–14) portray John as a preacher, calling all Israel to repentance. Many people responded to him, especially sinners such as tax collectors, prostitutes and soldiers. The theme of judgement is emphasized only in the Q material of Matthew and Luke, though it seems to be authentic. All four Gospels claim that John pointed to someone coming after him, described as 'more powerful' by the Synoptic writers (Mark 1:7; Matthew 3:11; Luke 3:16; cf. John 1.27). There is much debate about whether John was originally referring to a human representative of God, whom the Gospels believe to be Jesus, or to God himself. Certainly, John does not seem to have been convinced that Jesus was the one who was to come after him. From prison, he sent messengers to ask if Jesus was that figure, which implies serious doubts that he was (Matthew 11:3; Luke 7:19).

John the Baptizer believed in an imminent, cataclysmic, apocalyptic judgement. But Jesus saw an important and radical break between his work and John's. In Matthew chapter 11, Jesus reflects on the importance of John (cf. Luke 7:24–8, 16:16). In verses 7 to 11, Jesus affirms that John is a prophet and more than a prophet. This section is very early, since the sarcastic reference to 'a reed shaken by the wind' refers to coinage struck by Herod Antipas before 28, which had a reed on it. Unlike Herod, John is no pampered royal figure. Rather, he is the one who fulfils Malachi's prophecy (3:1, 4:5) of a preparatory messenger to the coming Elijah. Even so, Jesus goes on to say that:

Truly I tell you, among those born of women no one has arisen greater
than John the Baptizer; yet the least in the kingdom of heaven is greater
than he. (11:11)

Why should John be rebuked? Perhaps because 'martyr he may have
been, but he and his message lacked the dimension of gentleness, and that
made John's yoke hard to bear',[18] unlike the easy yoke of Jesus (11:30).

The differences between them must have centred on aspects of John's
message of judgement. Mark describes John's baptism as 'a baptism of
repentance for the forgiveness of sins' (1:4). The Baptizer baptized people
so they could escape from the imminent judgement of God. His ascetic
lifestyle (he ate locusts and wild honey, and wore clothing of camel's hair
girt with a leather belt) was modified by Jesus, who was condemned by
opponents as a 'glutton and a drunkard' (Matthew 11:19). In contrast to
John's more austere message of a catastrophic and imminent judgement,
Jesus developed a sense of God's present grace and goodness, with the
offer of forgiveness to the unbaptized sinner (such as Zacchaeus the tax
collector, recorded in Luke chapter 19, verses 1–10).

Mark straightforwardly records that Jesus was baptized by John in the
Jordan (1:9). Matthew makes John refuse to baptize Jesus, saying that
Jesus must baptize him. However, Jesus insists that John baptize him 'to
fulfil all righteousness'; this makes it clear that Jesus was not baptized as
a sinner (3:13–15). In John's account, Jesus comes to John bearing the
sins of the world, not his own sins. There is no baptism by John, who
witnesses to Jesus as the one who baptizes with the spirit (1:29–34). In
Luke, John has been arrested before Jesus is baptized; he records that
Jesus was baptized when all the people were baptized (3:18–21).

The evangelists' embarrassment about John's baptism of Jesus would
therefore have been to some extent a result of the fact that Jesus first
associated himself with John's radical message of judgement, before he
changed his mind and developed his own more gracious and hospitable
understanding of God's reign. Also, from their perspective about Jesus, it
seemed inconceivable that he should have submitted to a baptism of
repentance for the forgiveness of sins. For instance, although Mark and
Luke preserve a tradition that Jesus said that only God was good,
Matthew rather clumsily modifies it to play down the implication that
Jesus was no more a good person than anyone else (Mark 10:18; Luke
18:19; cf. Matthew 19:17).

Luke records a saying from Jesus that 'the law and the prophets were in effect until John came; since then the good news of the kingdom of God is proclaimed, and everyone tries to enter it by force' (16:16). This interprets the Baptizer as a figure of an age that is past, a point that is strengthened by another saying in Luke and in Matthew's: 'I tell you, among those born of women no one is greater than John; yet the least in the kingdom of God is greater than he' (Luke 7:28; cf. Matthew 12:11).

JESUS AND CHRISTOLOGICAL TITLES

Because the evangelists played down the importance of John so as to raise that of Jesus, it is unclear what role John himself or his followers thought he played. Despite the fourth evangelist's protestations to the contrary (1:21), it is quite likely that John was believed by many (maybe even by himself) to be Elijah, the figure heralding the end-times. Certainly, there are indications that John and Elijah could be spoken of in the same breath (Mark 8:28; Matthew 16:14; Luke 9:19).

It may be that, in rejecting or at least modifying John's somewhat baleful description of God, Jesus became wary of using titles about God's messengers, because titles overemphasize certain aspects of God's message and underestimate others. Furthermore, titles draw attention away from the message to the messenger. This is not altogether wrong, since it is natural to ask what sort of person does what kinds of deeds. But it can be a wrong emphasis so closely to characterize the herald that his proclamation is not precisely enough heard. To put this another way, to summarize the descriptions of people like John and Jesus himself as 'titles' may be, in certain important respects, misleading: even neat phrases like 'Lord', 'Rabbi', or others we shall shortly look at in some detail. As important as the status of the messenger himself, if not more so, is the message he brings or the role he fulfils.

Nevertheless, Jesus could hardly have avoided facing the fact that people would have asked who he was. The history of Israel had produced kings, prophets and priests, so his contemporaries would have drawn analogies with these and other aspects of their heritage when they came to ask 'by what authority' (Mark 11:28; Matthew 21:23; Luke 20:2) Jesus healed and taught. It may be appropriate, and even possible, to offer a convincing and coherent account of who Jesus thought he was, so long as we bear in mind just how provisional and equivocal such an estimate must be. That is so, not just because of the confessional nature of the early traditions but also because Jesus himself seems to have been deliberately ambiguous about accepting or rejecting people's appraisals of his function. There are no certainties here: not even the radical certainty that the sources can yield nothing trustworthy and believable about him. In order to frame an answer to the question, 'Who was Jesus?', we shall examine three designations of him in the Gospels: Son of God, Messiah and Son of Man.

JESUS: SON OF GOD?

The birth stories of Matthew and Luke indicate that Jesus is the Son of God. The very opening of Mark so designates him. Early in John's Gospel, the evangelist records that 'God so loved the world that he gave his only Son, so that everyone who believes in him may not perish but may have eternal life' (3:16).

The Synoptic Gospels affirm that, when Jesus was baptized, God designated him as his Son (Mark 1:11; Matthew 3:17; Luke 3:22), whereas John has the Baptizer bear witness that Jesus is the Son of God (1:34; though this is textually uncertain, and the original may have been 'the Chosen One of God'). After his baptism, the Synoptic Gospels record that Jesus withdrew to the wilderness, where he was tempted for forty days. For Matthew and Luke, these are the temptations of the Son of God. The devil tempts Jesus to turn stones into bread (Matthew 4:3f.; Luke 4:3f.) and to cast himself down from the pinnacle of the Temple so that angels can bear him up (Matthew 4:5–7; Luke 4:9–12). He begins these enticements with the words 'If you are the Son of God', an indication that this title could be interpreted in terms of naked power and wonder-working. Jesus refuses to play the devil's game.

There may be allusion to Jesus's divine Sonship in Mark's brief account of Jesus's temptation: 'And the Spirit drove him out into the wilderness. He was in the wilderness forty days, tempted by Satan, and he was with the wild beasts; and the angels waited on him' (1:12f.). When the Jews left Egypt, they wandered in the wilderness for forty years, where they were created God's people by the gift of covenant and law. Perhaps an echo of Hosea chapter 11, verse 1 lies behind Mark's account: 'out of Egypt I called my son'.

These references to Jesus as the Son of God at the beginning of his career may indicate only the evangelists' convictions and that of the traditions they inherited and used. The Synoptic Gospels' accounts of the beginnings of Jesus's career look highly stylized: the relationship of Jesus to John, Jesus's vocation to be God's son given in baptism, his temptation as the Son, and then the start of his teaching and healing. These events have been considerably edited, to the point where it is no longer possible to assert, with any conviction, that they record a factual outline of the beginnings of Jesus's ministry. Yet the accounts are not historically valueless. They indicate a real break between Jesus and the teaching of John, and it is very likely that others (even Jesus himself) asked Jesus how their teaching differed, by what authority he spoke and acted as he did, and who on earth he was to teach and heal as he did. Whether the authors preserve a real historical tradition that Jesus self-consciously acted as God's Son, and that this is how others regarded him, is more uncertain.

If so, this title would not have been interpreted along the lines of the Nicene Creed's affirmation of him as Son of God. In the Old Testament, the title 'Son of God' never appears, but 'son' was a metaphor for a special relationship between God and certain human groups. We have seen that Hosea refers to Israel as God's son. Angels or other supernatural beings are called God's sons (Job 38:7), and God referred to the dynasty of David, Israel's greatest king, as his son (2 Samuel 7:14; Psalm 2:7). The early church referred to Jesus as God's Son almost from its beginnings: for example, 1 Thessalonians calls Jesus God's Son (1:10).

Jesus characteristically called God 'Father'. Although Matthew very often has him say, 'My father', Mark never has Jesus say this, and the possessive pronoun appears in this phrase only four times in Luke. John records the risen Jesus saying, 'I am ascending to my Father and your Father' (20:17). The historical Jesus may have only said 'Father' and 'Your Father', rather than 'My Father', or he may have used this intimate designation only sparingly.

Joachim Jeremias has argued that Jesus distinctively called God *Abba* (Mark 14:36), an Aramaic word implying an intimate relationship, equivalent to the English word 'Daddy'.[19] Jeremias interprets this to mean that Jesus had a deep and personal relationship with God of a kind that was unknown to his Jewish contemporaries. This has been increasingly disputed. It is certainly the case that God was called 'Father' by other Jews, as he has been, and still is, by millions of people over the centuries in many of the world's religions.[20] Even so, it seems likely that Jesus's designation of God as Abba was particularly characteristic of him. It is attested only twice in rabbinic literature.[21] Moreover, Jesus also encouraged his followers to call God 'Father'. The Lord's Prayer, preserved by Matthew and Luke, begins 'Our Father' (Matthew 6:9) or 'Father' (Luke 11:2), possibly *Abba* in the Aramaic he and his followers would have spoken. Two references to *Abba* in Paul's epistles (Galatians 4:6, Romans 8:15) suggest that this form was used, possibly liturgically, even in the Greek-speaking churches from earliest times.

Paul's letter to the Galatians indicates that he interpreted Jesus's divine Sonship as crucial for human beings to become the children of God:

> But when the fullness of time had come, God sent his Son, born of a woman, born under the law, in order to redeem those who were under the law, so that we might receive adoption as children. And because you are children, God has sent the Spirit of his Son into our hearts, crying, 'Abba! Father!'. So you are no longer a slave but a child, and if a child then also an heir, through God. (4:4–7)

Paul's teaching that humans become children of God because Jesus was his Son is not so far from the Synoptic authors' emphasis that Jesus knew God as Father, and encouraged and enabled his followers to share in that relationship.

In John's Gospel, *huios* (son) is applied to Jesus (by itself or with the genitive, 'of God') over thirty times. Jesus is God's only Son (3:16), a title that implies a very high status, so that Jesus says, 'The Father and I are one' (10:30). However, John's many references to 'the Son' are more important as theological statements than as historical memories.

In addition to those in John, there are three references to 'the Son' in the Synoptic Gospels. One has Jesus say: 'All things have been handed over to me by my Father; and no one knows the Son except the Father, and no one knows the Father except the Son and anyone to whom the Son chooses to reveal him' (Matthew 11:27; Luke 10:22). Jeremias is possibly right that its original form was parabolic. If so, then Jesus was explaining that a son and father know each other intimately and so are best placed to explain each other's inmost thoughts.[22] Even as a parable, this would make the high claim that Jesus knew God very intimately indeed. However, this Matthaean passage has resonances from Ecclesiasticus, chapters 6 and 51, a book from Jewish wisdom literature, and may portray Jesus as being as much a teacher of divine wisdom as an intimate son.

Mark's statement that 'not even the Son' knows the hour when heaven and earth will pass away (13:31f.) occurs in a passage which betrays Mark's heavy editing of traditions, some of which seem inauthentic. Yet the parable of the tenants in the vineyard (Mark 12:1–12; Matthew 21:33–46; Luke 20:9–19) does have a historical core. In it, the owner sends servants to collect the rent, but they are beaten up. In the end, he sends his son, whom the tenants kill. The parable has no hint of resurrection in it, which one would expect if it were wholly a post-Easter creation.[23]

In neither of the two authentic Synoptic passages which refer to 'the Son' would Jesus have straightforwardly called himself by that designation. Rather, he may have been using parable and metaphor to denote what he did, and how he pictured God. Yet behind Jesus's characteristic reticence seems to lie a deep experience of God, lived and shared with his disciples. His designation as God's Son at baptism was probably a creation of the evangelists, but there is no reason to doubt that Jesus had a strong vocation, tied up with a close sense of his closeness to God, whom he called 'Father'. This is preserved in the story of his transfiguration. Jesus took Peter, James and John up the mountain, where he was transfigured before them, so that his face shone and his clothing became white. There, he talked with Moses and Elijah. A voice from a cloud designated him as 'my Son' ('my Son, the beloved' in Mark and Matthew; 'my Son, my chosen' in Luke).

This story makes an interesting comparison with Muhammad's night journey from Makka to Jerusalem, where he met and prayed with several prophets, including Abraham, Moses and Jesus. Then he was taken up into the seventh heaven. Reflecting later upon this experience, Muhammad is said to have uttered: 'I was a prophet when Adam was still between water and clay.'[24] In both cases, the status of the messenger is underlined, doubtless a later addition to each story. Even so, both narratives intend to underline God's call, to Sonship in Jesus's case but to Prophethood in Muhammad's. It is possible to dismiss both stories as historically valueless. However, there was possibly a kernel of historical truth in them. At the very least, they were told to explain their heroes' vocations as central revealers of the divine purpose.

So did Jesus ever call himself 'the Son of God'? Paul may suggest otherwise. He refers to:

The gospel concerning his [God's] Son, who was descended from David according to the flesh, and was declared to be Son of God with power according to the spirit of holiness by resurrection from the dead, Jesus Christ our Lord. (Romans 1:3f.)

This points to Easter as the time after which Jesus was designated 'Son of God' by God himself. But this reflects Paul's own experience as much as the views of other early Christians. Luke traces the title back to Paul's conversion (c.36) in Acts chapter 9, verse 20. Paul associated Jesus with the heavenly Son of God who had called him by a vision. He did not associate the title so much with the lowliness of Jesus's earthly life and Jesus's struggles to identify appropriate words to define how God cared for and related to himself and others.

On balance, it appears unlikely that Jesus ever directly called himself the Son of God, though he did experience God as Father, and shared that experience with others. Yet it was arguably a credible development or elaboration of Jesus's experience of God when Christians soon came to apply the concept of Sonship, with many different shades of meaning, to him whose strong conviction of God's fatherly goodness transformed the lives of so many people whom he met.

JESUS: MESSIAH?

Very early on, the young church believed that Jesus was the Messiah. The opening sentence of the earliest work in the New Testament refers to Jesus Christ (1 Thessalonians 1:1). *Christos* is the Greek translation of the Hebrew *mashiah*, meaning 'anointed'. The followers of Jesus soon came to be called 'Christians' (Acts 11:26). Fascinatingly, Paul characteristically uses 'Christ' almost as an extension of Jesus's name, rather than as a reflective Christological assessment of Jesus, who he was and what he did. His usage confirms both that 'Messiah' was a very early designation for Jesus, and that it soon lost any specific theological or historical meaning as the church spread into the Gentile world. Even for a Hellenized Jew like Paul, it may have carried little dogmatic freight.

Mark begins his Gospel with a reference to Jesus as the Messiah (1:1), and it was the conviction of all the other evangelists that so he was. Yet in their accounts of his words and deeds the application of the title is rather rare, and its appropriateness somewhat ambiguous. Only once, in the fourth Gospel, does Jesus claim in so many words to be the Messiah, and he does so privately to a Samaritan woman (4:25f.). He accepted the designation only on two occasions, and not forthrightly.

The first occasion is recorded by the Synoptic Gospels (Mark 8:27–31; Matthew 16:13–21; Luke 9:18–22), and is that outlined in the first paragraph of this chapter. Jesus asked his disciples what people were saying about him. He then asked what they thought. Peter replied, 'You are the Messiah.' After this point, Matthew differs from Mark and Luke. They record that Jesus gave them strict orders not to tell anyone about it. Matthew maintains that Jesus welcomed Peter's statement (Peter had, in this version, called Jesus 'the Son of the Living God' as well as 'Messiah'), but then went on (as in the two other accounts) to warn them against broadcasting this view. It is followed, in Mark's and Matthew's Gospels but not Luke's, by Jesus rebuking Peter as 'Satan' for not believing that the Messiah must suffer many things and be put to death. (A similar story in John has Peter refer to Jesus as the 'Holy One of God' [6:66–71]. This phrase has Messianic resonances, since an anointed one is thereby holy.)

This is a mysterious scene. Did Jesus actually accept the title or not? Yes, though with reservations, if we follow Matthew; in the other accounts, the most we can say is that he did not straightforwardly refuse it.

The other occasion takes place after Jesus is arrested and brought before the high priest, who asks him, 'Are you the Messiah?' Mark records that Jesus said 'I am' (14:61f.), whereas according to Matthew he replied, ambiguously, 'You have said so' (26:63f.). In Luke's account, the whole assembly asks Jesus the question, which he refuses to answer at all, saying enigmatically, 'If I tell you, you will not believe' (Luke 22:67f.). Here again, ambiguity and enigma prevail.

Both these stories have been worked over before each evangelist set them down (though there is probably a historical core to each). For example, Mark's account of Jesus's frank reply to the high priest leads the interrogator to tear his clothes (14:63). This is picked up by Mark when, as Jesus dies, the veil of the Temple separating the Holy of Holies from the Holy Place, through which passed the high priest, and he alone, only once a year, on the Day of Atonement, was torn in two from top to bottom (15.38). This frankly theological rather than historical record is part of Mark's theme of judgement on certain Jewish religious leaders for failing to recognize God's presence in Jesus. They, and the kind of Temple religion they represent, are doomed (Mark was probably writing shortly after the Roman army destroyed the Temple in 70).[25] Even if these accounts are located in the life of Jesus, rather than the developing early tradition about him, it is difficult to determine with any precision his attitude towards the designation of Messiah.

The puzzling fact that Jesus was called Messiah early on, yet seems to have used it of himself only cautiously and rarely, if at all, is compounded when we look at the world of Judaism in his day. Some biblical scholars hold that many people believed in a coming Messiah, but the evidence suggests that some did whereas others did not. Outside the New Testament, there are about thirty references to the Messiah in existent Jewish literature from the period of about 200 BCE to 100 CE.

The Old Testament offers two roots of Messianic expectation. One was a ritual of anointing, attested for historical figures (especially kings, but also high priests and prophets) but not for future redeemers. The second were Messianic figures who, to be such, needed to fulfil three criteria: they must usher in a definitive and new state in the world; they must bring salvation, certainly to Israel and often more widely; and they must differ from the general run of humankind by their closeness to God.

Although some New Testament writers refer to Jesus's Davidic descent, there is one indication in the Synoptic Gospels that, even if Israel's greatest king was his ancestor, Jesus did not think it to be of crucial import (Mark 12:35–7; Matthew 22:41–6; Luke 20:41–4). In as much as kingly associations had political consequences, even leading some to hope for the removal of Roman authority by force if necessary, Jesus would have had little time for the designation of Messiah. After all, God's universal fatherly goodness is rarely best expressed through the medium of violent revolution. Moreover, as we have argued, Jesus's break with John possibly led him to be careful about the use of titles. Titles can obscure as much as they reveal the import of the words and deeds of God's messengers. Jesus respected John, but had sharp disagreements with him whom some may have called the Messiah or Elijah or the Prophet (of the end-times?) (John 1:20f.). He probably suspected that when people called John or himself Lord, Messiah, Rabbi or whatever, they conformed them to their hopes. He would rather that such people were transformed by God's grace as he taught and lived it.

Even so, Jesus wanted a reaction to his words and deeds. This is indicated in many places in the Gospels, particularly by the parable of the sower in Mark chapter 4, verses 1–12 and parallels, to be discussed in chapter 3. So the ambiguities in the Gospel records may reflect not only the variant forms of the traditions as they were transmitted, but Jesus's own ambivalence towards people's assessments of him. His deliberately provocative and deceptively imprecise Christological utterances suggest that they may have been framed to urge his questioners to consider: you may think I am the Messiah and, in some senses I am, yet it is for you to work out in what ways I am and in what ways I am not.

There is an irony here for fundamentalist readers of scripture. What if we glimpse, through the records of the Gospels, a man who was more interested in encouraging people to think about God's way in his world and their possible responses to it, than he was in giving transparently clear guidance? The Quran, the holy book of Islam, describes itself as 'a Clear Sign' (98:1); though it has not always seemed so to its readers. The New Testament, certainly the Gospel records, aim at something rather different: the *struggle* to understand that commitment to God's kingdom is important,[26] more so than the self-satisfied and often shallow human certainties of some of Jesus's followers, from Peter onwards.

JESUS: SON OF MAN?

Perhaps the strangest of all designations attached to Jesus, if it was, is that of the 'Son of Man'. There is widespread controversy as to whether Jesus actually used the title of himself or of someone else; or whether, as some scholars think, it was entirely a creation of the early church. Those who believe it was part of the early tradition about Jesus have to answer the question of why it is so often on his lips in the Gospels. Compared with the rare uses of 'Son of God' and 'Messiah' ascribed to him, the title 'Son of Man' occurs eighty-two times in the Gospels, in almost every case as a self-designation by Jesus. He never explains its meaning. Nowhere is Jesus ever directly called the Son of Man by anyone else. Elsewhere in the New Testament, it occurs only four times and only in one of these cases (Acts 7:56) does it contain the definite article. So far as we can tell, it was not a title used in worship by the early church. No wonder, then, that in John 12:34 the crowd say to Jesus, 'Who is this Son of Man?'; their bewilderment has been shared by many readers of the Gospels to this day.

There are three kinds of Son of Man sayings in the Gospels: present activity, suffering, and future coming. Let us take Mark as an example. He includes fourteen 'the Son of Man' sayings. Two of these denote present activity: chapter 2, verse 10 (cf. Matthew 9:6; Luke 5:24 – 'the Son of Man has authority on earth to forgive sins') and chapter 2, verse 27 (cf. Matthew 12:8; Luke 6:5 – 'the Son of Man is Lord even of the sabbath'). There are nine sayings that speak of Jesus's suffering, death and rising again, including three so-called Passion predictions, for example chapter 9, verse 31 (cf. Matthew 17:22f.; Luke 9:44 – 'The Son of Man is to be betrayed into human hands, and they will kill him, and three days after being killed, he will rise again'). There are three sayings that refer to a future figure, for example chapter 13, verse 26 (cf. Matthew 24:30; Luke 21:27 – 'Then they will see "the Son of Man coming in clouds" with great power and glory').

These distinctions are not as clear cut as has sometimes been assumed. For example, when Jesus says that 'the Son of Man came not to be served but to serve, and to give his life a ransom for many' (Mark 10:45; Matthew 10:28), this includes both his present activity and his suffering.

The designation must come from a Jewish background, since the phrase 'the Son of Man' is stilted Greek. Exactly, or even approximately, from where has proved controversial. In the Old Testament it is used as a synonym for a human being (e.g. Psalm 8:4). Throughout Ezekiel and in Daniel chapter 8, verse 17, the prophet of the book is referred to as 'Son of Man'. Indeed, in ordinary conversation, the Aramaic equivalents would mean human beings generally, some indefinite person or (though this is disputed) 'I' as a circumlocution. Certainly, according to Jeremias, there are many Son of Man sayings which can simply be replaced by 'I'.[27] Although Jeremias does not believe that the Aramaic is a periphrasis for 'I', Geza Vermes has argued otherwise.[28] However, it seems odd and inconsequential to think that Jesus used this rather convoluted designation just to mean 'I', rather like the royal 'we' or 'one'.

The term can also be found in visionary language, especially in Daniel chapter 7, which can be dated between 167 and 164 BCE. In a vision, animals representing successive world powers are destroyed by God. Then, the writer records:

I saw one like a Son of Man coming with the clouds of heaven. And he came to the Ancient One and was presented before him. To him was given dominion and glory and kingship, that all peoples, nations, and languages should serve him. His dominion is an everlasting dominion that shall not pass away, and his kingship is one that shall never be destroyed. (7:13f.)

How to interpret this figure, the Son of Man, is uncertain. He could stand for a collective entity of Israel, just as the beasts stood for other nations, or else he could be an individual, not necessarily a man but possibly an angel (as in Daniel chapter 8, verses 15f.). Two later Jewish accounts, the Similitudes of Ethiopic Enoch 37–71 and IV Ezra 13, developed Daniel chapter 7 along apocalyptic lines. The latter can be dated to the end of the first century, though the former's dating is disputed. In different ways, these passages turned the Son of Man into a Messianic and primordial figure of the end-time; an apocalyptic judge, if you will.

A number of New Testament scholars have depicted the Son of Man figure in the Gospels along the lines of these two Jewish interpreters of Daniel chapter 7. Many German scholars have argued that Jesus spoke about a coming, eschatalogical figure and that the early church then identified Jesus with this figure after the resurrection. In due course, other 'Son of Man' sayings about his present activity and suffering were created by the community and placed on Jesus's lips. Quite why this should have happened is unclear.

Perhaps a better starting point is to recognize that Daniel chapter 7, verses 13f. need not be developed along the lines of the Similitudes of Ethiopic Enoch 37–71 and IV Ezra 13. They establish that it was an important source for reflection by Jews around or a little after the time of Jesus's life and the development of the early Christian traditions about him. It may be that Jesus used this Danielic designation of himself in his own eccentric way. That seems more likely than that the church made it up about him, considering its almost total absence in early Christian writings outside the Gospels. However, if this is the case, it means only that we can be moderately sure that Jesus used it of himself, not that we know for certain what he meant by it. The evangelists could have misinterpreted the appellation, or developed it inappropriately. Certainly, they do not offer us a straightforward and coherent interpretation of what it meant for Jesus.

Even so, a reasonable estimation of what it meant to him can be attempted. If he drew on images of 'man' in the Psalms, Ezekiel and Daniel, a credible picture can be drawn of a human being, born to suffer and die, as are all people, yet one who is called and vindicated by God. Psalm 8, verses 4f. describes the Son of Man as, from the perspective of God's handiwork in creation, very little indeed; yet from another perspective, he is a little lower than God (or divine beings, or angels). So Jesus might be indicating that it is as a man, born to die, that he is able to proclaim and embody God's kingly rule. Perhaps he saw his identification with 'the Son of Man' as a useful corrective to more powerful and violent interpretations of the designation of Messiah. When Peter called him Messiah, Jesus told the disciples to keep silence but then proceeded to talk quite openly about the sufferings of the Son of Man. Peter could not accept this, so Jesus named him 'Satan', the 'adversary' who tempts him away from his destiny as suffering Son of Man towards the misconceived goal of a more political and brutal restoration of Israel.

'WHERE DID THIS MAN GET ALL THIS?'

The titles of 'Son of God', 'Messiah' and 'Son of Man' not only arise out of Israel's past, but also claim for Jesus a role in the future of the people of God. There is another interesting indication of this. It is likely that the stories that Jesus called twelve apostles (Mark 3:13–19; Matthew 10:1–4; Luke 6:13–16) contain a kernel of historical truth. No doubt he had in mind the twelve tribes of Israel, and therefore chose a group of people who would bring about the restoration of Israel (for ten of the tribes had long before disappeared, after the fall of the Northern Kingdom in 722 BCE). It is remarkable that he does not include himself among them, but stands outside their number. What an extraordinary and impressively implicit claim to authority is being made here.

Mark records that Jesus went to his home town of Nazareth, and began to teach in this synagogue. Many were astounded by his teaching, and said:

> 'Where did this man get all this? What is this wisdom that has been given to him? What deeds of power are being done by his hands! Is not this the carpenter, the son of Mary and brother of James and Joses and Judas and Simon, and are not his sisters here with us?' And they took offence at him. (6:2–3)

No wonder Jesus was amazed at their unbelief (6:6). Familiarity breeds contempt or, as Jesus put it, 'Prophets are not without honour, except in their home town, and among their own kin, and in their own house' (Mark 6:1–6). However, the opening question that the Nazarenes ask poses the issue of Christology. The Greek is *pothen touto tauta*: literally, 'whence to this [man] these things?, or, as the New Revised Standard Version more idiomatically has it, 'Where did this man get all this?'

From God, Mark would say; and with him, the other evangelists and writers of the other documents of the New Testament, and countless millions of Christians since. Yet this was not the only deduction, as Mark well knew. In Jesus's lifetime, some refused to believe that a person they had known from childhood could speak authoritatively from God. Others assumed the origin of his teaching and deeds was evil rather than good (Mark 3.22). Why should what he said and did, and the origin of these, arouse such strong feelings? To his words and actions, we turn in Chapter 3.

Notes

1. I have used 'Baptizer' rather than the more usual 'Baptist', since that word describes what John did. He was certainly not a member of a relatively modern Christian denomination.
2. Schweitzer 1954, 4.
3. Räisänen 1997, 177.
4. J. M. Robinson, 1959, 12-19.
5. Funk et al., 1993, 34–7; Borg 1997, 4f.; Shorto 1997, 5–8.
6. This and much more information can be garnered from the website of the Jesus Seminar at http://religion.rutgers.edu/jseminar. The article there by Robert J. Miller on *The Jesus Seminar and its Critics* is particularly informative and thought-provoking.
7. Funk et al. 1993, 550.
8. Ibid., 549.
9. M. Grant 1994, 3-50.
10. The division between BC (Before Christ) and AD (*Anno Domini*, 'the year of the Lord') was first made in the sixth century by Dionysius Exiguus. Previously, the usual way of dating had been from the foundation of Rome. He chose the year 754 from Rome's founding as Jesus's birth year. This is most likely too late, because Herod probably died in 750.
11. Jeremias 1964, 36–41.
12. Stauffer 1960, 36–43. He offers a most interesting but, to me, unconvincing defence of the historicity of the birth stories.
13. Forward 1997, 9, 116.
14. Borg 1997, 6.
15. Eliot 1954, 98f.
16. Josephus 1965, 93.
17. Ibid., 81–5.
18. Jones 1994, 73.
19. Jeremias 1971, 61–8.
20. Cracknell 1986, 85–98.
21. Theissen and Merz 1998, 308.
22. Jeremias 1971, 59–61.
23. Theissen and Merz 1998, 429f.
24. Forward 1997, 43–5.
25. On the Sadducees, and their involvement in the death of Jesus, see Chapter 4.
26. Struggle (Arabic: *jihad*) is important for the reader of the Quran too. (See Forward 1997, 60.) My purpose in making comparisons is not to score points, but to suggest differences of emphasis.
27. Jeremias 1971, 258–76.
28. Vermes 1973, 160–91.

3

THE KINGDOM OF GOD HAS COME NEAR

A t the beginning of Jesus's vocation, Mark summarizes his teaching
thus: 'The time is fulfilled, and the kingdom of God has come near;
repent, and believe in the gospel' (1:15). This could be Jesus's own
summary, but it is more likely to be Mark's, placed at the beginning of
Jesus's ministry as a concise interpretation of it.

It proclaims Jesus as the climax of God's promises, which are now
accomplished in his ministry. It interprets the sort of God that God is:
kingly, demanding and caring. It establishes the gospel, or good news, as
a gracious and alluring claim upon all who hear it. It requires a response:
not to respond is to make a negative answer to God's offer of forgiveness.
This chapter looks at Jesus's teaching of the kingdom.

THE LORD'S PRAYER

It is possible to detect traces of Jesus's own summary of his teaching in
the Lord's Prayer. Although a few scholars have argued that this prayer
was created by the early church to correspond to the Jewish daily prayer,
the *shema*,[1] this is most unlikely. True, Matthew interprets it as a more
appropriate prayer for Christians than the long-winded pieties of certain
pagans of his day. His version has a liturgical form, reflecting its use in
Christian worship. Luke's is more succinct, but this does not mean it is
the earlier form. It is impossible to be absolutely sure of the original
prayer. Probably each evangelist inherited a different version, so that it is
now impossible to locate its precise form on the lips of Jesus.

In its context in Luke's Gospel, the Lord's Prayer is a model prayer for disciples. One of his followers asks him to teach them to pray, as John the Baptizer taught his disciples. In response:

> He [Jesus] said to them, 'When you pray, say: Father, hallowed be your name. Your kingdom come. Give us each day our daily bread. And forgive our sins, for we ourselves forgive everyone indebted to us. And do not bring us to the time of trial.' (11:2–4).

Luke has already emphasized that Jesus is a man of prayer (6:12; 9:18, 29). Prayer is to characterize those who are his disciples. His version offers five petitions in memorable form: two about God; three concerning the needs of those who follow him.

The petitions about God combine two metaphors for him: father and king. These designations are to be found in the Judaism within which Jesus grew up. The juxtaposition of both images, father *and* king, should warn those who pray with this prayer against sentimentalizing the concept of father as daddy or some other such childish designation. There are indications in the Gospels that discipleship requires one to be child*like* in one's trust in and dependence upon God as parent, but that does not imply a child*ish* mawkishness (Mark 10:13–16; Matthew 19:13–15; Luke 18:15–17).

However, Jesus's emphatic usage of the word 'father' does betoken an unusual degree of intimacy, which he shares with his disciples. Even so, unlike Matthew's version of this prayer, Luke's does not say '*Our* Father'. It is possible to argue that, because the context in Luke is a prayer for disciples, the word 'Our' is redundant. Or else one could infer that the word is inclusive rather than exclusive, not a private possession to be jealously guarded, but an insight into God's nature, potentially open to all to know and share.

God's name is to be hallowed: that is, he is to be revered as holy, and his kingdom is to be prayed for. Jesus emphasized the kingdom of God. Outside the Synoptic Gospels and Acts, the phrase is mentioned in John chapter 3, verses 3 and 5. It is also found in Paul and occasionally elsewhere in the New Testament, but sparingly. The petition, 'Your kingdom come' raises questions about when it will come.

The meaning of the next request, 'Give us each day our daily bread', has been the subject of much discussion. The word Greek word for 'daily' (*epiousion*) has been variously understood as, among other interpretations, 'spiritual' or 'necessary'. Luke's request for this daily bread 'each day' is probably his gloss for the original 'today'. Elsewhere, he emphasizes the need for daily discipleship: followers must take up their cross 'each day' (9:23; cf. Mark 8:34 and Matthew 16:24, where there is no 'daily'). No doubt Luke's audience discerned an allusion to the Eucharist in this reference to bread given 'each day' as one of the means of sustaining ceaseless commitment.

Luke does not imply that divine forgiveness is dependent upon human clemency. Rather, it is only in the trust and perception of God as forgiving that we are enabled to forgive and seek forgiveness. The petition that God should not bring us to the time of trial, or put us to the test, implies that God may test us as he did Jesus in the wilderness (4:1–13). If so, this is not a punishment (any more than Jesus was punished thereby) but a testing of our vocation (cf. Luke 8:13), in which God empowers us to withstand the evil hour.

So the Lord's Prayer is a pithy summary of the Christian vocation. Despite the interpretative evaluation by Luke (possibly even more by Matthew), it is likely that one comes close to Jesus himself in the prayer. This is a thoroughly Jewish prayer. Indeed, one occasionally hears comments that it could be a point of understanding and even common spirituality between contemporary Jews and Christians. This misses two important points. First, although the elements of the prayer can be located in Judaism, the emphasis is Christian. Second, the prayer has a two-thousand-year history as a means of defining who is a Christian and who is not.

THE KINGDOM: NOW OR THEN?

Should there have been a two-thousand-year history after Jesus? Some of his earliest followers believed that the end of this present reality was about to engulf them. Paul's first letter, 1 Thessalonians, responds to a question about those Christian believers who had died (4:13–5:11). Paul answers that they have hope of resurrection on the day of the Lord, along with those Christians who are still alive. This indicates that Paul and many early believers thought that the Lord was soon to return, even though Paul pointed out that the day was not known and would come like a thief in the night.

Jews at the time of Jesus were interested in eschatology, matters concern the *eschata* or last things of this earth. It is important to distinguish between eschatology and apocalyptic (*apokalupsis*: Greek, 'revelation'), though it is not very easy to find an adequate definition for apocalyptic. One definition of apocalypticism, from the Jesus Seminar, is:

> The view that history will come to an end following a cosmic catastrophe and a new age will begin. Such views are frequently expressed in an 'apocalypse': a revelation through a heavenly vision of events to come.[2]

Most members of the Jesus Seminar, and some other scholars, hold fast to a non-apocalyptic Jesus. In their view, a future apocalyptic emphasis in the Gospel narratives, such as is found in some of the Son of Man sayings, is inauthentic. Rather, Jewish notions of wisdom, rather than apocalypse, are the basis of Jesus's teaching of the kingdom. For example, Dominic Crossan contends that 'sapiential eschatology . . . emphasises the *sapientia* [Latin: 'wisdom'] of knowing how to live here and now today so that God's present power is manifestly evident to all . . . In apocalyptic eschatology we are waiting for God to act, but in sapiential eschatology God is waiting for us to act.'[3] Members of the Jesus Seminar do not doubt that some Jews in the first century, such as members of the community that produced the Dead Sea Scrolls, were influenced by apocalyptic. But they do doubt that it was widespread and that Jesus must have been influenced by it. Indeed, since his audience mainly consisted of Galilean labourers, fishermen, shopkeepers, scribes and the like, rather than members of an isolated and disaffected sect, it is doubtful whether he and they would have had much time for such esoteric and life-denying views.

The question is whether the Jesus Seminar's definition of apocalyptic is adequate. To find and agree on a satisfactory definition is a minefield in current New Testament research. Christopher Rowland has carefully argued that a definition of apocalyptic should not be too restricted. He believes that 'apocalyptic seems essentially to be about the revelation of divine mysteries through visions or some other form of immediate disclosure of heavenly truths'. Apocalyptic is not a synonym for eschatology, for apocalyptic is concerned with the revelation of a variety of different matters, not just with the end or ends of things. Rowland suggests that the baptism of Jesus may denote an apocalyptic experience. He possibly had other such experiences, such as that recorded by Luke: 'I watched Satan fall from heaven like a flash of lightning' (10:18).[4]

In the present state of research, it may be that eschatology provides us with a better key than apocalyptic for unlocking the meaning of Jesus's words and deeds. Whether many Jews were interested in apocalyptic visions is debatable. However, many more Jews would have been interested in the end or ends of things, because (unlike Hindus and Buddhists, as we shall see in Chapter 5) they believed in a linear view of history. But not all saw the last things in an apocalyptic way, though some Jewish writings of the period did.

It is also possible that groups could have seen the transformation of the present world order in apocalyptic terms, yet believed that the result would be a reformed world rather than its winding up. In other words, the world would not be destroyed; rather, the present world order would be replaced by a 'converted' one. It may be that more Jews believed in the transformation of the world than in its destruction. Some would have seen the defeat of the Romans and the restoration of God's rule over Israel as desirable and achievable goals. Others, however, would have held the world to be so evil that it had to be destroyed.

What did Jesus think? In the Lord's Prayer he taught his disciples to pray for the coming of the kingdom. The gloss of Matthew's account 'Your will be done, on earth as it is in heaven' (6:10), emphasizes the important fact that God's rule is secure in heaven, but not on earth, where individual and structural evil was and remains rampant. Nevertheless, as a Jew, Jesus would have been perfectly aware that, in one sense, God rules here and now. The fact that God 'makes his sun rise on the evil and on the good, and sends rain on the righteous and on the unrighteous' (Matthew 5:45) indicates a present environment in which God takes an interest in people, is gracious towards them, and makes demands upon them. Even so, Matthew's addition to the Lord's Prayer indicates a tension between God's present and future rule.

Sometimes, Jesus points forward to the kingdom as a state to be entered upon in the future, perhaps after death. For example, Matthew chapter 7, verse 21 records Jesus saying, 'Not everyone who says to me, "Lord, Lord", will enter the kingdom of heaven, but only the one who does the will of my father in heaven.' Another variation on future statements is that God's rule, now in heaven, will one day transform the earth. So, for example, Matthew's addition to the Lord's Prayer; and also Mark's account of Jesus's saying that 'there is no one who has left house or brothers or sisters or mother or father or children or fields, for my sake and for the sake of the good news, who will not receive a hundredfold now in this age – houses, brothers and sisters, mothers and children, and fields with persecutions – and in the age to come eternal life' (Mark 10:29f.; cf. Matthew 19:29; Luke 18:29f.). Some of the Son of Man sayings, and others too, describe a future cataclysmic event. Mark chapter 13, and its parallels in Matthew and Luke, describe stars falling and the like (vv. 24f.). This does not necessarily betoken the end of the world. Contemporary Western people know that this world would not survive such a calamitous upheaval. People in the ancient world, to whom the stars appeared much nearer than they actually are, may have seen it as a dramatic spectacle, in which the kingdom would come to an earth that would stay in existence, though greatly changed. (I remember a charming occasion when, in India, I was travelling in a car with an elderly Indian peasant woman from a remote village. Suddenly and rather unexpectedly, a parachutist from the Indian army landed nearby. The woman asked me, in all seriousness, whether he was the man from the moon.) Some hearers may even have interpreted Jesus's words for their dramatic and poetic rather than their literal sense!

Jesus's teaching of the coming of the kingdom has led scholars to a number of different interpretations. Some have held that Jesus believed in the future but imminent arrival of the kingdom. Albert Schweitzer thought that he expected it in his own lifetime, and was disappointed when it did not happen. So troubled was Jesus that he hastened to bring it about by going to Jerusalem, there to accept the 'Messianic woes' that he believed would hurry it in.[5] In reaction to this view, C. H. Dodd suggested a 'realized eschatology' in which all eschatalogical expectations were realized in Jesus. In his view, 'nothing in . . . [the teaching of Jesus] is more clearly original than his declaration that the kingdom of God is here. It meant that a hope has become a reality. You no longer look for the reign of God through a telescope; you open your eyes to see.'[6]

Dodd has not convinced people of his interpretation. Against his view is the fact that most of the sayings about the kingdom have a reference which seems to lie in the future, beyond this earthly existence. To be sure, Luke chapter 17, verses 20f. records Jesus saying about the coming of the kingdom, 'The kingdom of God is not coming with things that can be observed; nor will they say, "Look, here it is!" or "There it is!" For, in fact, the kingdom of God is among you.' Yet this passage is within a context of sayings about the future coming of the kingdom, so it is unwise to build too much upon it. Many recent commentators emphatically deny that this saying can be 'spiritualized' to mean that the kingdom is not so much 'among you' as 'within you', a private, inner glow of goodness. Yet such denials may protest too much. The words may intend a recognition by Jesus that every person has an innate capacity for faith, to discern the inner presence of God and let it grow.

Also against the view of those who refute a future reference to kingdom language is the witness of Paul and other early Christians. In 1 Thessalonians chapter 4, verses 13–18, Paul may have had a very 'end-of-the-world' view of the coming of the Lord, when he and all other followers who were alive would be caught up in the clouds, together with the dead, to meet the Lord in the air. It could be that Paul seriously misunderstood Jesus's teaching. If so, it seems more probable that he would have mistaken the *details* of a coming of the Lord than its *fact*. Paul's words could be interpreted instead to mean that Jesus will meet believers in the air and return with them to earth.

Most likely, Jesus had a strong view that his work would ultimately be vindicated by God, when the kingdom would come in power. Either because he was characteristically reticent about spelling that out in detail, or else because early followers poured his words into the moulds of their own hopes and desires rather than his (or for a mixture of both), it is difficult to pin down what precisely he believed. My own belief is that, during his lifetime, Jesus used future, eschatalogical language, anticipating that God would vindicate him soon after he obediently went to Jerusalem as the suffering Son of Man. From our perspective, we can see what he could not know: he was vindicated in resurrection. Many of Paul's contemporaries, although they believed in the resurrection, were sufficiently impressed by other beliefs of their day to look for a further, final coming, to ratify the resurrection. We who live two millennia later can see that they were mistaken. Modern Christians have no need to believe in a second coming, though many do.

Jesus himself saw a link between the present rule of the kingdom and its future full inauguration. His observation, 'If it is by the finger of God that I cast out the demons, then the kingdom of God has come to you' (Luke 11:20; cf. Matthew 12:28), suggests that though the kingdom is a future state, it is anticipated in his words and deeds. Jesus also said:

> From the days of John the Baptizer until now the kingdom of heaven has suffered violence and the violent take it by force. For all the prophets and the law prophesied until John came; and if you are willing to accept it, he is Elijah who is to come. (Matthew 11:12 f.)

It is difficult to determine who are those taking the kingdom by force. They could be wickedly violent men like Herod Antipas or Herod the Great, or religious and political figures of Jesus's day who strive to overpower the rule of God when its message does not suit them. Or, more likely in the context of a wholly new dimension now that the kingdom is proclaimed, Jesus could be urging people to seize the kingdom violently, lest they fail to join the new age it heralds.

This difficult passage does not mean that all previous generations are excluded from the promises of God. Rather, it is a dramatic summons to make a decision about what God is offering in Jesus's words and deeds. Probably Jesus thought it more important for people to recognize what God was actually accomplishing through his agency than to speculate when the kingdom would come in all its fullness. Even so, that future dimension cannot reasonably be excluded from his hopes and his teaching.

We may sum up Jesus's attitude towards the coming of God's kingdom like this. Because he was a Jew, he believed that the kingdom of God was present to some extent, for God created the world and takes an interest in it. He saw the kingdom of God at hand in the outcome of his own preaching and healing. His was a message more gracious and forgiving than John's. Although John was a remarkably important figure in God's purposes, he belonged to the old order. Jesus's works and deeds portended a new age. He believed that the kingdom would come in immeasurably greater power and grace at some point in the future. He probably linked that future moment with his vindication by God. We shall explore this further in the final section of this chapter.

THE STORIES OF JESUS

A characteristic of Jesus's teaching, as of the Lord's Prayer, is that it is memorable. This notable distinction derives from his use of figurative speech. In the Synoptic Gospels, there are short, pithy statements, and parables of the kingdom.

The Synoptic Gospels call all forms of Jesus's figurative discourse, parables, whether they are proverbs, imagery or more extended narratives. This corresponds to the terminology of the Septuagint, which translates the Hebrew *mashal*, which has a similar range of meanings, by the Greek *parabole*. Jesus took up a form that was already known in Judaism yet which flowered in great and peerless profusion in his teaching.

There has been a developing understanding of the meaning of parables. Dodd and Jeremias drew a sharp distinction between parables and allegories. They argued that a parable usually makes one point, often subversive and certainly not commonplace. An allegory overemphasizes the details of the story and makes them equate, in a painstaking and pedantic way, with what they are believed to represent in real life. This position is now very much qualified. John Drury has argued that parables should not be seen as a genre in themselves, unique to Jesus. Indeed, he demonstrates that the Old Testament and other Jewish literature have a number of parables, some of which are strongly allegorical.[7]

It would seem that some of Jesus's parables are allegories, or at least have some allegorical components, whereas others resist allegorization. Some Christian commentators have muddied the water by inappropriately allegorising non-allegorical parables. Take, for instance, St Augustine of Hippo's contrived interpretation of the parable of the good Samaritan. This story (recorded in Luke chapter 10, verses 25–37) tells of a man who went from Jerusalem to Jericho. He was set on by thieves and left for dead. A priest and then a Levite saw him and passed by. Finally, a Samaritan came by, bound up his wounds, put him on his beast and took him to an inn, where he paid for him to be looked after. Augustine's one-for-one match includes, for example: the man is Adam himself; the thieves are the devil and his angels; the priest and Levite signify the priesthood and ministry of the Old Testament, which (in Augustine's view) can profit nothing for salvation; the Samaritan is Jesus; the beast is the flesh in which Jesus came, so the setting on the beast is belief in the incarnation; the inn is the church and its keeper is St Paul.[8] This ingenious elaboration misses the point, which is that the necessary deed of love comes from an unexpected, perhaps despised, source, the Samaritan.

However, in over-reaction to an overtly allegorical interpretation of those parables which are resistant to such an interpretation, some have underestimated the allegorical details of certain parables. Sometimes a parable does seem to have obvious resonances with real life. A parable involves a comparison, and once a comparison is made, then it is natural to compare someone or something in the parable with someone or something in the real life setting. So, in another parable peculiar to Luke, that of the prodigal son (15:11–32), it is probably not unreasonable, in some respects (though, as we shall see, not in all), to interpret the father as God. Further, some parables do, intrinsically, have a strong allegorical component. Mark records three seed parables together (4:1–34). The second tells how God's kingdom can be like the seed that has its own power and will ripen in its own time (vv. 26–9). The third compares the kingdom with the mustard seed which, from small beginnings, flourishes and grows dramatically (vv. 30–2). The first and longest parable is of the sower sowing the seed (vv. 3–8), a story that certainly seems to have an allegorical base.

Some seed fell on the path where the birds ate it, some on rocky ground where it sprang up too quickly, some among the thorns where it was choked, and some in good soil where it brought forth a harvest. The interpretation of the parable (vv. 13–20) has often, on linguistic and other grounds, been seen as a creation of the early church. Certainly, all three parables, both by the way Mark artificially puts them together and in some of the interpretative comments, betray a fairly strong editorial hand. Drury has shown that that the interpretation of the parable of the sower is reflected in incidents later in the Gospel. So Satan's removal of the word that has been sown (4:15) is mirrored in Peter's attempt to remove Jesus's prophecy of his own death. For this reason, Jesus calls Peter 'Satan' (8:31–3). Those who fall away when tribulation comes (4:17) turn out to be the disciples, forsaking Jesus at his arrest (14:43–50). Those who are entranced and led astray by the world's cares and its riches (4:18f.) include the rich young man (10:17–22). The one striking exception is that the good soil, with its abundant crop, is not reflected later in the Gospel. Mark may be 'looking beyond his book, with its famously abrupt ending, to the life of his church; hoping for better things after the resurrection than happened before it'.[9]

Still, despite this setting in Mark's own creative imagination, it may be possible here to detect an echo of Jesus's own reflection on his ministry. The point of the parable of the sower is that some people respond, though many do not or, if they do, have no staying power. Jesus knew this, yet withal remained hopeful, for, by God's grace, his work grew and would flourish. If there is such an echo here of Jesus's understanding of his work, we have a strong implicit Christology: the kingdom is supremely important, yet he brings and proclaims it.

At the end of this section, Mark offers this editorial observation:

> With many such parables he [Jesus] spoke the word to them, as they were able to hear it; he did not speak to them except in parables, but he explained everything in private to his disciples. (vv. 33f.)

This indicates the delicate role of parables. To those who have ears to hear, they unlock meanings about God's kingdom. To those who do not, they are opaque. There is a hint here, and a more clear indication in verses 10–12, that the parables were deliberately misleading. These verses contain a reference to part of Isaiah chapter 6, verses 9f., in which the prophet is told by God that his mission will be unsuccessful. Yet the words of Isaiah should be interpreted as bitter irony rather than with pedantic literalness. Why should God send a prophet whom he knows cannot succeed? Rather, God is saying that his unresponsive people will hear without hearing, and see without seeing; otherwise, perish the thought, they might actually repent!

So Mark, perhaps echoing the historical Jesus himself, was saying to his disciples, 'For God's sake, listen, understand, respond!' The irony is that, in Mark's Gospel (Matthew and Luke tend to tone this down), the disciples are an uncomprehending bunch, while some outsiders show remarkable faith. So, for example, the disciples flee at the crucial moment of Jesus's arrest (14:32–42, 47, 50, 66–72) whilst the Roman centurion at the foot of the cross recognizes that Jesus is God's son (15:39). The saying about the lamp to which people must come, tucked away in the midst of the three seed-parables (4:21f.), shows that Jesus's purpose was to clarify, not to obfuscate.

Moreover, in Mark chapter 12, verse 12, some people realize that Jesus had directed a parable against them: they could well see, and disapprove of, its import. This particular verse comes at the end of the parable of the vineyard (12:1–12), which has a strongly allegorical component. Jeremias tries to account for this and maintain his rather hard distinction between parables and allegories by deeming this parable 'unique'.[10] Clearly, this parable is an allegory: the man is God, the vineyard Israel, the tenants are certain Jews, as any reflection on Isaiah chapter 5, verses 1–7 would indicate. The servants are Old Testament figures, and the son and heir is Jesus himself. In it, the wicked tenants beat up or kill successive servants sent to collect the man's dues. Finally, the man sends his son, who is killed and thrown out of the vineyard. It is difficult to suppose that the entire parable is a post-Easter creation. For Jesus was not killed by certain Jews but by the Romans, as we shall see in Chapter 4, and his body was not thrown out of the vineyard unburied, but was given a burial. Here, we may be in touch with Jesus's own reflection upon Isaiah's passage, and what it portends about his own fate and the fate of many of those who would bring God's message to a recalcitrant and hard-hearted audience.[11]

Perhaps a more important indicator of the efficacy of each story than the recovery of its pristine form, free from allegory and elaboration, is its capacity to shock and challenge people about the nature and values of the kingly rule of God. To those who heard the parable of the prodigal son, it would be shocking for a father to make a spectacle of himself by running to greet his wayward younger son, as it would be for both sons to question his authority in their different ways. This is particularly so in the society in which Jesus lived, where all three characters in the story offend against the concept of honour of a Mediterranean village society. There is a fond and foolish father who divides his estate. There are two shameless sons who accept this shocking decision, which could, in such a time and place as first-century Galilee, imply that they wished he were dead. At the end of the story, their scandalized neighbours would, by coming to the feast held by the father to celebrate his younger son's homecoming, have accepted both back into the solidarity of the community. Yet what of the elder son? He accuses his brother of squandering money on prostitutes, though the story has not previously indicated this (the translation in the New Revised Standard Version, 'dissolute living', in verse 13 is mistaken; the Greek *zon asotos* means 'living wastefully'). He therefore slanders his brother and publicly insults his father; as the elder son, he should have greeted the guests, not stayed away, sulking. At the end of the story, he is the one who is marginalized by his shameful behaviour. And what of the mother? The story is puzzlingly silent about her. What did she think of her sons' actions, and of her husband's? What was her status in this dysfunctional family, and what was the effect of its problems on her acceptance in the community at large?[12]

Even on a more traditional reading of the text, there are some nice incidental points to shock the conventional hearer: for example, a Jewish boy, at the end of his tether, is reduced to working with 'unclean' animals like pigs. Furthermore, it is a very matter-of-fact view of repentance that makes the young man return to his father on the grounds that even his father's hired hands are better off than he. His pretty little speech to his father about have sinned against heaven and before his father is a rather shabby way of ingratiating himself, rather than a statement of deep penitence. Indeed, the term 'repentance' is never mentioned in the story. An important emphasis of the parable is that the lad has no idea of the depth of his father's love, and that his father is interested only in the fact that he has returned, not in the reasons for it. Elsewhere, Luke shows an interest in the sincere repentance of sinners (for example, the story of

Zacchaeus in chapter 19, verses 1–10), but not here. The emphasis is on the father's shocking love, mirroring God's abundant grace for undeserving sinners. This ought to make the hearer puzzle over the real meaning of repentance. Even if, as with Zacchaeus, it implies a change of heart and direction of life, it requires a hard-headed appraisal of the advantages that accrue from such a decision. To some hearers, this rather calculating, self-interested, unsentimental view seems shocking.

Still, it is a feature of Luke's interpretation of Christian faith that it starts from a shrewd assessment of its advantages. The parable of the unjust steward makes this point (16:1–13). In this outrageous story, the manager of a rich man is called to account for squandering property. So the manager summons his master's debtors and dishonestly lessens what they owe him. In this way, he makes himself friends against the evil hour of his dismissal. The parable ends: 'The master commended the dishonest manager because he had acted shrewdly.' A number of embarrassed interpreters point out that the manager is commended for his shrewdness, not his dishonesty. Fair enough; but perhaps they underplay the story's offensive tone, scandalous content and, above all, its humour. If Jesus's audience was largely peasant and poorer rather than richer, would they not be amused at the canny manager's willingness to thumb his nose at a wealthy man who seems to have been rich at other people's expense? And what a surprisingly topsy-turvy world it is, in which a grasping, prosperous man can, in one sense, be compared to God, who approves of those who, from enlightened self-interest if for no better reason, have a radical change of heart. Just as it is a confused, upside-down world in which God's grace can be shown in the dishonourable behaviour of a dysfunctional family.

It is impossible to know the original context of each parable in the life of Jesus (perhaps, like any sensible storyteller, he told the choice ones rather often, to different groups), and quite difficult to separate the words of Jesus from their development in, or even creation by, the early traditions. The parables of the prodigal son and the unjust steward are found only in Luke, and fit that Gospel's emphasis upon the right use of wealth and social position. This does not mean that they are Luke's creations. The fact that the latter story offers a number of different interpretative conclusions (vv. 8b–13), suggests that it has a prehistory and is not simply a creation of the evangelist.

Parables also contain implicit Christologies. Jesus's behaviour matches his words, so that his table-fellowship with sinners (Luke 15:2) is like the father's behaviour in the parable of the prodigal son, which Jesus tells to justify his practice. Yet the major purpose of parables is to underline Jesus's teaching that the kingdom of God (or the kingdom of Heaven as Matthew prefers to call it; in typical Jewish fashion, he chooses not to speak of God directly) has drawn near, and to underline what it entails.

THE MIRACLES OF JESUS

Heirs of the Enlightenment have rather taken against miracles. They have believed in a closed universe, bound by laws of nature which forbid the unwanted intervention of the supernatural. Yet it is clear that Jesus of Nazareth was remembered as a healer and exorcist. Indeed, his Hebrew name, Yehoshua, means 'God is salvation', or even 'God is healing'. Tales of Jesus's abilities as a healer are found in all strands of the traditions about him. What, then, to do?

Some have rationalized the miracles. So, for example, when Jesus walked on the water (Mark 6:45–52; Matthew 14:22–33; cf. John 6:15–21), he stepped on logs of wood he knew were there. When the storm raged above the boat and he said, 'Peace! Be still' (Mark 4:35–41; Matthew 8:23–7; Luke 8:22–5), stillness descended into the hearts of the disciples, which they then psychologically transferred, as it were, to the elements. When Jesus fed the five thousand, it was not with five loaves and two fishes (Mark 6:35–44; Matthew 14:15–21; Luke 9:12–17; cf. John 6:4–14), but with a message that compelled people to share their food with those who had failed to bring any. Such explanations are always trite, often moralizing and sentimental, and occasionally imply that Jesus deliberately set out to trick people by the equivalent of conjuring tricks. It is easier to believe that he healed than that he was such a person.

Some scholars have pointed to widespread stories of miracles in the Hellenistic world. They believe that the stories of healing, exorcism and wonder-working accrued to accounts of Jesus's life and death as early Christianity made its way into the Gentile world.

In the 1970s, two Jewish scholars relocated the miracles within the historical setting of Jesus's life. Geza Vermes pointed out that Honi was a Palestinian rainmaker of the first century BCE, and that the rabbi Hanina ben Dosa, of the first century CE, performed miracles. Both these, like Jesus, claimed a close relationship with God that was, to some extent, independent of the Law. All worked within a charismatic milieu. Morton

Smith argued that Jesus had probably received training as a magician in Egypt. He had been possessed by Beelzebub, had recovered by summoning up the spirit of John the Baptizer from the dead (an eccentric interpretation of Mark chapter 6, verse 6), and used them as mediums to perform magical miracles. Smith also recorded other reasons why Jesus was a magician: he had miraculous foreknowledge, knowledge of demons and spirits, he distributed bewitched food to unite those who ate it.[13]

Smith's argument is unconvincing, as are some of the details of Vermes's. However, they underline that point that Jesus worked within a setting far from that of rationalist modern and postmodern Europe and America. Indeed, social anthropologists have drawn attention to how societies identify miracle from magic, health from sickness and so on. Certainly, the difference between religion and magic is, in large part, a matter of social labelling rather than demonstrable reality.[14] So, the Enlightenment project, literally, to disenchant the world, strip it of mystery and magic, may prevent sophisticated Westerners from understanding how a society like first-century Galilee operated. There, the telling of miracles gave, in certain circumstances, power to the powerless, and offered hope to the dispossessed. Societies that weave stories of the miraculous and the magical can, of course, risk appealing only to the credulous. Yet this need not be so. If the possibility of the miraculous is controlled by social constraints about what it intends to achieve, there may be limits to what it can and cannot accomplish. So what, in the telling of miracle stories, do the Synoptic Gospels intend should be conveyed about Jesus's life?

It is significant that Mark describes Jesus, at the beginning of his ministry, teaching on the sabbath, but does not give details of what he taught. Instead, he tells of Jesus healing a man with an unclean spirit. The response of those standing by was: 'What is this! A new teaching. With authority he commands even the unclean spirits, and they obey him' (1:21–8). So for Mark, miracles could be a kind of teaching. Rather like certain prophets of the Old Testament (e.g. Ezekiel eating a scroll that tasted like honey, then speaking to the people [3:1–11]), teaching could be as much an acted parable as verbal instruction of a doctrinal or ethical kind.

So, perhaps miracles can be described as acted parables. They offer the life of the kingdom just as does the more straightforward teaching of Jesus. Also, like other teaching of Jesus, they contain implicit Christologies. According to Matthew (11:2–6) and Luke (7:18–23), John the Baptizer sent two disciples to him asking:

'Are you the one who is to come, or are we to wait for another?' Jesus answered them, 'Go and tell John what you hear and see: the blind receive their sight, the lame walk, the lepers are cleansed, the deaf hear, the dead are raised, and the poor have good news brought to them. And blessed is anyone who takes no offence at me.'

Even if it be argued that this is tradition about, rather than the words of, Jesus, it shows that, from early days, miracles were imputed to him and interpreted as signs of the kingdom breaking in and of the significance of its messenger.

Miracles can be broken down into different categories. Examples include exorcisms like the removal of the unclean spirits from a man in the country of the Gerasenes to a great herd of swine (Mark 5:1–34; Luke 8:26–39; cf. Matthew 8:28–34), and deliverance miracles, specifically, the stilling of the storm (Mark 4:35–41; Matthew 8:23–7; Luke 8:22–5) and the walking on the water (Mark 6:45–52; Matthew 14:22–33; cf. John 6:15–21). It has been argued that exorcisms can plausibly be located in the ministry of Jesus, whereas deliverance or nature miracles retroject the glorified, post-Easter Christ back into milieu of Galilee. From our modern perspective, that seems credible. It may, however, miss the point of the strangeness of both Jesus and his setting to those of us who inhabit a very different world and wish to accommodate him within it.

The growth of healing ministries is a feature of modern Christianity. Many charismatic churches in Black Africa make a great deal of healing miracles (anthropological and theological reflections from there might cast fascinating light upon first-century Galilee). Even in the Western world, healing ministries abound. Some of these are of dubious moral and theological worth, yet it is difficult to believe that of churches which offer the laying-on of hands and healing Eucharists: misguided, maybe; disreputable, hardly. The insights of Freud, Jung and others into the human unconscious ought to have made rigorously mechanistic and deterministic views of human behaviour seriously questionable. They and their disciples have uncovered the human potential for communicating with the mysterious and the profound within and maybe even outside oneself. If this is so, then at least two aspects of the miracle stories of Jesus might cause modern persons to pause and ponder. The first is whether healing ought to be taken seriously as a sign of God's gracious power. The second is whether Jesus could be described as a psychic. 'Psychic' is a difficult word, with resonances of charlatanism, magic and superstition for many contemporary people. Any interpretation of it must intend to evoke telepathic gifts and deep intuitive skills.

Both aspects of miracle stories might be illustrated by the story of the healing of the woman who had an issue of blood (Mark 5:25–34; Matthew 9:19–22; Luke 8:43–8). Mark's account of this has been tidied up and abbreviated by Luke and, especially, Matthew, at the cost of some fascinating detail. This is a miracle within the miracle of the healing of Jairus's daughter. Jesus is on the way to cure the girl. A woman had been haemorrhaging for twelve years, and had exhausted her wealth and her hopes on many physicians, to no avail. She touched Jesus's cloak, believing it would make her well. Not only did her flow of blood cease, but she felt in her body that she was healed. Jesus knew that power had flowed from him and asked who had touched his clothes. The disciples, exasperated, pointed out that the crowds were pressing against him. The woman came to him in fear and trembling, fell before him and told him the truth. Jesus said: 'Daughter, your faith has made you well; go in peace, and be healed of your disease.'

There are a number of important elements in this story. It is significant that, after we are told that she was healed, Jesus pronounces her so. Here is a link between word and creative power; a Jewish theme going back to the opening of the book of Genesis, and also picked up in the prologue of John's Gospel. More important is the painful reminder of the woman's lack of status. She may have had enough money to waste on physicians, but she is nameless and, until the end of the story, voiceless. In religious terms, her illness made her ritually unclean, though the story does not make an issue of this point. So her lowly status as a woman in a man's society pervades the story. (Interestingly, Jairus is named in Mark and Luke – though not in Matthew – but his daughter is not.) Hearers of the story might find shocking Jesus's description of her action as one of faith. It seems, rather, credulous and irrational. Indeed, later interpretations of this story became so; there used to be a belief among English people that the monarch's touch could heal the sick. However, this judgement may simply betray our contemporary perspective. Within Jesus's (and, for that matter, medieval and early modern English) society, her actions may have been perfectly understandable. Unquestionably, Jesus was sure of her faith. What are the characteristics of such faith? When all else failed, she knew that hope and healing were invested in Jesus, and his promise of God's kingly, healing rule. As in the parable of the prodigal son, she, like him, had reached the end of her tether and, at that point, knew what she must do. Faith is that mixture of desperation, risk and decision.

As for Jesus, he has an intuitive awareness, maybe telepathic gifts, by which he discerns that power has flowed from him as a result of that need and faith. There are other Gospel stories which show his foresight. Some of these are probably creations of the evangelists, to denote his authority and great gifts. Jesus's foreknowledge that a man would ask his disciples why they were taking the donkey (unless the banal explanation is that Jesus contrived this situation), could be such an example (Mark 11:1–6; Matthew 21:1–7; Luke 19:29–35). Yet it is not beyond the bounds of possibility, indeed it is entirely credible, that Jesus possessed deep intuitive and telepathic gifts, even if they have been exaggerated. Such endowments are not proof of Christological status, yet they may denote a man who, by virtue of possessing and exercising them, had the ability to gather people to hear and respond to other things: specifically, the healing, restorative kingdom of God.

Indeed, although some scholars call Jesus a charismatic (Vermes and Theissen, for instance), it may be nearer the mark to deem him a psychic, if one can rid that description of its negative connotations. Certainly, Jesus was charismatic in the sense that he lived in the power of God's spirit (so Luke, at least, would affirm). But charismatic can often be a rather woolly word. So-called charismatic figures have often made very sure of audiences ready to greet them and of acolytes to spread their word, and have a shrewd idea of how to harness social forces.[15] There is simply not enough knowledge about Jesus to know if he was so well organized.

JESUS AND WOMEN

Many books about Jesus point to the surprisingly free and open way in which he related to women, compared with many of his contemporaries and, indeed, compared with men in many different times and cultures. Luke records that women accompanied and financially supported him and the twelve disciples during his travels through Galilee (8:1–3).

Even so, to a large extent the Gospel accounts betray a patriarchal perspective. The anonymity of the woman with the issue of blood is matched by the story of the woman who poured ointment on Jesus's feet (Mark 14:3–9; Matthew 26:6–13; Luke 7:36–50; cf. John 12:1–8, where the woman is named as Mary, sister of Martha and Lazarus). Mark and

Matthew tell us that Jesus was in the house of Simon the Leper, about whom nothing is known but his name. Ironically, the woman is to be universally remembered, not for her name but for her deed: 'She has done what she could; she has anointed my body beforehand for its burial. Truly I tell you, wherever the good news is proclaimed in the whole world, what she has done will be told in remembrance of her.' Similarly, the Canaanite woman whose quick-witted faith caused Jesus to change his mind and heal her daughter is not named, nor is her daughter (Mark 7:24–30; Matthew 15:21–8). Further, we know the name of Jesus's brothers, but not his sisters (Mark 6:3; Matthew 13:55f.).

We do not know whether the seventy (or seventy-two) disciples whom Luke records that Jesus sent out to places as harbingers of his arrival contained women (10:1–16). Given Luke's recognition that Jesus had women followers, it is an intriguing possibility that these twosomes were married couples.

Is the anonymity of these women indicative of the fact that Jesus was more open towards women, not only more open than many of his contemporaries but also than the evangelists and much of their material? If so, early Christian men did not see the full implications of his words and deeds. To establish this point, we need to know something of the attitudes towards women in Galilee. It is likely that many peasant women worked in the fields alongside men, to sow, care for and bring in the harvest. Full seclusion would only have been possible for women of fairly wealthy families. In these families, men may have restricted their women's movements in order to show others that they could afford to. Religious obligations for women were different from those of men. For example, in the Temple, they could go only so far as the Court of the Women. There is no need to make depreciative comments about Judaism. The religious duties of and possibilities open to women have been dictated by men (sometimes with dubious reference to divine sanction) from time immemorial, and still are, including within many Christian circles. Moreover, the onus on women to teach religious precepts and practices to young children in most faiths, illustrates that women did have their sphere of influence. What Jesus seems to have done was to open up possibilities to women that many men and women may have thought inappropriate, and to interact with women who were marginalized by society.

Jesus's healing of the woman with the issue of blood is an example of the latter point. Luke's account of Mary and Martha may be illustrative of the former. Martha welcomed Jesus into her house, and then set about her many tasks. These are not spelled out but no doubt included the preparation of food and drink, since hospitality was an important social custom. Her sister Mary sat at Jesus's feet and listened to him. Then Martha complained to Jesus that Mary was not helping her, and Jesus rebuked her, telling her that her sister had chosen the better part (10:38–42). It is easy to trivialize this story, by pointing out that Martha was fulfilling the expected woman's role whereas Mary was listening and learning. The account is more intriguing and radical than that. Martha welcomed Jesus into her home, so had her own household: no man is mentioned in the story, so presumably the sisters were widowed or unmarried, yet not dependent on male members of their family: a shocking situation. Martha was an unusual woman, but perhaps, in Jesus's eyes, not unusual enough! Her freedom from convention was considerable, but not absolute. The most important of all things, even more important than the obligation of hospitality, is to hear of the kingdom and enter it.

Significantly, in Jesus's parables of the kingdom, women appear alongside men, sometimes (to the chagrin of some proponents of women's rights) in gender-specific roles. For example, take the parables of the lost sheep and the lost coin (Luke 15:3–7, 8–10). Jesus is portraying the world he knew and observed. In it, women were not shepherds nor did men do household chores; if a man had lost a coin, no doubt he would have got his wife, sisters or daughters to search for it. Yet women were not ignored by Jesus's teaching but included in it.

So was Jesus himself an ardent feminist? This is to contemplate anachronistic possibilities. He was a child of his times and culture. That culture, although highly patriarchal, was not immune to change. The impact of Hellenism and Roman rule, the presence of Gentiles as well as Jews in Galilee, at least in the urban centres, was unsettling, yet also raised new possibilities for social transformation. So Jesus would not have been alone in interpreting his religious tradition in socially innovative ways. Furthermore, alongside his remarkably open attitude towards women should be mentioned such things as: twelve male apostles; images in his teaching of women as the object of men's lust (Matthew 5:28) or of patriarchal practices (Matthew 24:38; Luke 17:27). Defenders of a radical Jesus could interpret these, to some extent, conventional attitudes as the creation of the early traditions. It is just as possible, indeed very likely, that Jesus no more saw all the extraordinarily far-reaching possibilities of his attitudes and actions towards women than did his male followers and interpreters. Such a judgement is not to diminish his importance, but simply to locate him as a real human being in a real context.

In Jesus's day and culture, most divorced or childless women would have returned in disgrace to their father's or eldest brother's household. A widow with children would have been looked after by her eldest son, if he was married. Otherwise, her dead husband's family would take her in. A number of stories about Jesus describe him dealing with women who were, uncharacteristically, without male protection. They did not fit into a traditional extended family pattern. What then was Jesus's attitude towards the family?

JESUS AND THE FAMILY

Jesus seems to have forbidden divorce. Its prohibition appears once in Paul (1 Corinthians 7:10f.) and four times in the Synoptic Gospels (Mark 10:2–12; Matthew 5:31f., 19:3–9; Luke 16:18). The Gospels have a long form (Mark and Matthew 19), and a short form (Matthew 5 and Luke); Paul's account is nearer to the short form. It is impossible to know which is more authentic. The short form more or less condemns remarriage of divorced people as adultery. The longer form has Jesus argue that marriage is an act of creation, and Moses permitted divorce only because of the hardness of human hearts. At any rate, like the shorter form, it forbids divorced people to marry again. It would be trite to domesticate Jesus's teaching in the way some church people do. Arguments about the bringing up of children in the security of a married relationship betray a commitment to the nuclear family which would have been foreign, or at least of secondary importance, to Jesus. It is best to note that this perfectionist ethic is characteristic of one strand of Jesus's teaching. It expresses the ideal of the kingdom, breaking in now, hereafter to come in its fullness. In the kingdom to come, families will be harmonious and united.

Jesus faced the fact that the ideal of the kingdom was not yet actualized. His disciple Peter had a mother-in-law, whom Jesus healed (Mark 1:30f.; Matthew 8:14f.; Luke 4:38f.). Was his wife dead, did she stay at home or did she travel around with her husband, following Jesus? It is impossible to tell. Paul records that Peter's wife accompanied him on his travels as a leader of the early church (1 Corinthians 9:5). Was this a new wife? If the same one, was this a continuation of the practice that happened during Jesus's ministry? Again, it is impossible to tell. However, given the diverse scattering of texts on this subject, it would seem most likely that some married couples followed Jesus (with their children?), whereas other people embraced chastity to do so. Certainly, despite his prohibition against divorce, Jesus made responding to the kingdom a greater priority than normal family life. He said to one man, who offered to follow him after his father's funeral, 'Follow me, and let the dead bury their own dead' (Matthew 8:22; cf. Luke 9:60). Jesus's contemporaries would have found this a shocking thing to say, as would a lot of people in many societies these days.

Indeed, Jesus's own family were at odds with his teaching so, scandalously, he rejected them when they came to see him. In a pointed rebuke, he said 'Here are my mother and my brothers! Whoever does the will of God is my brother and sister and mother' (Mark 3:20, 31–5). Both Matthew (12:46–50) and, especially, Luke (8:19–21, 11:27f.) tone this down. It could therefore be that he saw the group of disciples, men and women, who accompanied him, as a kind of substitute family. If so, he must have been frustrated by their inability truly to understand what he had to do, as when, just before his arrest in Gethsemane, Peter, James and John went to sleep instead of supporting him (Mark 14:32–42).

Jesus cannot have been an easy person to follow, to understand or even to like; an obvious fact that much Christian piety underestimates. He quite literally put the fear of God into his close followers. Mark's Gospel in particular emphasizes their slowness in understanding him and their reverence, even fear, at his powers. Indeed, the original ending of the Gospel has the three women who went to anoint his body keep quiet about the resurrection, for they were afraid.

There has been some fascinating though speculative psychological work done about Jesus and his family. Joseph seems absent from Jesus's adult life, so he had probably died before Jesus left his home to follow John the Baptizer and then branch out on his own itinerant ministry (although he could have divorced Mary; if so, perhaps this was responsible for Jesus's vehement attitude towards divorce). Was Jesus's description of God as ideal father forged out of his unresolved relationship with his own father, which ended abruptly? Was his relationship with Mary as idealistic as Luke makes it? Hardly, one imagines. It cannot have been easy for Mary as a mother to see her son leave the family home for the insecure 'career' of a wandering teacher and healer. Further, in the eyes of her neighbours it would have been shameful for her that he did so, since it was the eldest son's role to look after his mother when her husband died or disappeared. Maybe, then, there was a great deal of Jesus's personal agenda invested in, for example, his parable of the prodigal son, in which the elder as well as the younger son break social taboos, and in which the family is deeply dysfunctional. Jesus's brother James was undoubtedly an important figure in the early church, so the family cannot have been irretrievably fractured.[16] Even so, out of the crucible of a family context of bereavement, misunderstanding and fear of social stigma, Jesus may have forged some of his central teaching about God and his kingdom. All this is highly speculative, but it is not foolishly so. From our vantage point after the psychological insights of Sigmund Freud and Carl Jung, it is possible to interpret even ancient material with tools not previously accessible.

Some have gone further, speculating about Jesus's sexuality and his sexual orientation. His capacity to touch, to heal and to empathize cannot cohere with any notion of him as pale, bloodless and asexual, despite the rather odd sentiments of Matthew chapter 19, verses 10–12 about eunuchs who have made themselves eunuchs for the sake of the kingdom. (This exemption could be an extreme way of saying that the need to obey God's rule overrides normal family responsibilities.) It is impossible to know if Jesus was celibate or married (perhaps he was a widower by the time of his teaching and preaching career). If he was celibate, that need not indicate that he was gay. His attractive relationships with both men and women do not indicate a sexual preference for one or the other or, indeed, both. It has sometimes been asserted that his friendship for the beloved disciple (John 13:23) was homosexual in nature and even practice, but in many societies, affectionate and touching (in both senses of the word) male friendships do not betoken physical passion.

It is just possible that passages in the Secret Gospel of Mark imply that Jesus inducted his male disciples in a homosexual initiation rite. The only known fragment from this work is a quotation in a letter of Clement of Alexandria (d. c.215), a copy of which was discovered in 1958 by Morton Smith in the Mar Saba monastery, twelve miles south-east of Jerusalem. Some, but not all, scholars doubt its authenticity.[17] Crossan believes it to be an early version of Mark, dating from the early 70s.[18] At any rate, it contains a story rather close to John's account of the raising of Lazarus. Jesus raises from death the brother of a woman of Bethany. The young man was in the tomb. Jesus went in and revived him by grasping his hand. The text records that they went to the house of the young man, who was rich. There is an addition to the story in the Secret Gospel of Mark that has no parallel in John's Gospel:

> And the young man, looking at Jesus, loved and began to beseech him that he might be with him . . . And after six days Jesus gave him an order; and when the evening had come, the young man went to him, dressed with a linen cloth over his naked body. And he remained with him that night, because Jesus taught him the mystery of the kingdom of God.[19]

Morton Smith argues that this was a secret baptismal rite, illustrating an early libertarian as opposed to legalistic strain within Christian faith and practice. He draws attention to Paul's baptismal language, which he interprets as a ritual for union with Jesus. Although baptism was widely practised in the ancient world, Smith believes that this concept of union with Jesus is unusual and must have come from Jesus himself. He believes that 'by unknown ceremonies', the mystery of the kingdom of God was administered in water baptism by Jesus, and the disciple was possessed by Jesus's spirit and united with him. He comments:

> Freedom from the law may have resulted in completion of the spiritual union by physical union. This certainly occurred in many forms of gnostic Christianity; how early it began there is no telling.

The reader is left to infer that homosexual practices in baptismal initiation can be traced to Jesus himself, and were certainly adopted by some later Christians.[20]

Understandably, many religious people think it shocking, prurient or at least improper to discuss the sexual preferences of a great hero of faith. Perhaps a more astute judgement is that it is a pointless exercise. We have no means of knowing the truth of this matter. Nor is it particularly important that Jesus did not mention homosexuality, either in condemnation or affirmation. He failed to talk about (or at least to persuade others to record his thoughts on) many subjects, and arguing from silence is rarely a useful or worthy endeavour.

Perhaps there is a more credible implicit reference to Jesus's attitude towards human sexual orientation than the lubricious implications of Morton Smith's theory. He healed the Roman centurion's servant (Matthew 8:5–13; Luke 7:1–10). It has been argued that it would have been common gossip that such relationships were sexual. But the text does not afford information on this point, even though it is willing to concede the offensive enough fact (to some) that Jesus would heal for an agent of foreign oppression. Even if the centurion and his servant were lovers, Jesus's act would not necessarily show that he condoned their affair. The Gospels often, indeed usually, portray him dealing with wounded, frail, imperfect humans in deep need; he had no need to heal the whole and the holy (Mark 2:17; Matthew 9:12f.; Luke 5:31f.).

Questions of human sexuality are a matter of concern to the contemporary West, rather than to Jesus's society. Although we might like him to offer a word for all seasons, he does not oblige us. However, we can affirm two things. He was a flesh-and-blood figure: he loved, had compassion, healed, had extraordinarily close and sometimes socially unusual, if not unacceptable, relations with people, subverted usual norms. Because of this, attempts to portray him as an upholder of conventional heterosexual values are as misguided as those that would turn him into a gay icon.

DEATH

The next chapter will consider who was responsible for Jesus's death. This section will examine whether Jesus foresaw and even hastened his own death, and what happened thereafter.

Theological interpretations of Jesus's death were formulated early on. Paul, writing to Christians in Corinth in about late 53 or early 54, observed that 'Christ died for our sins in accordance with the scriptures' (1 Corinthians 15:3). Paul maintains that he is passing on what he has received, so the tradition is somewhat earlier than the date of the letter. This information means that Jesus's execution was not fortuitous, but part of God's purposes. Paul and other writers in the early church thought so. Did Jesus?

The Synoptic Gospels record that Jesus foretold his Passion and resurrection three times (Mark 8:31–3, 9:30–2, 10:32–4; Matthew 16:21–3, 17:22–3, 20:17–19; Luke 9:22, 43b–45, 18:31–4). Although these passages have been worked over by the early church, it is very likely that Jesus realized that his attitude towards the Torah and the Temple, which were deeply offensive to many of his Jewish contemporaries (as we shall see in chapter 4), would set him on a collision course with his co-religionists. When he overthrew the tables of the money changers (Mark

11:15–17; Matthew 21:12–13; Luke 19:45–6; cf. John 2:13–17), this would have drawn the attention of the Roman authorities, especially around the time of Passover when many pilgrims were in Jerusalem and the opportunity for insurrection was high. If Jesus's entry on a donkey had Messianic overtones, or if his enemies could claim to the Romans that it had, he would be at even greater risk of arrest and execution. In Jericho, just before his entry into Jerusalem, he healed blind Bartimaeus, who called him 'Son of David', a title with kingly, Messianic overtones (Mark 10:46–52). By the last week of his life, he was hailed by at least some people as Messiah. Probably, he accepted a Messianic role for himself, even if he wished to reinterpret it so that he was a suffering Son of Man whom, he believed, God would vindicate. Jesus's Last Supper with his twelve disciples had a symbolic and eschatological meaning. He had said that many would come from east and west, and north and south to feast in the kingdom of God (Luke 13:29; cf. Matthew 8:11). Now he said that he would not drink the wine again until he drank it anew with them in the kingdom of God (Mark 14:24f.; Matthew 26:27–9; Luke 22:17–19).

It seems, then, that Jesus believed that God would vindicate him, after which the kingdom would come. There is no reason to suppose that he had a clear idea of what form that vindication would take. The detailed knowledge of the three Passion predictions seems like pious retrojection by early Christians who, from their vantage point, knew what had happened and assumed that Jesus had known in advance what they now knew. Although there are some passages of the Hebrew scriptures which suggest that suffering falls only on the wicked, there are many more that do not. Jesus himself had rejected the notion that there was a straightforward connection between sin and suffering by pointing to two events: Pilate had killed some Galileans at a festival, and eighteen people had died when a tower fell on them at Siloam. Jesus candidly denied it was the fault of the victims (Luke 13:1–5). The events of the last week of his life also show that Jesus knew God's messengers were often killed (e.g. Mark 12:1–12; Matthew 23:34–9); so, it was likely that he, too, would die.

He went his death uncertain how he would be vindicated by God. In Paul's and Luke's accounts of the Last Supper, Jesus said, 'Do this in remembrance of me' (1 Corinthians 11:24f.). Jeremias has argued that Jesus was thereby telling his disciples to implore God to remember the Messiah and bring in the kingdom; until he did, his work was not complete.[21] This is a fascinating possibility but has not gained wide acceptance, though I am inclined to accept it. Perhaps Jesus hoped God would intervene before he died (Mark 14:36; Matthew 26:39; Luke 22:42).

God did not. Jesus was betrayed by a disciple, Judas Iscariot. He was deserted by most of his disciples, except for a few women. He was hastily nailed to a cross to complete his death before the festival of Passover. He died a failure, a broken, frustrated and abandoned man. His last coherent words were quite probably, 'My God, my God, why have you forsaken me?' (Mark 15:34; Matthew 27:46). These come from the opening of Psalm 22, which ends in hope. That psalm was important in the early construction of the Passion narrative. It refers, for example, to the casting of lots for the victim's clothes (v. 18), a theme which is taken up by all the evangelists (Mark 15:24; Matthew 27:35; Luke 23:34; John 19:23f.). This part of the crucifixion story was no doubt created on the basis of the psalm. Yet it seems very likely that Jesus did utter these or some other words of desolation, and that they conveyed his sense of failure, rather than the hope of ultimate triumph. God had not intervened to defend and vindicate him.

RESURRECTION

God's vindication of Jesus came in an unusual way. His closest followers soon came to believe that God had raised Jesus from death. In 1 Corinthians chapter 15, Paul cites what had been the content of his preaching to the people of that Greek city. In short: Christ died for our sins according to the scriptures, he was buried, he rose on the third day according to the scriptures, he was seen by Peter, then by the twelve, then all at once by five hundred believers, then by James and all the apostles, and finally by Paul. This was, Paul wrote, 'the good news that I proclaimed to you, which you in turn received, in which also you stand' (v. 1).

The burden of this passage is that Jesus appeared to people in a visionary experience, such as Paul had had (Acts 9:1–9; Galatians 1:13–17; 2 Corinthians 12:1–10). Some people have denied that these experiences were grounded in a historical reality. They are explained, for example, as mass hypnosis or communal self-deception. Some writers have noted that Paul does not mention an empty tomb, so regard that part of the resurrection story as a later fabrication. Instead, the origins of the Easter story lie in visions by disciples in Galilee, far away from

Jerusalem. There, they could indulge their wishful thinking in flights of fancy. Against this dismissive attitude towards the narratives of the empty tomb, it could be argued that Paul was handing on a solemn, abbreviated, formulaic, perhaps even liturgical summary of the resurrection, not an exhaustive historical overview of it.

However, important theological points were certainly made by the evangelists in the Synoptic Gospels' accounts of an empty tomb. In Mark, the resurrection is the last of three important yet veiled manifestations of God's presence: the baptism, the transfiguration and, finally, the angel at the tomb. Matthew, who tells of attempts by the priests and elders to conceal the resurrection, emphasizes the wickedness of the present generation of Jewish leaders, so that the risen Lord sends his disciples to teach and baptize the Gentiles. Luke places all the Easter events near Jerusalem and, in the story of the walk to Emmaus, the risen Lord interprets himself as the Messiah who needed to suffer to fulfil scripture. Significant differences between the accounts can be explained on the basis of the important theological component in their composition.

Does this mean that there is no historical basis to the accounts of the empty tomb? All four Gospels record that women were the first to witness the resurrection (Mark 16:1–8; Matthew 28:1–10; Luke 23:54–24:12; John 20:1–18). Interestingly, in Luke's account (24:11) the disciples refused at first to take their word. This may, of course, have been because of the extraordinary nature of the claimed event. It could also reflect patriarchal prejudices. Indeed, if there is no historical truth to the accounts of the empty tomb, it seems odd that women were portrayed as witnesses to it rather than men, whose testimony would be more likely to be convincing. For this reason, the accounts of an empty tomb seem credible.

This does not make them true, though it does suggest that the evangelists believed them to be true. Some sceptics have argued that the women went to the wrong tomb where no body had yet been placed. Others have suggested that Jesus was not dead when he was taken from the cross, though he appeared so. He was revived and fled the scene. Members of the Ahmadiyya movement, a heterodox Muslim group, have asserted that he eventually went to the region of Kashmir (nowadays split between India and Pakistan), where what is claimed as his tomb can be visited to this day.

These suggestions are at least as implausible as the plain belief of the evangelists that the tomb was empty because God raised Jesus from the dead. Certainly, Paul affirmed that 'if Christ has not been raised, then your faith is futile' (1 Corinthians 15:17). This does not prove that the resurrection happened. It does indicate that Paul, and no doubt other early Christians, sincerely believed that God had raised Jesus from the dead, and would not have tolerated any deceitful way of 'proving' that event.

From our modern or postmodern perspective, the resurrection seems impossible. Because it is a unique, or at least very rare, claim that a man should be raised by God from death, some have argued that it cannot be a historical event at all, since there is nothing to compare it with. This seems an excessively theoretical position to take, because, unique event or not, if it happened, it occurred within history. More credible are those who deny a physical resurrection because they hold to an Enlightenment belief in an enclosed universe, bound by laws that God would not capriciously break. It is perfectly possible to stand in such a tradition and yet remain a Christian. One interesting and recent explanation of the resurrection along Christian yet strictly rational and Enlightenment lines avers that Peter experienced the risen Christ in a vision and this led to a chain reaction. Since he was overcome with guilt at having abandoned and then denied Jesus, this vision came in the form of an assurance of forgiveness. This therefore became the basis of the early apostolic preaching, found also in Paul, that Christ died for our sins. So although Jesus's resurrection was a verdict of faith, it was not a historical fact. In fact, Jesus died, and his body rotted in the tomb. But, the gospel message goes on, that unity with God, experienced through faith, continues beyond death.[22] This is an impressive hypothesis, but it looks excessively and implausibly rationalistic. Religion does not bypass rationalism, but it challenges and, many of its adherents would say, surpasses it.

The Christian belief in the resurrection of Jesus contends that the ways of God in his world are more seductive, diverse, and enigmatic than either blind credulity or an equally blind iron logic based on premises that are too mechanistic to explain the creation and re-creation of the world and its inhabitants. It also suggests that God honours faith in unexpected and wondrous ways. Further, it has furnished the Christian religion with powerful images for the overcoming of suffering and death. Once again, Paul is a powerful witness:

> We are afflicted in every way but not crushed; perplexed, but not driven to despair; persecuted, but not forsaken; struck down, but not destroyed; always carrying in the body the death of Jesus, so that the life of Jesus may also be made visible in our bodies. (2 Corinthians 4:9f.)

Jesus proclaimed that the kingdom of God had drawn near. He went to Jerusalem, knowing that he was courting death yet believing God would vindicate him. Probably he hoped that God would intervene before he died, and bring in the kingdom in its fullness. This kingdom would not be commensurate with political freedom from Rome. It would be based on a small renewal group who shared a Messianic meal and the hopes for God's rule of peace, justice and goodness. Yet he died, abandoned by his closest followers, and seemingly by God. The resurrection was his unexpected vindication.

NOTES

1. 'Hear [*shema*], O Israel, the Lord our God, the Lord is One' (Deuteronomy 6:4). To this basic verse are added Deuteronomy 6:4–9; 11:13–21; and Numbers 15:37–41.
2. Funk et al. 1993, 542.
3. Borg 1997, 34f.
4. Rowland 1982, 70–2, 358–68.
5. Schweitzer 1954, 328–89.
6. Dodd 1973, 123f.
7. Drury 1985, 1–38.
8. For further details of Augustine's allegory, see Dodd 1961, 13f.
9. Drury 1985, 51f.
10. Jeremias 1972, 70.
11. Theissen and Merz 1998, 429f.
12. Shillington 1997, 141–64.
13. Vermes 1973, 58–82; Smith 1978, *passim*.
14. Crossan 1991, 303–53.
15. For a fascinating modern example, I suggest Mohandas Karamchand Gandhi, the *mahatma* or 'great soul' of modern India. His administrative flair and capacity for self-advertisement in order to promote his cause should not be lost by denoting him as charismatic, which, at least on one reading of the word, he was. I admire him greatly. My point is not to cheapen his memory as one of the great men of the twentieth century. Rather, it is to say that 'charismatic' is a word that needs to be spelled out; like 'psychic', perhaps (cf. J. M. Brown 1972, 356f.).
16. Trocmé 1997, 22–8, 78–81.
17. Koester 1990, 293–303.
18. Crossan 1991, 429f.
19. Koester 1990, 296.
20. Smith 1973, 97–114.
21. Jeremias 1966, 237–55.
22. Lüdemann with Özen, 1995, 132–7.

4

JESUS THE JEW

J esus was born and died a Jew, not a Christian. Yet a strong history of
anti-Jewishness[1] has pervaded Christian teaching for much of
Christian history, leaving its mark on how Jews and Christians view
Jesus. This chapter will briefly indicate that history. It will then look at
Jesus's attitude to the Torah, Jewish religious law, to ask whether he
spurned, modified or accepted it. It will consider whether the Jews killed
Jesus. Afterwards it will examine whether contemporary Jews and
Christians can forge a more mature relationship, suited to the diverse
world we inhabit, and what role, if any, Jesus might play for both
communities within it.

THE ORIGINS OF THE SHOAH

Many Jews prefer to use the word 'Shoah', Hebrew for 'catastrophe',
rather than 'Holocaust', which is descriptively true, in that the crematoria
contained many 'burnt-offerings' of Jewish bodies, but is theologically
controversial, with its notions of sacrifice offered to and accepted by God.
At any rate, the Shoah has cast a dark shadow over the twentieth century.
It indicates the murder of six million Jews under Germany's Third Reich,
mainly between 1942 and 1945. When the war ended in 1945, so had a
whole way of life for Central and Eastern European Jews. Their
communities were destroyed. Of the pre-war Jewish populations of
Poland, Latvia, Lithuania, Estonia, Germany and Austria, less than ten
per cent survived; and less than thirty per cent of Jews in occupied Russia,
Ukraine, Belgium, Yugoslavia, Norway and Rumania.

Emil Fackenheim has offered the following list of five basic facts about the Shoah, which are unique in their combination:

1. One in three of all Jews were killed, putting the future of Jewish survival as a whole into doubt.
2. If Hitler had won, few if any Jews would have survived. His intention was their utter extermination.
3. Jewish birth was the grounds for torture and death. Except perhaps for gypsies, other groups which were killed, such as Poles and Russians, had committed the crime, in Hitler's eyes, of being too many in number, not of existing at all.
4. The 'final solution' was an end in itself, not a pragmatic project serving economic or political ends. Indeed, as Nazi power crumbled in 1944 and 1945 it became the only end that remained, as when Adolf Eichmann, who administered the 'Office for Jewish Emigration', diverted trains from the Russian front, where they were needed to protect Germany's eastern border. Instead, they were commandeered to take Jews to the death camp at Auschwitz.
5. Few of the perpetrators were sadists. Most were ordinary people with an extraordinary and perverted ideal.[2]

The term 'anti-Semitism' was first used by Wilhelm Marr, a German journalist, as late as 1879. Before him, discrimination against Jews had been coloured largely by Christian religious perceptions of them as killers of Christ. However, Marr saw them as biologically different to model blue-eyed, fair-haired, white Teutons. He asserted that Semites could not be assimilated to the majority race, and were a threat to them. Adolf Hitler despised Jews for racial reasons, but was prepared to give Christian religious colouring to justify his prejudice and his actions. In a devastating list, Raoul Hilberg has shown how specific Nazi measures against the Jews had equally specific antecedents in medieval canon law. For example, book burnings, the forbidding of Christians to use Jewish doctors, the prohibition of the building of synagogues, and the designation of Jews by items of clothing were all measures foreshadowed in Christian Europe's Middle Ages.[3]

Christian anti-Jewishness goes back further than the High Middle Ages. Among the church fathers, there was a veritable litany of bile directed against Jews. For example, the so-called 'golden-tongued' preacher of Antioch, John Chrysostom (344–407), who ended his days as Patriarch of Constantinople, wrote six sermons entitled *Adversus*

Judaeos (Against the Jews) in c. 386–7. He observed, among other things: the synagogue is a whorehouse and a theatre, and also a den of thieves and a haunt of wild animals; the Jews live by the rule of debauchery and inordinate gluttony; they murder their own children, sacrificing their sons and daughters to devils. God hates the Jews, Chrysostom averred, and so must Christians: for his part: 'I hate the Jews, for they hate the Law and insult it.' And he urged his audience:

> Instead of greeting them and addressing them so much as a word, you should turn away from them as from the pestilence and as the plague of the whole world.[4]

According to Jules Isaac, the fate of Israel did not take on a truly inhuman character until the end of the fourth century, the era of John Chrysostom. Isaac coined the phrase, 'the teaching of contempt', to denote the process of anti-Jewishness, which truly begins at this time. This teaching of contempt has seven major points,[5] which had gradually developed in the church up until that time, and depicted Jews as:

1. belonging to a degenerate Judaism, ossified upon the coming of Christ;
2. a sensual people incapable of spiritual insight;
3. the persecutors of Jesus;
4. a people denounced by God himself;
5. a deicide people;
6. justly dispersed from the Holy Land and exiled from Jerusalem;
7. forming a synagogue of Satan.

Perhaps the gravest charge was that the Jews were guilty of deicide; that is, they were killers of God. The earliest known form of this charge is in the writings of Melito, Bishop of Sardis in his *Homily on the Pascha*, the coincidence of Passover and Good Friday, c. 190.

> He who fastened the universe has been fastened to the tree
> the Sovereign has been insulted
> the God has been murdered
> the King of Israel has been put to death by
> an Israelite right hand.[6]

Such anti-Jewishness has survived into the twentieth century, and it can be illustrated from much popular English literature. The caricature of the hook-nosed, swarthy Jew can be found in many authors who once were popular, such as G. K. Chesterton, author of many books including Christian works and the Father Brown detective stories, and John Buchan, the thriller writer. A particular example is Agatha Christie, the so-called Queen of Crime, whose publishers declare that she is the world's best-selling novelist, writing works which have been translated into every major language. In her *Three Act Tragedy*, first published in 1935, Mr Satterthwaite, an elderly snob, yet an acute observer of the human condition, contemplates a young man named Oliver Manders:

> A handsome young fellow, twenty-five at a guess. Something, perhaps, a little sleek about his good looks. Something else – something – was it foreign? Something unEnglish about him . . .
> Egg Lytton Gore's voice rang out:
> 'Oliver, you slippery Shylock – '
> 'Of course,' thought Mr. Satterthwaite, 'that's it – not foreign – Jew!'[7]

Actually, the great Belgian detective, Hercules Poirot, is benevolently disposed towards the young man, who gets his girl in the end. Yet Christie uses barbed language about Jews not only in that book, but also in many more. The point is not that Agatha Christie was a particularly virulent exponent of anti-Jewishness, or even consciously anti-Jewish. Worse in a way, her casual comments illustrate the stereotypes and caricatures widespread in British society of her day. Similarly, yet ironically, it has affected many who have studied the pages of the New Testament, to locate a Jew.

Certainly, for all the brilliance of many German biblical scholars of the recent past (who have greatly influenced scholars from other countries), the scholarship about Jesus that emerges from their works is often strongly anti-Jewish. They depict Judaism at the time of Jesus as 'late Judaism' (*Spätjudentum*), as if Jewish religion had ended after 70 or should have. This position was based on the conviction that post-exilic Judaism had ossified and betrayed the prophetic faith of Israel. Jesus stands outside such a hardened, legalistic religion, a stranger to it, condemning the scribes and the Pharisees who were the fathers of Rabbinic Judaism and who have thus misled modern Judaism into perpetuating this sterile, legalistic religion. It is somewhat disquieting that German biblical scholars as important, interesting and (in many ways) perceptive as, for example, Martin Noth, Rudolph Bultmann, Martin Dibelius, Günther Bornkamm and Joachim Jeremias should have depicted Judaism of the time of Jesus in this way.[8] This is particularly so, since most lived through the Holocaust years but still seem oblivious to the Christian teaching of contempt about Jews, which watered the roots of anti-Semitism, and which persists, even if only as an unconscious and instinctive habit, in their works.

One of the tools by which some Gospel scholars assess the genuineness of a saying or deed of Jesus is the criterion of dissimilarity, which focuses on those words and works of Jesus that cannot be derived from the Judaism of his day (or, indeed, from the early church). For example, Matthew records his sweeping prohibition of all oaths (5:34, 37, but cf. James 5:12). Yet (among other objections to it), this tool divorces Jesus totally from the Judaism of his day. He was a Jew, deeply influenced by its unusual emphasis upon belief in one God and his gift of the Torah to his people. Jesus was not an alien intruder in first-century Palestine. Whatever else he was, he was a reformer of Jewish beliefs, not an indiscriminate fault-finder of them.

Can we take a step further, and admit that anti-Jewishness is a feature of the New Testament itself? Jules Isaac believed that Christians justified this 'teaching of contempt', because of its coherence and continuity with themes in the New Testament. Anti-Jewish polemic in early Christian literature has been admitted by many Christian scholars, ever since the pioneering book by James Parkes, first published in 1934, *The Conflict of the Church and the Synagogue*. Yet many such scholars do not go back beyond the church fathers of the second century onwards to the New Testament itself. Even Parkes, for most of his life, argued that anti-Jewishness was a distortion of the meaning of the New Testament, though he later changed his mind. However, the Jewish theologian of the Holocaust, Eliezer Berkowits, disagreed with those who refuse to admit that Christian scripture itself is a cause and the source of a history of the teaching of contempt. In an article entitled 'Facing the Truth', published in the summer 1978 edition of *Judaism*, he wrote:

> Christianity's New Testament has been the most dangerous anti-Semitic tract in history. Its hatred-charged diatribes against the Pharisees and the Jews have poisoned the hearts and minds of millions and millions of Christians for almost two millennia. No matter what the deeper theological meaning of the hate passages against the Jews might be, in the history of the Jewish people the New Testament lends its support to oppression, persecution and mass murder of an intensity and duration that were unparalleled in the entire history of man's degradation. Without

Christianity's New Testament, Hitler's *Mein Kampf* could never have been written. (pp. 323f.)

This is a grave charge. We must turn, then, to the pages of the New Testament.

THE DIVERSITY OF JUDAISM AT THE TIME OF JESUS

There were many ways of being Jewish at the time of Jesus. Josephus mentions Pharisees, Sadducees, Essenes and Zealots. Both he and the Gospels had axes to grind in their accounts of Judaism in the first century, so those who would understand its nature and complexity must proceed with caution.

There are two further grounds for caution. Jesus spent more time interacting with ordinary people than with religious or political groups. Anyway, the groups whom he met may not have been as structured as we are led to imagine, because of certain Gospel caricatures of them. The second is that, for all the differences within the divergent interpretations of Judaism of that time, there also was much in common between them. Two convictions especially bound Jews together. The first was a belief in the one and only God, who brooked no rivals. God made behavioural demands of his people, so Jewish faith could be described as ethical monotheism. The second was that God had entered into a special covenantal relationship with Jews. In the call of Abraham, the exodus from Egypt and the giving of the Law on Sinai, God had elected and chosen his own people.

The Law or Torah has been much misunderstood by Christians; particularly by Protestant Christians who have read Paul through the eyes of the sixteenth-century reformers, a rather narrow though extremely influential perspective. It is a false notion to infer that for Jews, works of the Law make a claim on God. Rather, the Torah is a gift from God, tracing how his people can live within the covenant.

Until 70, the Temple was at the heart of Judaism. God was to be worshipped only in one place, at the Temple in Jerusalem. The Temple had no image of God. Alongside the Temple, synagogues grew up, both in Palestine and in lands of the Diaspora (in Hebrew, *golah* or *galut*, which means exile) wherever Jews lived. Usually in Palestine, these were private rooms for the community to use. There was a priesthood in the Temple, but not in the synagogues where a lay religion developed. So the synagogue was an important focal point of local Jewish religious life, but it was still the desire of many Jews to go to Jerusalem for Passover, to worship in the Temple. The Temple was the centre of a sacrificial cult, whose focal point was the Day of Atonement, when the high priest entered the Holy of Holies to bring about atonement for the people. In the synagogues, a form of worship without sacrifice developed. There, scripture was read and expounded. Most of what Christians call the Old Testament (Jews do not, since for them it has not been supplemented with a New Testament) formed part of the Jewish scriptures, though they were (and still are) in a different order, and the books of Ecclesiastes and the Song of Solomon only later gained widespread acceptance as part of scripture.

With which of the groups did Jesus have dealings? There has been much scholarly debate about the relationship of the Essenes to the Qumran community of the Dead Sea Scrolls (it seems probable that they were identical), and how, if at all, Jesus was influenced by either or both groups. Any influence is highly speculative and rather unlikely. The Gospels never mention the Essenes. Their sense that they were different from other Jews because they were true sons of the covenant whom God alone had called, which inculcated a strong sense of separateness from a wicked world, is far removed from Jesus's message of grace to sinners and his acceptance of their hospitality.

In Josephus, Zealots appear as a group only after the outbreak of war in 66. Yet Luke includes Simon the Zealot among the twelve disciples (6:15). Some scholars who have associated Jesus strongly with resistance movements opposing Roman power make much of this. It is likely that Luke is correct, but since Jesus also called a tax collector, it seems best to interpret him as creating an inclusive group whom he hoped would catch his vision. Jesus was not endorsing a particular revolutionary stance against Rome.

Jesus's major dealings were with Pharisees and Sadducees. Who were they? Both these groups (and, indeed, the Essenes) began as attempts to define how to be authentically Jewish in a pluralistic milieu. They originated in the second century BCE. By that time, Greek influences had begun to percolate through into Jewish life and thought. The widening of Hellenistic influences had begun after Alexander the Great's conquests; he captured Palestine from Persian rule in 332 BCE. One of the immediate successors to Alexander's empire, Ptolemy I, had entered Jerusalem in 320 BCE, made himself master of the city and deported some people to Alexandria.

The spread of Greek influence can hardly have abated when, for a short period of time, under the Maccabaean dynasty, the Jews were self-governing. The Jewish patriot, Judas Maccabaeus, conquered and purified the Temple in 164 BCE, after a successful revolt against the deranged Syrian king Antiochus IV Epiphanes, who forbade the practice of the Jewish religion and established the cult of Zeus Olympius or Baal ha-Shamayim in the Temple. Even if there was a modest respite after 164 BCE, the capture of Palestine in 63 BCE by the Roman general Pompey, who also desecrated the Temple, would have heralded another wave of Hellenization.

The Diaspora of Jews abroad was also an important factor in forcing Jews to deal with the process of Hellenization. In Alexandria and other cities abroad, but also in Palestine itself, Jews had to face serious questions about how they could obey God in a pluralistic milieu. The Pharisees and Sadducees offered very different answers to these questions.

The Sadducees were an aristocratic, priestly (and therefore small) party who controlled the Temple. They believed that the true Jew was bound to God through worship there. The maintenance of the Temple cult, established by Ezra and Nehemiah after the return from exile in Babylon in the fifth century BCE, was essential for the well-being of the nation and for Israel's covenant obligations to God. Rather like the Jews of the Diaspora, they believed that it was necessary to come to terms with foreign rule so that they could be granted the space to organize their lives according to their convictions. Since many Jews from Palestine and beyond flocked to the Temple for the festivals, it must be assumed that the Sadducees were tolerated by the vast majority of Jews; indeed, that their work was believed to be necessary and important. However, the desecration of the Temple in 167 and 63 BCE, and again just after the death of Jesus, by order of the mad Roman emperor Caligula (who ruled from 37 to 41), meant that many discerning Jews must have wondered how secure Temple worship could be as a central and abiding symbol of Jewish purity and covenant identity.

The Pharisees probably first emerged as a political party, opposing the rule of John Hyrcanus (134–104 BCE). Yet they soon moved from politics to pietism, locating the centre of Jewish life on home and synagogue rather than Temple. They became chiefly concerned with the Law, preserving Jewish identity by obedience to its commands. Thus they distinguished themselves from the Gentiles.

How did Jesus relate to the Sadducees and the Pharisees? He seems to have been closer to the latter than to the former. The Sadducees did not hope for the resurrection of the dead, though the Pharisees did and so did Jesus (Mark 12:18–27; Matthew 22:23–33; Luke 20:27–40). Moreover, there were Pharisees who were members of the Sanhedrin, the supreme Jewish legislative assembly, who were sympathetic to him: Nicodemus (John 7:45–52; 19:39) and perhaps even Gamaliel (Acts 5:33–40). No sympathetic Sadducees are named.

This seems perplexing, given the Gospel accounts of Jesus's opposition to the Pharisees. The evangelists' antagonism arose out of the developing conflict between church and synagogue after the Jewish war against Rome. To a great extent, it has been read back into the dealings of Jesus with the Pharisees. Despite the centrality of the Temple, the establishment of the synagogues meant that not all forms of Judaism would perish when it was razed to the ground. The Pharisees survived and, based at Jamnia in Galilee, began an impressive and comprehensive reconstruction of Judaism. This became Rabbinic Judaism, the progenitor of the varieties of contemporary Judaism.

The Sadducees, the Essenes and the Zealots failed to survive 70. The destruction of the Temple smashed both the power base and the *raison d'être* of the Sadducees. The quietist philosophy of the Essenes was never likely to drive a popular movement. Although there were other Jewish uprisings against Rome after 70, the violent, revolutionary option suffered irreparable damage.

JESUS, THE EARLY CHURCH AND THE PHARISEES

So, among Jewish groups, only the Pharisees and the Christians survived the war against Rome. At first, influential leaders of the Christians were Jews, many of whom were committed to a Jewish form of Christianity, including Torah observance. But Paul's mission to the Gentiles, and their freedom from the necessity for circumcision and other aspects of the Jewish Law (Galatians 2:7–10; Acts 15:1–29), led to Christianity becoming a largely Gentile movement, certainly after the murder of James, the brother of Jesus, in 62. He had been the leader of Jewish Christianity. After his death, it became a small group, though there were still Christians who observed the Torah for many centuries thereafter. The Christian message that Gentiles and Jews were incorporated in the church would not have gone down well with post-70 Pharisees, who were trying to rescue a Jewish way of life from the wreckage of rebellion against Rome. For this reason, and because of the Christological claims made for Jesus, Jews began to expel Christians from the synagogues after 70.

According to John's Gospel, Jesus, during his farewell discourse, said to his disciples: 'They will put you out of the synagogues. Indeed, an hour is coming when those who kill you will think that by doing so they are offering worship to God' (16:2). Although John's Gospel appears to overestimate the capacity of Jews to perpetrate malevolent actions against Christians, this may have been the only period in the history of Jewish–Christian relations when Jews were able to exercise power over Christians. Many Christian scholars have argued that, from their centre in Jamnia, the Pharisees promulgated the *Eighteen Benedictions*, which anathematized Christians (*notzrim*) and heretics (*minim*). The twelfth benediction, the *birkat ha-minim*, runs

> For the apostate let there be no hope
> And let arrogant government be speedily uprooted in our days
> Let the *notzrim* and the *minim*
> be destroyed in a moment
> And let them be blotted out of the Book of Life and not
> Inscribed together with the righteous
> Blessed art thou, O Lord, who humblest the proud.

There is a theory that the fourth Gospel was written as a response to local Jewish–Christian difficulties caused by the promulgation of the twelfth benediction. Yet this prayer may have been directed against other Jewish sectarians, not Gentile Christians. Indeed, there is some evidence that Christians were welcome in the synagogues, even after 70, despite the passage in John's Gospel. So the *birkat ha-minim* was possibly not a watershed in Jewish–Christian relations (Hilton 1994, 224–6). Maybe no single edict caused an irrevocable separation between Judaism and Christianity, but rather a long process dependent upon local situations and the growing power of the church.[9]

After 70, the Pharisees were rivals with Christianity for the authentic meaning of Judaism. No wonder, then, that the evangelists, writing shortly after that event, should have depicted Jesus's relations with the Pharisees darkly. Although he disagreed with them on certain important issues, there are hints in the Gospels (such as his relations with Nicodemus) that he had cordial and even close relations with some

Pharisees. The fact that, broadly speaking, two Jewish interpretations of how to be faithful to God survived 70, should also alert Christians against making condescending and untrue, even if well-meaning, statements along the lines of modern Judaism being the mother of Christianity. Both are heirs of late Second-Temple Judaism; different interpretations, indeed. One developed through Mishnah,[10] Talmud,[11] synagogue and a sense of specific Jewish identity. The other evolved through a New Testament, church and a sense of universal mission.

Ed Sanders is one of a number of recent scholars who have contributed to the recovery of the Jewishness of Jesus. His great achievement has been to paint the story of Jesus against a wider background of Jewish belief and practice. His *Judaism: Practice and Belief 63BCE–66CE* is an unusual treatment from a New Testament specialist, rather telling in that it is a book which is not dominated by Jesus, as Christians falsely assume that Jewish faith in that period must have been. In an epilogue to that work, Sanders confesses:

> I rather like the Pharisees. They loved detail and precision. They wanted to get everything just right. I like that. They loved God, they thought that he had blessed them, and they thought that he *wanted* them to get everything just right. I do not doubt that some of them were priggish. This is a common fault of the pious, one that is amply demonstrated in modern criticism of the Pharisees. The Pharisees, we know, intended to be humble before God, and they thought that intention mattered more than outward show. These are worthy ideals.[12]

Sanders believes that Jesus offended his Jewish contemporaries in certain respects. First, he included the 'wicked', who were outside the law, within the scope of God's kingly rule, even though they remained outside rather than repenting and becoming observant. A second offence was the commandment to the prospective disciple to leave his dead father (Matthew 8:19–22; Luke 9:57–60), which conflicted with the law to honour one's parents; this was probably a one-off occasion rather than an indication that Jesus intended to oppose, root and branch, the Deuteronomic legislation. Thirdly, Jesus's prohibition of divorce (Matthew 19:3–9; Mark 10:2–9) was a radical indication that the Mosaic Law was not strict enough. In particular, his attitude towards the Temple was probably sufficiently offensive to bring about his arrest and execution (as we shall see in the next section). Nevertheless, in *Jewish Law from Jesus to the Mishnah*, Sanders concludes that 'the synoptic

Jesus lived as a law-abiding Jew'.[13] This means that, of the material depicting legal conflict between Jesus and others, very little goes back to him. There is just the whiff of a suspicion that Sanders' interpretation of Jesus the faithful Jew (as, elsewhere in his writings, of Paul, also a dutiful but rather more eccentric Jew) too easily dismisses or plays down material which causes offence between Christians and Jews.

Even so, the evidence suggests that Jesus accepted the Jewish Law. Matthew records that Jesus said: 'Do not think that I have come to abolish the law or the prophets; I have not come to abolish but to fulfil. For truly I tell you, until heaven and earth pass away, not one letter, not one stroke of a letter, will pass from the law until all is accomplished' (5.17f.) It is quite possible that Jesus said something like the second of these sentences. Such a statement may have been hyperbolic but not ironic. Jesus grew up believing the law to be a gift and a blessing. He interpreted but did not abandon it. Yet his interpretation was radical.

He was particularly radical in interpreting the commandment about cleanness (Mark 7:1–16; cf. Matthew 15:1–11). This is a curious passage, since Jesus accuses the Pharisees of failing to keep the Torah, then apparently abrogates its teaching. It may be that Jesus is closer to the conservative Sadducees on this point than to the Pharisees, whom he accuses of holding to human tradition rather than the commandments of God. If so, what is at issue is how to interpret the law, not how to undermine and revoke it.

It is probably misleading to claim, as many do, that Jesus put people above the Law's demands. Rather, since Jews of his day believed that the Law was a gift of God, he would be more likely to have assumed that people interpreted it erroneously. His rather basic and earthy analogy with bodily functions (Mark 7:14) shows his recognition that mere observance of the Law means nothing: 'Listen to me, all of you, and understand: there is nothing outside a person that by going in can defile, but the things that come out are what defile.' Indeed, the Law needs to be so accepted and lived that it reforms and improves its adherents, and is not simply observed. As so often, Paul was an astute interpreter of Jesus when he claimed that 'the letter kills but the Spirit gives life' (2 Corinthians 3:6). This is precisely the point that Jesus made, and that would have antagonized many sincere people who, from his perspective, mistook the means for the end.

There are other illustrations of Jesus's relaxed attitude towards questions of cleanness. In the healing of the woman with the flow of blood, Jesus was not embarrassed by her touch. Since she presumably suffered from vaginal bleeding, she was ritually unclean (Leviticus 15:25–30).

This attitude towards cleanness suggests that Jesus differed from the Pharisees in his opinion about the scope of God's grace and peoples' reactions to it. It could be said that the Pharisees made a hedge around Torah. Within the 'field' bounded by this hedge, Jewish life could flourish in an identifiable way. Jesus believed that everyone could and should become holy: 'Be perfect, therefore, as your heavenly Father is perfect' (Matthew 5:48).

Nevertheless, Jesus was certainly not a lone Jew in preaching God's love. Luke's parable of the good Samaritan is told after a Torah scholar confesses that eternal life is inherited by those who love God, and their neighbour as themselves (Luke 10:25–37). The scandal of the parable lies in its interpretation of the scope and distribution of God's love, and therefore of one's own. God's love can work through a Samaritan, when a priest and a Levite fail in their obligations. The Gospels record many occasions when Jesus offended the religious susceptibilities of some of his contemporaries: for example, healing on the sabbath (Mark 3:1–6; Matthew 12:9–14; Luke 6:6–11). The report of Mark and Matthew that the Pharisees determined thereafter to kill Jesus may be doubted, but it is not intrinsically unlikely that over-scrupulous people found his interpretation of the Law unacceptable, and even threatening.

We may sum up like this. Jesus was in many ways close to the Pharisees. Both wished to hallow everyday life, and did so in the context of living faithfully within Torah. However, Jesus was a remarkably free interpreter of the Law. He saw that its purpose was to transform people's lives, not to be burdensome: if it was a divine gift, it was a gift for good, not for evil, to enhance rather than diminish people's lives. No doubt many Pharisees and other Jews thought so too. Others, no doubt, irritated him by their pedantic interpretations of the Law, which made the mechanics of the Law more important than its end to transform lives by God's generous, forgiving love.

Many people, not just pedants, may have found his reading and living of the Law too free, sovereign and unfettered. Did he actually say, 'You have heard that it was said . . . but I tell you', or was this a creation of the early traditions, as tales of his authority grew in the telling? Whichever, Jesus treated the Law with sovereign freedom: tightening it in some respects (especially divorce), but relaxing it in others. The fact that he may have agreed with the Sadducees against the Pharisees on certain issues illustrates that interpreting the Law was an essential occupation for many Jewish intellectuals, so as to root it in the realities and possibilities of people's lives. Nobody would have worried about the principle of interpreting the Law; some may have worried a great deal about the details of how it was interpreted.

As the Gospels stand, much of the material about Jesus's dealings with the Pharisees reflects the controversies of the generation following the destruction of the Temple in 70. Even so, there is no reason to doubt that Jesus had serious disagreements with many of his contemporaries about the scope and distribution of God's covenant grace; he interpreted the Torah to maximize God's forgiving and generous love. Others may have been more cautious, though that is no reason to regard all his opponents over the issue of the Law as Pharisees and extreme exclusivists. However, many such antagonists would have been Pharisees, for the Law was very important to them. It is as possible to underestimate the anger of some Jews, including many Pharisees, with Jesus, as it is possible to exaggerate and caricature it.

THE DEATH OF JESUS AND THE SADDUCEES

The Passion narrative, from arrest to burial, forms the longest consecutive account of Jesus's life in each Gospel. Some scholars hold that it was the earliest fixed connected account that circulated about Jesus, well before Mark's Gospel was written. They may well be right, because of the central importance of Jesus's death to the apostolic preaching, not least to Paul's theology.

Its pathos has been recorded in art, drama and music. Millions of ordinary Christians find it the centre of their spiritual lives, evoking prayer, meditation and wonder. It has provided Christian theologians, especially of the Western churches, with their most fruitful ground for reflection.

That process of theological reflection can be seen in the accounts of the evangelists. Mark and Matthew depict Jesus as one who is abandoned by his followers (Mark 14:50; Matthew 26:56), and even, so it would seem, by God himself (Mark 15:34; Matthew 27:46). Even so, he is the Messiah (Mark 14:61f.; Matthew 26:63f.), and by his willingness to drink the cup of suffering to the full (Mark 14:36; Matthew 26:39), he is vindicated by God, as the resurrection stories affirm.

Mark's Gospel, which consistently underlines the failure of Jesus's closest followers to understand him, emphasizes that failure in his account of the Passion and even the resurrection. Not only the disciples but also an unnamed young man flee at the moment of Jesus's arrest (14:51f.), and the women at the empty tomb flee, for they were afraid (16:1–8). It seems probable that Mark's readers knew about suffering and even failure. They needed to be reassured by Jesus's commitment, anguish and sense of abandonment. They also required to be challenged to be as indomitable as their Lord had been.

Matthew's account is haunted by a sense of who is responsible for the death of Jesus. Judas, who betrayed him, tries to evade responsibility by returning the thirty pieces of silver. The priests buy the 'Field of Blood' with it, attempting thereby to distance themselves from this blood money (27:3–10). Pilate's wife, spurred by a dream, warns her husband not to have anything to do with 'that innocent man', Jesus (27:19). Pilate washes his hands of the deed of execution (27:24). The crowd answer 'His blood be on us and on our children' (27:25). No one can evade accountability, but the real responsibility falls on 'the people as a whole'. Clearly, Matthew's account is to a great extent constrained and created by the apologetic concerns of his own day, as he and his audience struggled to understand why the majority of Jews failed to believe that Jesus was the Messiah and expelled Christians from the synagogues as deviants from the faith of Israel. Matthew believed they were perversely responsible for the death of the innocent Messiah. No doubt the destruction of the Temple in 70 led him to believe that it was just punishment on a recalcitrant people. He was not to know that his condemnation of Jews would reverberate, appallingly, down the centuries.

Luke interprets Jesus as a martyr, willing to die for a just cause. Jesus trusts God to vindicate him. He finds time to forgive those who crucified him, and a penitent thief hanging alongside him (23:34, 39–43). He dies, not in abandonment, but with the confident and serene words, 'Father, into your hands I commend my spirit' (23:46). Alone among the evangelists, Luke records a trial before Herod Antipas (23:6–12) as well as Pilate, just as Paul will appear before a Jewish king and Roman governor (Acts 24–6). This parallel may be a hint from Luke to his readers that Paul (whom Acts leaves imprisoned in Rome) is to bear martyrdom serenely, as did Jesus and Stephen (Acts 7:54–60) before him. Even if Luke's is a somewhat romanticized account, it is not quite sentimental: it is, after all, a story about martyrdom written for people who had to be reminded to take up their cross 'daily' (Luke 9:23).

If Luke's picture of dying Jesus is serene and trustful, as opposed to Matthew's and especially Mark's portrait of Jesus as anguished and abandoned, the Jesus of John's account is even more in control of matters. He tells Pilate, 'You would have no power over me unless it had been given you from above' (19:11). His last words are 'It is finished' (19:30), signifying both the end of his earthly life and the accomplishment of its purpose; namely that 'I, when I am lifted up, will draw all people to myself' (12:32). So he dies, not just serene but triumphant.

This brief summary hardly does justice to the theological subtleties of the different accounts of the Passion narrative. Its point is to underline that these accounts are replete with theological meditation. Here, as much as, if not more than, anywhere else in the Gospels, history and faith-full reflection are bound together in a creative, dramatic and moving symbiosis.

One important historical question is: how many trials were there? A conflated account of the Gospels would produce something like a trial before the Sanhedrin, then before Pilate, who sent him to Herod, who then returned Jesus to Pilate. It is uncertain whether Jesus appeared before Herod. Luke may preserve the memory of a real event (23:6–12). Herod would probably have known that Jesus had been a follower of John the Baptizer, whose death he had ordered. Herod's followers may also have long wanted Jesus out of the way (Mark 3:6; 12:13). If Herod was in Jerusalem for the Passover festival, Pilate may very well have sent Jesus to him, since, as a Galilean, Jesus could be held to come under Herod's jurisdiction.

Whether Jesus appeared before the Sanhedrin is even more problematic, and has produced wide disagreements among scholars. The word comes from the Greek *sunedrion*, 'sitting in counsel'. Jewish sources indicate that it was a supreme court of seventy (or seventy-one) members which sat in the 'chamber of hewn stone' in Jerusalem until 70, and thereafter in various other cities.[14] (However, some scholars, both Jewish and Christian, cast doubt about whether this 'supreme court' met in the pre-70 period and, if so, who sat on it, representing what groups.[15])

The Synoptic Gospel accounts of Jesus's death tell a different story. Here, the High Priest, in his palace, presides over Jesus's condemnation (Mark 14.53-65; Matthew 26.57-68; Luke 22.66-70). Until recently, Christians and Jews tended to claim that their own view was right and the other's was wrong. Now it seems more convincing that both preserve ancient traditions of a supreme legislative assembly that once existed in Judaism, but both have read back into it their own concerns and ideas.

In John's Gospel, however, there is no trial before a council. Instead, Jesus is interrogated by Annas, erstwhile high priest, who then sends him to the high priest, his son-in-law, Caiaphas (18:13, 19–24). If this is a reliable and independent source, it may indicate that Jesus first appeared before informal Sadducaean representatives of the Temple establishment. There are grounds for believing this to have been the case, rather than that he was subjected to an interrogation before a formally constituted religious court. For one thing, although Jesus's capture was no doubt planned, it is hard to conceive that a large group of people, possibly including some of Jesus's sympathizers, would be on hand in the middle of the night to meet and judge him.

Even more telling, Jesus's death by crucifixion was a Roman punishment, not a Jewish one. It is difficult to know precisely what happened before Pilate, but it is virtually certain that the most important confrontation was between Jesus and the Roman governor. Probably what really happened after Jesus was apprehended at night was that he was questioned by a Temple authority or authorities, who then dragged him before Pilate, who administered a swift and severe punishment.

We have noted that Matthew's Gospel involves the Jews in the death of Jesus as the chief of those who were guilty of it. At the time when the Gospels were being written, it was in the interests of every evangelist to emphasize the Jews' rather than the Romans' involvement in the death of Jesus. A number of reasons would have operated: to explain the scandal (as they saw it) of Jewish resistance to belief in Jesus as the Messiah; to distance themselves from those Jews who had rebelled against Roman rule; and to establish Christians as loyal citizens of the Empire.

Yet, historically, the Roman authorities had at least as much reason to want Jesus dead, as did certain Jews. He had entered the city in a way that carried Messianic overtones and he had caused a scandalous flurry in the Temple at a time when many Jews were in the city for the festival of Passover. Pilate would no doubt have taken the view that a man who might focus the political and religious discontent of swollen crowds was best expeditiously killed. So the Roman governor executed a Palestinian troublemaker: a common enough occurrence. Some scholars have suggested that, by his own lights, Pilate was right to do so, since Jesus had an overtly political agenda: namely, the overthrow of Roman imperial authority and its replacement by a Jewish theocratic government. This is much to misplace Jesus's ambitions.

Can his attitude towards political sovereignty be gauged from the story, in the last week of his life, when Pharisees and Herodians (Mark 12:13–17 and Matthew 22:15–22), or agents of the Chief Priests and Scribes (Luke 20:20–6), asked him if it was lawful to pay tribute to Caesar? Jesus seems in a 'no win' situation. Either he condemns Roman rule, thus courting immediate arrest and death, or else he connives at hated foreign occupation. He asks them to bring a coin, then asks whose head is on it and whose title; he then says: 'Give to the emperor the things that are the emperor's, and to God the things that are God's.' Strictly speaking, the engraving of any human likeness was offensive to Jewish beliefs, yet his opponents had such coins about them. Jesus gave a brilliantly evasive answer to a trick question, from which little can be deduced.[16] Even so, Luke records the charge against Jesus at his trial before Pilate that he forbade people to pay taxes to the emperor. This may well have been made.

Jesus had no such coherent political strategy to replace Roman by Jewish power. Nevertheless, his message of God's kingdom, and his own role in it, was subversive both of the political *status quo*, and of the ideals of Jewish patriots who hoped to supplant it by home rule.

Among Jewish groups, it was certain Sadducees, who had a vested interest in and a deep commitment to Temple worship, who most sought and achieved Jesus's demise. Significantly, the Passion narratives do not record any confrontation with Pharisees. The Sadducees more or less disappeared after 70. With no Temple cult to administer, and tainted by association with a vengeful conquering foreign power, they fell into historical oblivion. Yet at the time of Jesus, it was precisely their willingness to collaborate with the Romans and their cultic function that led them to seek his silence, by death if necessary.

Some scholars have argued that Galilee and Judaea were political powder kegs, waiting only for a fuse to detonate Jewish rebellion against Roman government. This seems overstated. Nevertheless, anything Jesus did which had political implications could destroy the delicate balance the Temple authorities had achieved with Roman rulers. Collaborators are only welcome so long as they serve an occupying power's deepest interest in keeping the peace and cracking down on potential as well as actual dissidents. The Sadducees knew this, and were willing to bring Jesus down. It is likely that some laid charges which contained political overtones against him before Pilate.

Furthermore, Jesus's teaching about the Temple struck at their belief about the centre of Jewish faith. When he overturned the tables of the money changers, this was as much a symbolic gesture about the end of Temple worship as a criticism of immoral practices there. At his trial before the Jewish council (more likely, I have suggested, before a few high officials, probably including Caiaphas), both Mark and Matthew state that false witnesses accused him of saying he would destroy the Temple and build another within three days (Mark 14:57f.; Matthew 26:59–61). This sounds like special pleading by the evangelists. After all, they and Luke record that Jesus predicted the destruction of the Temple to his disciples (Mark 13:1f.; Matthew 24:1f., Luke 21:5f.). Probably Jesus believed that when God intervened and brought the kingdom in, in all its fullness, the Temple would not survive, since it would not be needed, given the glory of God's presence (rather like the view of the author of the book of Revelation, in chapter 21, verse 22). Or else (if the reference to three days is authentic, and has not been created to refer to the resurrection) he may have looked for a new, more perfect Temple. Since many religious people mistake the means for the end, this iconoclastic hope would have shocked them. It would certainly have disturbed the Sadducaean authorities, whose religious authority derived from the maintenance of the existing Temple. To be fair, they would have been genuinely shocked by Jesus's views, as well as, human nature being what it is, mindful of their own status and importance.

Jesus died, executed by order of the Roman procurator because he was a threat to peaceful rule. But some Jews conspired at his death, to suit their own deepest convictions and also their self-interest. This does not mean that all Jews then, still less all Jews since, were guilty of his death.

A much more acceptable way for Christians to internalize and relive the story, as many do each Holy Week before Easter Sunday, is to see it addressed to everyman and everywoman. A hymn often sung then starts 'Were you there when they crucified my Lord?' The obvious answer is, no. It all happened long ago, in another time and age. But those who devotionally re-enact the story, as many do, are most engaged with its deepest meanings when they place themselves, not perfidious Jews, as the central characters. After all, Jews could not help being there, given the place and the circumstances! This is a narrative about human nature, not about racial typology. And, from a Christian theological perspective, even if *some* Jews delivered Jesus up to the Roman procurator to be executed, it was within the eternal purposes of God (e.g. 1 Peter 1:17–21), who redeemed the world by a crucified Jew.

JEWISH RESPONSES TO CHRISTIAN ANTI-JEWISHNESS

For most Jews, Jesus is irrelevant as an authentic exponent of Judaism. The rabbis rejected the interpretation of Jewish faith that Christians drew from his life, death, resurrection and teaching. Starting from the New Testament itself, Christians have often seen this as culpable error. Yet this is not how it seems to Rabbinic Judaism. Rather, for its adherents, Christian belief in Jesus as the Son of God, even in its New Testament meanings but particularly as it developed in the official and Trinitarian formularies of the early church, is incompatible with Jewish belief. So is the belief that Jesus is the Messiah. Followers of Jesus are called *minim*, 'sectarians', in the Talmud, but so are all schismatic groups. Only rarely is there a direct attack by a Jew or Jews on Jesus or on Christian belief.

This silence is deafening, as though the majority of Jews simply turned their backs on this deviant interpretation of true faith. It is matched by the absence of early Jewish reflection on many parts of the Jewish heritage of faith which Christians used to illuminate the meaning of Jesus. For example, the Suffering Servant passages, particularly Isaiah chapter 52, verse 13–chapter 53, verse 12, though potentially an enormously fruitful resource for understanding the sufferings of Israel, were hardly ever explored by Jews until the medieval period. The most convincing explanation of this is that these passages were used by Christians to define the meaning of Jesus (e.g. Mark 10:45; Acts 8:26–40) and therefore, Rabbinical Judaism steered clear of them.

In the medieval and early modern periods, the centuries of European Christendom, inasmuch as many Jews considered Jesus at all, it was as the lord and master of Christians who persecuted them in his name. Although the European Enlightenment brought Jews out of the ghetto, it did not always gain them wide acceptance. Many converted to Christianity so as to be accepted by polite Christian society. So, for example, the German musician Mendelssohn (1809–47) and the British politician Disraeli (Prime Minister in 1868 and from 1874 to 1880) came from converted families. Yet, by and large, this attempt failed. Anti-Semitism remained a potent force throughout much of Europe. Many Christians of Jewish background, including Christian clergy, ended their lives in one of Hitler's death camps. Thus the religion of Jesus the Jew is hardly an attractive option for most Jews.

Even so, the story of Jesus has had powerful resonances for many Jews. No doubt many who have converted to Christianity have done so for religious, rather than economic or social reasons. In recent years, there have been a number of Jews by background who have sincerely converted to Christianity, and so believe that Jesus was the Messiah. These are 'Jews for Jesus' or 'Messianic Jews'. There are said to be four thousand such in Israel itself (including many immigrants from Russia), where they hesitate to use the title 'Christian' because of so much past Christian anti-Semitism.[17] There are many more such converted Jews in the USA, Britain and elsewhere. They raise pastoral issues for other Christians. For example, they are rejected as Jews by the vast majority of other Jews, so should Christians treat them as Jews or as Christians who once were Jews?

In recent years, some committed Jews, as well as converts, have examined Jesus's life and achievements. The first biography of Jesus by a modern Jewish scholar, Joseph Klausner, was published in 1925 (its English translation is entitled *Jesus of Nazareth*). In it, Klausner observed that

> In his [Jesus's] ethical code there is a sublimity, distinctiveness and originality in form unparalleled in any other Hebrew ethical code; neither is there any parallel to the remarkable art of his parables. The shrewdness and sharpness of his proverbs and his forceful epigrams serve, in an exceptional degree, to make ethical ideas a popular possession. If ever the day should come and this ethical code be stripped of its wrappings of miracle and mysticism, the Book of the Ethics of Jesus will be one of the choicest treasures in the literature of Israel for all time.

Indeed, generously, Klausner concedes that 'Jesus surpassed Hillel [the foremost teacher in Palestine in the first century BCE] in his ethical ideals', by changing the Golden Rule from a negative form ('What thou thyself hatest do not unto thy neighbour') to the positive form ('What thou thyself wouldest that men should do unto thee, so thou also do unto them'). Even so, Klausner observes that Jesus's ethical teaching 'has not proved possible in practice'. (Less than ten years after this book was published, Hitler came to power in Germany, ironically reinforcing Klausner's judgement.) Klausner argued, as have many Jews (and some Muslims, as we shall see in Chapter 5), that Paul distorted the message of Jesus by Hellenizing it.[18]

Parts of this thesis depend on a branch of early nineteenth-century biblical scholarship which depicted Paul as the founder of a Christianity that betrayed or at least deviated from the ideals of Jesus of Nazareth.

This was not particularly convincing then, and has become even less so. Despite his disapproval of Paul, Klausner recognizes that he paved the way for unfolding the will of God to all people. He believed, though, that Judaism and not Christianity would become the universal religion.

This is not the view of Pinchas Lapide. Among recent Jewish writings on Jesus his is one of the most interesting, from a Christian perspective. He believes that the resurrection actually happened, though he is a practising Orthodox Jew. He is unconvinced by the 'strange paraphrases' of many modern Christian theologians about the resurrection. He believes them 'all too abstract and scholarly to explain the fact that the solid hillbillies from Galilee who, for the very real reason of the crucifixion of their master, were saddened to death, were changed within a short period of time into a jubilant community of believers'. Only resurrection could have accomplished that. Lapide built on the thought of Franz Rosenzweig, an agnostic humanist Jew from the beginning of this century. For both, Christianity is the Judaizing of the pagans. Lapide quotes approvingly the words of Clemens Thoma, a Catholic theologian, that 'through the resurrection of Jesus, an access to faith in the one, until then unknown, God of Israel was opened to the Gentiles'. Jesus is the way for the Gentiles; the Jews, who already know God, do not need Jesus.[19] This conviction has not gained wide acceptance among either Jews or Christians, though it is an intriguing one.

Martin Buber (1878–1965), author of the classic book *I and Thou* (first English edition 1937), which interpreted the Bible and relations with God in a personal and existential fashion, has had a huge impact on modern Protestant theology, though he has been rather less influential in Jewish circles. In one of his books, entitled *Two Types of Faith*, he argued that Jewish faith, *emunah*, is in the history of a nation, whereas Christian faith, *pistis*, is in that of individuals. This is not an especially convincing distinction, but his book is quietly memorable for its avoidance of any apologetic tendency. Buber wrote:

> From my youth onwards I have found in Jesus my great brother. That Christianity has regarded and does regard him as God and Saviour has always appeared to me a fact of the highest importance which, for his sake and for my own, I must endeavour to understand . . . I am more than ever certain that a great place belongs to [Jesus] in Israel's history of faith.[20]

Neither Klausner, Lapide nor Buber were persuaded by Christianity's doctrinal claims about Jesus, for all the positive things they found in aspects of his teaching.

Neither is Geza Vermes so persuaded. His *Jesus the Jew*, first published in 1973, opened the eyes of many to the Jewishness of Jesus, whom Vermes depicted as a Galilean *hasid*, holy man, rather than a Pharisee, Essene, Zealot or Gnostic. More problematic for Christians was the careful examination of titles claimed for him: prophet, Lord, Messiah, Son of Man, and Son of God. Vermes concluded, controversially, that none of the claims and aspirations of Jesus link him with the Messiah, that no titular use of 'Son of Man' is attested in Jewish literature, and that 'prophet', 'Lord' or even, figuratively, 'Son of God' could be easily applied to holy men in the Judaism of Jesus's day. In two works since, *Jesus and the World of Judaism* (1983) and *The Religion of Jesus the Jew* (1993), Vermes has developed his picture of Jesus as a charismatic teacher, healer and prophet.

What then of the Christian church or churches, of the phenomenon of Christianity itself? According to Vermes, this owes more to the Hellenizing theologies of John and Paul than to Jesus the Jew, to its migration to the Graeco-Roman, Gentile world than its Jewish origins. But he observes that, through the three ancient witnesses of Matthew, Mark and Luke, Jesus the Jew emerges to challenge traditional Christianity of the Pauline–Johannine variety. In Vermes's opinion, the decline in the numbers of Torah-observing Jews who followed the teaching of Jesus, without believing in the virgin birth or the deification of Christ, allowed the dominant Hellenized Christianity a free run. Indeed, by the beginning of the fifth century, important figures in the church had ruled that it was heretical for Christians of Jewish origin to keep the Law. Vermes observes:

> Despite all this, in fairness, it must be emphasized that notwithstanding all its alien dogmatic and ecclesiastical features, Christianity still possesses fundamental elements of the piety of Jesus, such as his emphasis on the purity of intention and generosity of heart, exemplified in a Francis of Assisi who relinquished wealth to serve the poor, and even in our century, an Albert Schweitzer, who abandoned fame to heal the sick in God-forsaken Lambaréné, and a Mother Teresa who, age-old, cares for the dying in the filthy streets of Calcutta.[21]

Vermes's representation of the meaning of Jesus is insightful. His work can also be interpreted, to some extent, as a brilliant piece of polemics: he himself converted to Christianity and was a Roman Catholic priest, then eventually reverted to Judaism.[22] His works are an implicit response and answer to the traditional Christian claim that it knows what Jewish faith should be and that Jews have got it wrong, by insinuating that Jews know what Jesus's faith would have been and that Christians have got it wrong. Despite its confrontational nuances, Vermes's work on the Jewishness of Jesus has profoundly influenced Christian writers like his former colleague at Oxford, E. P. Sanders, whose work we have noted, and it will no doubt long endure. Christians, as well as others who would locate Jesus against his historical background, have reason to be grateful for Vermes's books on Jesus.

However, other Jewish responses to Jesus have had more of a sting in the tail. Some contemporary Jewish scholars of Jesus seem to be as motivated by polemics as by other more praiseworthy purposes. Hyam Maccoby is a particular example. In his recent (1992) stimulating book *Judas Iscariot and the Myth of Jewish Evil*, he outlines Judas's burgeoning role in Christian mythology as the 'sacred executioner', whose vices of envy, greed and ultimate disloyalty have been transferred to all Jews. Yet this is a speculative overstatement. Moreover, he uses the same controversial distinction as does Vermes, that the Jerusalem church represented the teaching of Jesus, but became a persecuted minority, traces of whom can still be found in the tenth century though they disappeared as an effective organized body by the fifth century. Finally, his works ignore the positive links between Christians and Jews: what, after all, were Christian Jews doing and saying to their co-religionists about relations between the two faiths in this long period of time?

It is good for Christians to receive the interpretations of Jewish 'spin-doctors', to import a political term, rather than have the field open to their own prejudice and anger. Yet it is hard to see that the polemical aspects of Maccoby's and even Vermes's work are an adequate substitute for their, and others', more patient and impartial academic endeavours.

It is clear that Christian history is indebted to its Jewish past, a point painstakingly made by many scholars. After all, Christians have 'borrowed' from the Jews: scripture, the history of ancient Israel, the idea of covenant and so forth. Sometimes, it looks as if all the borrowing went one way. Yet Rabbi Michael Hilton's *The Christian Effect on Jewish Life* argues that Jews learned from Christians just as much, if not more, than Christians from Jews. Indeed, you would expect it to be the case that minority groups would learn more from majorities than vice versa.

Hilton's examples are fascinating. How is it that Jews and Christians share the same Hebrew scriptures, even though Christianity emerged before the Jewish canon was fixed? Most Christian scholars have assumed that Marcion's rejection of the Jewish scriptures in the middle of the second century encouraged Christians to hurry up and accept them. Hilton argues rather that Christians and Jews needed an agreed textual basis for the many disagreements with which they were riven in the early centuries of the common era.

Hilton also contends that the *seder* meal, the Passover meal, arose in response to the Christian celebration of the meal which Jesus shared with his disciples on the evening before his death. This raises the startling and ironic possibility that all the meals eaten in churches on Maundy Thursday in imitation of a Jewish feast are in fact imitating a meal which, in certain essential details, was fashioned in response to, and incorporated actions of, the Christian celebration of Jesus's last meal. This example, and others, have proved controversial but fascinating.

CHRISTIAN RESPONSES TO CHRISTIAN ANTI-JEWISHNESS

Since the end of World War II, Christian relations with the Jewish people have undergone a transformation. The Roman Catholic Church and many other churches have spurned the charge against Jews that they are guilty of Deicide. Liturgies have been purged of anti-Jewish sentiments. The question of the ethics and even the necessity of Christian mission to the Jews has been debated. This is not a time to give easy answers to Christian questions about the continued existence of the Jewish people and their religion. What is important is that the questions have been asked in a much more amicable, agreeable and collaborative way than in the past.

For example, the vast majority of Jews do not believe that Jesus was the Messiah. In their view, the Messianic age will bring in the worship of the true God, an end to warfare and the reign of peace. This has always been conspicuous by its absence from the world, and Jesus's own fate was counter to central Jewish beliefs. A suffering Messiah is teaching unique to Jesus.

Yet Jesus was early on called Christ or Messiah, and the vast majority of Christians believe him to be that figure. Certain Christians doubt whether Jesus did refer to himself as the Messiah, but that hardly means that Jews and Christians can, after all, agree on the fact that he was not. That would be a trivial consensus. It is best to acknowledge that Jews and Christians do not agree about Jesus. Many older Christian scholars who lived through the time of the Holocaust have understandably been so concerned to improve Jewish–Christian relations that they have sometimes sought harmony where none exists, or simply avoided difficult questions. It may be that this or a future generation of Jewish and Christian scholars can explore a more exciting and diverse interpretation of a Jewish and Christian Jesus, suitable for the needs of world citizens of the new millennium.

Finally, there remains the issue of whether the New Testament itself, and not just many of its interpreters, is profoundly anti-Jewish. Certainly, the evangelists condemn Jews for not believing in Christ. John even records Jesus saying to 'the Jews who had believed in him' (but no longer did?) that their father was the devil, a murderer from the beginning who does not stand in the truth (8:31–46). Some readers will see this as implicitly teaching that the Jews killed God about a century before Melito of Sardis explicitly charged the Jews with deicide. Others will ask: who are the Jews in John? (All Jews? A particular group, such as Judaeans as opposed to Galileans?) Moreover was not John a Jew himself, like most, if not all of the New Testament writers? If so, is it meaningful to speak of anti-Jewishness or is this an example of a family quarrel from which Gentile Christians should disengage themselves. There are no easy answers, but at least the questions are now being honestly and painfully asked.

NOTES

1. I prefer this term to 'anti-Semitism' which is relatively modern and, strictly speaking, emphasizes racial rather than religious prejudice against Jews. I also prefer it to anti-Judaism, since prejudice was not only against a religion but against a 'people' (however difficult it is to define that term) who practised that religion. Professor Yehuda Bauer and others have argued for antisemitism rather than anti-Semitism, since there is no such phenomenon as Semitism that it opposes. See O'Hare 1997, 5.
2. Fackenheim 1994, 12.
3. Hilberg's list is found in Hilberg 1985, 11f.
4. For a sympathetic appraisal of Chrysostom and the Jews: Kelly 1995, 62–6.
5. His book *L'Enseignement du mépris* was published in Paris in 1962; then in English in 1964. His more exhaustive list of eighteen points is

   detailed in O'Hare 1997, 7–9.
6. Wilson 1986, 92f.
7. A. Christie, *Three Act Tragedy*. London, Fontana, 1935, 19, 21.
8. Klein 1978, *passim*.
9. Cf. J.L. Martyn, *History and Theology in the Fourth Gospel* rev. ed., Nashville, Abingdon, 1979, and R.E. Brown, *The Community of the Beloved Disciple*, New York, Paulist Press, 1979.
10. The digest of oral Torah, compiled around the end of the second and beginning of the third centuries.
11. In reality, there are two Talmuds, containing the teachings of rabbis in Babylon and Palestine, in the form of a running commentary on the Mishnah. They date from, respectively and approximately, 500 and 400.
12. Sanders 1992, 494.
13. Sanders 1990, 90.
14. Jacobs 1995, 442.
15. E.g. Sanders 1985, 311–18.
16. Bammel and Moule 1984, 241–63.
17. Coughlin 1997, 177–90.
18. Klausner 1928, 63f., 414, 397.
19. Lapide 1984, 129, 153.
20. Buber 1951, 12f.
21. Vermes 1993, 214.
22. His spiritual journey is recorded in his autobiography, *Providential Accidents* 1998.

5

JESUS AMONG THE RELIGIONS

J esus is inescapably located in one religion other than Christianity: Islam. He has also found a home in Hinduism and, to a lesser extent, Buddhism and some other faiths. This chapter will examine aspects of Jesus's appropriation and estimation by other religions, especially Islam, and how significant this is in our global village at the beginning of the third millennium of the Common Era.

The widespread modern interest in the figure of Jesus has been linked to the movements of Western imperialism, particularly in the last two centuries. The British, French and Dutch empires conferred some benefits on the people and lands they ruled: education and law, for example. But 'empire' has proved a controversial phenomenon, and it is probably still too early to assess its importance, negative and positive, with an impartial attitude. To a great extent, views of Jesus among people of other than Christian faith (and even by many colonialized Christians) have been coloured by his association with the beliefs of members of often overweening and dominant foreign governments.

CHRISTIANS AND MUSLIMS

Christian relations with the world of Islam have been particularly uneasy from the very beginning. Within five years of the death of the Prophet Muhammad, the holy city of Jerusalem had been captured from Christian Byzantine rule and, apart from a short period thereafter (1099–1187), it remained in Muslim hands until the twentieth century. That short period marked the first stage of the Crusader movement of the

High Middle Ages, when Muslims and Jews were slain in the name of Christ, for earthly reward and heavenly glory. The Crusader period and the modern imperial age when many Muslim lands were under Western, Christian rule has left its mark upon many Muslims, who associate Christianity with violence, treachery and bitter hatred of its sister monotheistic faiths.

Conversely, for over one thousand years Christian Europe lived in fear of Muslim conquest. Exactly a century after the death of the Prophet Muhammad, Charles Martel defeated Muslim forces at the Battle of Poitiers in France in 732. But for that event, it is likely that most Europeans would today be Muslims, like the inhabitants of the Middle East and North Africa, many of whose ancestors were once Christian. Indeed, throughout most of the European Middle Ages, parts of Spain were under Muslim rule. The ancient Christian city of Constantinople fell to Muslim rule in 1453. As late as 1683, Muslim Turks laid siege to the gates of Vienna.

Paranoia has gripped both Muslims and Christians about the ill-intent of the other and in our post-Cold War world, it is easy for Christians to depict Muslims as the major enemy, and vice versa. For the last two hundred years, Christian scholars have cast the same cool and appraising eye upon Islam as they have upon their own religion. Recently, many Muslims have dismissed this as 'Orientalism', the romanticization and demonization of Eastern ways and beliefs by voyeuristic Westerners.[1] In doing so, they have sweepingly dismissed any criticism as negative and unworthy of consideration.

Yet the figure of Jesus binds Christians and Muslims together, whether they wish him to or not. He is not just the central Christian figure but is claimed by Muslims as a prophet, appearing in Islam's holy scripture, the Quran. So it is important to discover whether he is potentially a figure to heal divisions between the two religions or one who merely adds fuel to the furnace of their disagreement. Past history has, sadly, suggested the latter.

The distinguished Christian Islamicist, Kenneth Cragg, in his earliest book, *The Call of the Minaret* (1956), identified five difficult areas for Christian–Muslim mutual understanding: the authority of scripture; the person of Jesus; Jesus's crucifixion; the doctrine of God; and the Christian church and society. All of these, explicitly or implicitly, raise issues about the controversial and divisive meaning of Jesus, and of the God to whom he points (as both religions would say) or embodies (as only Christians affirm).

JESUS IN THE QURAN

What then does Islam teach about Jesus? He figures in fifteen chapters and ninety-three verses of the Quran, or 'recitation', which Muslims believe God revealed to the Prophet Muhammad in piecemeal fashion from c.610 until 632, through the agency of the angel Gabriel (in Arabic, *Jibril*). Much important information is given about Jesus therein.

His mother, Mary, was the daughter of Imran. His wife was upset at giving birth to a girl but implored God's help for her and her offspring. God concurred and, when Mary grew up, Zechariah was chosen by lot to be her guardian. Whenever he went into the sanctuary, he found that Mary had been fed with food she said had been provided by God (Q3:33–7, 44). The story of the Annunciation is told twice (Q3:42–7; 19:16–22). She had withdrawn towards the east, and was concealed behind a curtain. Either angels came to her, or else God's spirit came in the reassuring form of a perfect man. Mary asked how she could have a son since she had not been impure. She was told either that God brings into being what he wills simply by commanding it, or that such a thing is easy for God and that her son would be a sign for humankind, a mercy from God and a manifestation ordained.

She removed herself to a far place; then, when the birth pangs came, went to the trunk of a palm tree, where she complained that she wished to be dead and forgotten. A voice told her to cease grieving, to drink from a stream the Lord had provided there and to eat dates which would fall from the tree when she shook it (Q19:22–5; 23:50). She was told to speak to nobody. She brought the boy to her kith and kin, who called her 'sister of Aaron' and exclaimed that her father had not been a wicked man nor her mother a strumpet. She pointed to the child who spoke in her defence, saying that he was God's slave and that God had given him a scripture and designated him a prophet. He further said that God had made him blessed, had commanded him to pray and give alms for all of his life, and that peace was upon the day of his birth, the day of his death and the day he was to be raised to life (Q19:26–33).

Mary was told that Jesus would speak to humankind when in the cradle and when grown up (Q3:46). He was strengthened by the Spirit, and taught the scripture and wisdom, the Torah and the Gospel. He breathed life into a clay bird by God's permission, and also, by divine permission, healed the blind and the lepers, and brought forth the dead (Q5:110). He witnessed to the truth of what was in the Torah, but made lawful some things that had hitherto been forbidden (Q3:50). He warned that heaven was barred to those who ascribed partners to God (Q5:72), a barbed condemnation of both Arabian paganism and Christian Trinitarianism; also, perhaps, of the Jews' overemphasis, as Muslims see it, on the details of religious law (Q9:30). He taught that he was sent to establish the religion that had been Noah's, Abraham's and Moses', and was also Muhammad's (Q42:13), particularly the unity of God. Christians are wrong to designate God as three (Q5.72f.). When God questioned him, Jesus denied that he told humans to take himself and his mother as gods apart from God, and said that although God knew what was in his, Jesus's mind, he does not know what is in God's mind (Q5:116). Jesus told of a messenger after him who would be called Ahmad ('the praised one'; Q61:6).

Jesus's disciples asked him whether God could send down a table filled with food to eat so that they could be certain he spoke truly. Jesus asked God to do so, as a feast but also as a sign. God agreed, but stated that after that he would punish in a singular way any who disbelieved (Q5:112–15).

At the end of Jesus's life, the Quran records two events that are difficult to interpret: the death of Jesus and his return to herald the last day. Most Muslims believe that Jesus did not die, but was taken up by God and will return as a sign of the last day. However, that is probably not the meaning of the Quran but, rather, how many Muslims have interpreted it.

It can be argued that the weight of the Quran, as opposed to many interpretations of it, is in favour of a real death. For example, Quran 19:33, 'Peace is upon me [Jesus], the day of my birth and the day of my death', indicates that Jesus died and that his raising up is at the general resurrection of all people when the world ends. Jesus's return to God is mentioned in Quran 3:55 and Quran 5:117, verses which are most naturally interpreted to refer to his death. The first of these passages runs:

> So God said: 'Jesus, I shall take you up and draw you to me, and make you pure from those who disbelieve, and place those who follow you ahead of those who disbelieve until the day when all are raised. Then your return will be to me, and I shall arbitrate among you all about the disagreements between you.'

The Arabic word *mutawaffika*, employed in these passages of Jesus, is used of people dying in Quran 2:240 and, in Quran 6:60, of believers being called to God in the night, raised up to complete a stated term and returning to him. The most contentious passage between Muslims and Christians about Jesus is Quran 4:157, which most Muslims see as a denial of the crucifixion. This in turn has led them to interpret Quran 3:55 against its natural sense, to mean that Jesus did not die. Quran 4:157 comes in a section (Q4:155–9) which runs:

> So for their breaking their [the Jews'] covenant, and disbelieving the signs of God, and killing the prophets without right . . . and for their unbelief, and their speaking against Mary a great slander; and for their saying: 'We killed the Messiah, Jesus the Son of Mary, the messenger of God' – though they did not kill him, and did not crucify him, but only a likeness of it was shown to them. Truly, those who have gone in different ways about him are in doubt about him; they have no knowledge of him and only follow speculation; though they certainly did not kill him. No, to be sure, God raised him to himself. God is almighty and wise. And there is no People of the Book but will surely believe in him before his death, and on the day of resurrection he will be a witness against them.

The most widely held view among Muslims about this passage is that the Jews tried to kill Jesus but were unable to do so. Many believe that there was a substitute who suffered in his place. The canonical Gospels affirm that Jesus truly died and have no suggestion of a replacement figure. Against them, Muslims have slender support in the teaching of the second-century CE Egyptian Gnostic and Christian Basilides, whose views only survive in rather diverse interpretations by his opponents. The idea of a substitute, perhaps Judas Iscariot or Simon of Cyrene, has been accepted by some notable Muslim commentators of the Quran. For example, Tabari (d. 923) believed that a Jewish chief called Joshua, whom God gave the form and appearance of Jesus, died in his place. However the passage hardly demands this interpretation, which does not seem its obvious import. I have rendered the Arabic *shubbiha la-hum* as 'only a likeness of it was shown to them'. It is possible that the Arabic words mentioned should be attached to the crucifixion and not Jesus. Then the meaning of a very difficult passage could be that the Jews did not kill Jesus, rather than that he did not die. Such an interpretation could perhaps lead to interesting dialogue between Muslims and Christians.

The Muslim Egyptian surgeon and educationalist Kamel Hussein has argued that:

> No cultured Muslim believes . . . nowadays [that someone substituted for Jesus on the cross]. The text is taken to mean that the Jews thought they killed Christ but God raised him unto Him in a way we can leave unexplained among the several mysteries which we have taken for granted on faith alone.[2]

Christians, of course, would not feel able to leave this simply as a mystery. Along with Paul, most believe that 'in Christ God was reconciling the world to himself, not counting their trespasses against them, and entrusting the ministry of reconciliation to us' (2 Corinthians 5:19). Naturally, Christian scholars like Kenneth Cragg and Geoffrey Parrinder who have examined the Quranic accounts of the death of Jesus offer their own estimates of how this event might be fruitful for conversation between Christians and Muslims.

Cragg in particular offers much food for thought. He affirms that Muhammad is a prophet, but that the deepest needs of humanity cannot be met by a prophet but only by a suffering Messiah. His affirmation shows how an assessment of Jesus between the two faiths cannot be made independently of a Christian interpretation of Muhammad, often hitherto lacking, partly because Muhammad has no place in Christian scriptures, as Jesus does in Islam's. This lack is not just for that reason. The difficult history between Christianity and Islam has not led the former to be generous towards the latter. Further, as Cragg himself has ventured to suggest: 'How is the Christian to contemplate positive acknowledgement of Muhammad when his prophetic significance [for Muslims] involves such crucial disavowal of truths Christian [not least that Jesus is the suffering Messiah]?'[3]

Muslims are reluctant to be drawn into such a discourse. Though an important figure, Jesus himself is not central to their faith. Muhammad is, and both he and the Quranic Jesus emphasized rather different attitudes to faith and practice than did the Jesus of the New Testament and Orthodox Christian doctrine.[4]

THE QURANIC OR THE SYNOPTIC JESUS?

We have seen that much modern Western scholarship about the historical Jesus has embraced the tools of Enlightenment knowledge to uncover his life and meaning. Islamic learning is different. The vast majority of

Muslims have believed and still do believe that the Quran is precisely the word of God. Muhammad is the vessel through which it flowed to humankind in the last two decades or so of his life. The contextual meaning of the Quran was then established through traditions (Arabic: *ahadith*; singular, *hadith*) of the Prophet's words and deeds that were recorded by his earliest and most devoted followers, collected in compilations and often incorporated in biographies and other works about him, and also through various commentaries (some of these are still being written).

What, then, of the differences between the Synoptic Gospels' and the Quranic accounts of Jesus? For the writers of the New Testament, Jesus was the most important of human beings, the central figure in God's gracious dealings with humankind. Not so, according to the Quran. To be sure, in the Quran Jesus is a much honoured figure, more so than any other figure of the past. He is called Jesus, Messiah, Son of Mary, Messenger, Prophet, Servant, Word, and Spirit of God. Even so, Muhammad is the 'seal of the prophets' (Q33:40); and Abraham and, arguably, Moses are more important Quranic figures than Jesus is. Moreover, the titles by which Jesus is called are emptied of any significant theological meaning. For example, the Quran does not have any inkling of either Jewish or specifically Christian interpretations of what or who the Messiah is.

Ironies abound as Christian and Muslim academics interpret Muhammad in various books and scholarly colloquies. For many Christians, the historical and even theological value of the virgin birth of Jesus is questionable, whereas Muslims will strongly defend this teaching since they interpret it as in accord with the Quran's teaching. In this instance, it is Christian sceptics who are treating the material historically (even if not all would accept their conclusions), whereas Muslims are making a pious, unquestioning commitment on the basis of a straightforward and uncritical reading of their sacred text.

Moreover, many Christians are doubtful of the value of the sources of the Quranic portrayal of Jesus. For example, the story of Jesus making clay birds can be found in the Arabic Infancy Gospel and other non-canonical works. It is also found in the *Toledot Yeshu*, a scurrilous Jewish appraisal of Jesus's life. Christians find these works worthless as historical or even as theological sources for understanding Jesus. They can even point to possible misunderstandings by the Quran in its accounts of Jesus's life. For example, Mary (in Arabic, Maryam) is said to be the sister of Aaron. Is this a confusion with the biblical story of Moses, who had a brother Aaron and a sister Miriam? Some Muslims take the phrase to mean 'descendant', rather than 'sister' of Aaron. Others hold that it was common to name children after a great and pious figure of the past. My own judgement, not polemical in intent but because it is the most obvious reading of the text, is that the Quran is mistaken on this point, and confuses different stories. Yet, for most Muslims, there can be no question of questioning the truth of the Quranic account, since God gave it, and to contemplate sources of the Quran, other than God himself, is manifest error.

Even where there is broad agreement between Bible and Quran about events in the life of Jesus, such as the fact that he performed miracles and healed the sick, the details of the stories point to very great differences between them. Sometimes, apparent agreements are nothing of the sort. For example, although Christians believe that Jesus acted in obedience to God, the Quran's insistence that he did nothing without God's permission is not really making the same point. Rather, the Quran is implying, and sometimes even explicitly insisting, that Jesus is simply a human being and not God. This is probably an anti-Christian point. Those scholars who tend to divide Christian commentators on the Quranic view of Jesus into either polemicists or apologists, but who fail to deal with the apologetic or even polemical character of Islamic views of Jesus are simply unconvincing; ironically, they come close to being apologists and polemicists themselves.[5] Playing down differences between faiths will not improve relations between them. This can only begin to be achieved by an attitude of respectful honesty.

As Julian Baldick has written, Muslims and Christians have very different views of the historicity of their original sources. He provocatively but forthrightly writes:

> The standard Muslim biography of Muhammad, composed well over a hundred years after his death, and edited in the ninth century [Ibn Hisham's (d. 833 or 828) revision of Ibn Ishaq's (d. c.767) work] is the earliest extended narrative that we possess. Today no serious student of early Christianity would imagine that its beginnings could be reconstructed, or the life of Jesus convincingly retold, if so lengthy an interval existed between our sources and the period to which they refer.[6]

Christians must respect Muslim attitudes towards their scripture, but it is pointless and untruthful to harmonize the different views. If Christians believe that their own scripture was written by human beings, then they can hardly with integrity hold that the scripture of Islam is wholly God's. If historical methodology is a tool to uncover the truth of one's own faith, it cannot logically be withheld from the assessment of another's. Yet it happens surprisingly often that Christian as well as Muslim scholars compare Muhammad or the Quran as Muslims uncover him or it, with Jesus as modern scholarship reveals him.[7] That procedure is, to overstate but emphasize the point, to compare the Jesus of history with the Muhammad or Quran of faith. It is to fail to compare like with like.

The fact that, from a Christian perspective, there are human sources of scripture, and that it will not do simply to privilege its information as God-given, would lead most Christians to deny that the Quran is of any historical worth as a source of information about Jesus. It came into being, humanly speaking, over half a millennium after the Synoptic Gospels. It appears to reflect the views of marginal Christian groups and works that were not accepted as part of the Christian canon.

How then, if at all, can Christians and Muslims proceed, if they are honest about this central distinction? Muslims believe that authentic scripture is wholly God's; Christians that it is mediated through fallible human beings, though inspired by God's spirit. For this reason, attempts by some Muslims to argue that 'present-day Christianity is a "mask" on the face of Jesus ... the Muslim believes in the Jesus of history and refuses to accept the "mask"'[8] do not ring true. The Muslim picture of Jesus is not a figure from the academic discipline of history, but is the product of a particular theology of revelation that Christians do not share; not, as many Muslims believe, of which they are ignorant.

Some Muslims are beginning to broaden the definition of revelation. A very few even believe that, in some sense, the Quran is Muhammad's, and indeed its many interpreters', as well as God's.[9] At any rate, not all Muslim proponents of the Quran's divine origin would argue for the historical accuracy of its stories. Stories can be God-given – yet as stories, not as historical narratives! The Bible and the Quran arose within a context of creative storytelling and myth-making, which were intended to change people's lives. The New Testament parables illustrates this. So may, for example, the two rather different Quranic accounts of the Annunciation. It is not always the literal sense of a story, still less whether it actually happened, that conveys its deepest meaning. Indeed, if I concentrate on judging the story's historicity, that may be a way of sidestepping its primary purpose of judging me!

History is, of course, important, but it ought not to be an absolute monarch, brooking no rivals. The creative imagination sometimes encourages us to be humble before myths and stories which lay bare the human condition as much if not more than any rational analysis is able to do.

It could be argued that some New Testament scholars lack a feel for the reverence in which sacred texts have been held by believers over many centuries. True, sometimes such reverence has been superstitious or, worse, led to the persecution of those who hold other points of view. It may also be true that popular piety has mistaken the signpost for the goal to which it points, by giving to scripture the veneration due only to God himself. Certainly, many Christian scholars have been careful to point out, on the basis of John chapter 1, verse 1–18, that Jesus is the Word of God in a primary sense, and the Christian scriptures are secondary witnesses to that primal Word. Maybe so, but the statement of some Christian academics about their scripture can give the impression that their central conclusions are, at best, disrespectful of a numinous document, or, at worst, impious.

Take a statement such as: 'Like the Bible as a whole, the Gospels are human, not divine, products. They therefore can be studied in the same way as other ancient documents.'[10] This, written by a member of the Jesus Seminar, may indeed be true, as far as it goes. Yet other ancient documents have not formed and sustained a life of faith for Christians over two millennia. They are not, therefore, fittingly the objects of awe and gratitude; nor are they iconic, windows of salvation into the heart and mind of God. Perhaps Christian biblical scholars should listen to voices from other faiths about how they reverence their holy writ. Muslims treat the Quran with the greatest of respect. It is often kept apart from other books and nothing is ever placed on top of it. Muslims never call it simply 'the Quran', but always use some honorary adjective. So they may call it 'Illustrious Quran', 'Noble Quran', or 'Glorious Quran'. They often wash their hands before they handle and read it. They know how important it is to read it in the original language of Arabic, rather than just in translation. Of course, this can become a formal and lifeless discipline. Equally, it can make the Quran into an idol, replacing God as the centre of a Muslim's worship. But it need not. Muslims know that their scripture is a different sort of work than any other, for in it God's will is recorded, and it has sustained the faith and devotion of millions of worshippers over many centuries.[11]

This does not mean that Christians must abandon the historical-critical method. They should not, however, see it as an end in itself. Rather, they should reckon with the possibility, even the likelihood, that, through the tools of historical methodology, God kindles and sustains the flame of faith. That surely ought to encourage reverence for the sacred text. Then perhaps Christians could encourage Muslims to have more regard and respect for the historical and other tools that unlock the meanings of the sacred text. Even though Christians and Muslims would, in all likelihood, continue to disagree about the aspects of the life and meaning of Jesus, Muslims might find it easier to take seriously the findings of historical Jesus research if they believed that it was a reverent rather than an impious enterprise.

JESUS BETWEEN CHRISTIANS AND MUSLIMS

The routes that Christianity and Islam trace through this world to the next are, in some respects, very different. Although many things are held in common between the two faiths, many other things are not. For this reason, some evangelical scholars have asked whether there is enough in common between Christian and Muslim ideas of God for us to be able to use the same word. It seems truer to argue, not that we believe in different Gods but that we believe in the One God differently. This is also closer to the Muslim conviction that Jews, Christians and Muslims are 'People of the Book', sharing some things in common even if they diverge significantly over certain beliefs and practices.

It is not surprising then that each religion conforms its heroes and heroines to its fundamental beliefs. For Muslims, Jesus teaches the unity of God and the certainty of judgement. For Christians, these concepts are also important, but they are very differently defined, and so the Jesus who supports the Muslim view of them often looks like an alien intruder, not an authentic spokesperson. Further, although Muslims honour Jesus, he is not so loved and revered as Muhammad, the last of the prophets. Sir Muhammad Iqbal (d. 1938), the great South Asian Muslim poet, summed up what most Muslims have felt about Muhammad over the centuries, when he wrote: 'Love of the Prophet runs like blood in the veins of his community.'[12]

From a Christian point of view, the Muslim honouring of Jesus is secondary to the esteem in which Muhammad is held, and therefore misleading as to his importance. To take an example from the rich and profound mystical Sufi tradition of Islam: Ibn al-Arabi (1165–1240; often called 'the Greatest Shaykh'), who is associated with the Sufi concept of 'the Oneness of Being', called Jesus 'the seal of the saints'. This is a puzzling designation, though it clearly parallels the Quranic description of Muhammad as the 'seal of the prophets'. The word 'saint' is rather different in Islam from its meaning in Christianity. In the latter, it suggests officially endorsed holiness or sanctity. In Islam, it indicates someone who is a client or protégé of God and who protects lesser Muslims. So we have an example of how a word (sometimes because of an inept linguistic or conceptual translation from one religion into another) can convey very different though not wholly unrelated impressions to members of different religions. Moreover, although Islamic mysticism greatly honours Jesus, it does not usually accord Jesus equality with (or, as Christians might prefer, superiority to) Muhammad. For example, the Persian mystical poet Iraqi wrote, in the thirteenth century, that:

> A pinch of his [Muhammad's] noble being
> Was placed in Jesus's breath,
> And from the radiance of the candle of his countenance
> Moses's fire was lighted.[13]

So we meet here the belief that previous prophets were partial aspects of the light of Muhammad: that, certainly; but no more than that. Dirini (d. 1297) forthrightly and lovingly expressed the superiority of Muhammad to his great predecessors:

> Certainly, Adam is God's special friend, Moses the one with
> whom God spoke,
> Jesus is even the spirit of God – but you [Muhammad] are
> something different.[14]

This is a perfectly natural view for a Muslim to express. Even so, Christians cannot be expected to share its sentiments about Jesus. Very often, Muslims express distress that Christians do not honour Muhammad at all, whereas they greatly respect Jesus. The problem is that Muhammad has no place in the Christian vision of ultimate reality and, from the Christian perspective, the Muslim view of Jesus is at best inadequate, and can be claimed to be seriously misleading. This is a serious issue for dialogue between the two faiths.

DISSENTING MUSLIM ASSESSMENTS OF JESUS

Although Jesus is honoured by most Muslims, some criticize him. The Ahmadiyya are a heterodox Islamic group founded in north India by Mirza Ghulam Ahmad (c.1836–1908), who declared that Jesus had not died on the cross but was rescued by his disciples and went to Kashmir, where he died and was buried. Ghulam Ahmad proclaimed that he himself was the spirit and power of Jesus. The Ahmadiyya accept him as Messiah and *mahdi* (Arabic: 'the one who is rightly guided'), contrary to the orthodox Islamic view that Jesus is the Messiah and Muhammad the last and greatest of the prophets. Writing in 1959 about their presence in Nigeria, the British scholar of religious studies, Geoffrey Parrinder, observed that they:

> have become exceedingly active in literature, education and propaganda, claiming converts among Christians as well as among animists ... In Lagos they print literature and journals, and a weekly column every Friday in the chief English newspaper (the 'Daily Times', with a daily circulation of over 80,000), is written by the chief Imam of the Ahmadiyya, and often contains anti-Christian propaganda, intended for literates.

It is likely that their missionary endeavours spurred him to write his book *Jesus in the Qur'ân*, to refute their allegations.[15]

A more centrally Muslim figure was Syed Ameer Ali (1849–1928), an Indian judge who argued that, unlike Jesus and all other previous prophets, Muhammad completed God's will by founding an obedient community. Basing his argument on certain early nineteenth-century Christian writers such as H. H. Milman, though drawing rather different conclusions, he asserted that Jesus's influence was least among his family and closest followers. Muhammad's family and friends, however, were warmly supportive of him. (This was by no means wholly true.) This proved to Ameer Ali's satisfaction that the later prophet was the greater religious figure. Also, drawing upon the sentimental portrayal of Jesus by the nineteenth-century Frenchman Ernest Renan, Ameer Ali argued that Jesus's failure to develop his teachings systematically led the way for Paul to infuse his simple teaching of the unity of God with neo-Pythagorean and other unwanted Hellenistic teachings. Thus Jesus's teachings, fulfilled in those of Muhammad, have become complicated and corrupted by Christianity.[16]

Although Ameer Ali's selective trawl through pages of the New Testament makes reference to Christian and secular scholars, the picture of Jesus he draws is controlled by central Muslim convictions of the unity of God, Islam as the final religion, and Muhammad as the seal of the prophets.

Ameer Ali's convictions have been taken up by other Muslims. In particular, the notion that Jesus failed to fulfil his mission, either because he died too soon or because Muhammad's life was intrinsically more meritorious, has often been reproduced in the writings of other South Asian Muslims. Occasionally, these writers come close to condemning Jesus in ways that many Muslims would feel inappropriate, on the grounds that all prophets are to be accorded honour. One relatively recent writer, Azhar, has vehemently objected to the Sermon on the Mount not only as 'pathetic and escapist', but also as reactionary, in that it appeased the Roman rulers, and made a virtue out of suffering and oppression, offering hope in the next world rather than in this. He sees turning the other cheek as demonstrating an 'utter lack of guts'. Since it is unreasonable and impractical, it has given rise to a history of torture and killing in Christianity, because 'Suppress an instinct completely, and you have laid sure foundations for the opposite instinct.'[17]

THE FUTURE OF JESUS IN ISLAM

What can be predicted about Jesus in Islam at the threshold of the third millennium? Perhaps the most obvious point to make is that it is for Muslims to determine, not for Christians and other outsiders. Christians do not have to agree with that determination, but to seek to control or maybe even to influence it could be interpreted by Muslims as another example of neo-colonialism and Orientalism.

One can guess that for many Muslims, Jesus will remain what he has always been: an important prophet, but not so important as some others, especially Muhammad. He will continue to be regarded by many Muslims as a witness against Christians for their belief in such unIslamic concepts as the doctrine of the Trinity. If the present climate of Islamophobia continues in the West, that will naturally encourage an equal fear of Christianity in Muslim lands. This would not encourage Muslims to consider a role for Jesus that would offer scope for more fruitful dialogue between Christians and Muslims.

However, one can be too pessimistic as well as too sanguine. The widespread migration of Muslims to Western countries since the end of World War II has led many (though by no means all) to remain both attached to their faith, yet also to the country in which they live. Many highly educated Muslims now live in the West. It may be that from their ranks, creative interpreters of Islam may come who will assess its relation to Christianity and its founder.

Scholarly colloquies, although they have their limitations, also serve to bring Christian and Muslim academics together for respectful dialogue. For the most part, womens' voices have been absent from these conversations between Christians and Muslims. This would seem a significant omission that should be rectified. The future looks exciting. The question of Jesus for Muslims, as indeed Muhammad for Christians, may look much more interesting and different in twenty years' time.

AVATAR AND INCARNATION

Although Islam has traditionally forbidden the incarnation of God, on the grounds that God alone is God, many Christians would want to argue that God may become incarnate as he wishes, since nothing is forbidden to him. It is unlikely that Christians and Muslims would agree on this point, though ironic that the same desire to let God be God points to such different conclusions.

However, Christians and Hindus might agree on the appearance of God in human form. One of the most interesting potential contact points between Hindus and Christians is the Hindu doctrine of *avatara*. According to the Bhagavad Gita, when righteousness declines and injustice floods the earth, God comes down (*ava-tri* means 'downcoming') to establish order. As a human or as an animal, God (usually Lord Vishnu) descends and rescues the needy. So, as a fish, he guides Manu through the great flood; as a man-lion, he slays a demon and rescues the young boy Prahlada; as Rama, he renounces his kingdom and, exiled, kills the demons of the forest; as Krishna, he fills his devotees with love.

In a Hindu home, one might enter a room set aside for *puja* (worship), and discover on the wall, pictures of Rama, Krishna and Jesus. Christians might be shocked by this juxtaposition. The Hindu might be similarly scandalized by the Christian claim that the incarnation occurred only once, long ago and in a far off place. Is this not a restriction on God's saving love?

Geoffrey Parrinder lists twelve characteristics of *avatara* doctrines. They are:

1. In Hindu belief the Avatar is real.
2. The human Avatars take worldly birth.
3. The lives of Avatars mingle divine and human.
4. The Avatars finally die.
5. There may be historicity in some Avatara.
6. Avatars are repeated.
7. The example and character of the Avatars is important.
8. The Avatar comes with work to do.
9. The Avatars show some reality in the world.
10. The Avatar is a guarantee of divine revelation.
11. Avatars reveal a personal God.
12. Avatars reveal a God of grace.

Parrinder undertook this summary to show Christian theologians what resemblances there might be between Hindu and Christian teaching. Because the epistle to the Hebrews, which invented the phrase 'once for all', places Christ in the succession of prophets and angelic messengers, Parrinder believes that there is a basis for comparing them.[18] Certainly, his list suggests some important similarities between avatar and Christian incarnation. He recognizes too that there have been Hindu critics of the avatar doctrines as philosophically or theologically naive or contradictory, or simply improper as a representation of God's being and his ways.

There may be more possibility for comparison between Hindu avatar doctrines and the Christian belief in incarnation than Parrinder suggests. The great medieval Christian theologian Thomas Aquinas (1225–74) considered the possibility of multiple divine incarnations in diverse forms in his *Summa Theologiae*. He argued that either the Father or the Son or the Spirit could become incarnate in one human nature or in several individuals.[19] However, Aquinas believed that God had in reality become incarnate only once, in Jesus. Yet his was not a purely theoretical discussion. At issue is the power of God to do as he wills. Aquinas knew nothing of Indian beliefs. One speculates what a contemporary Thomist theologian let loose in South Asia to explore this insight of his master might make of avatar and incarnation.

Parrinder, a Methodist minister and not a Catholic Thomist, although appreciative of *avatara* aims and instincts, nevertheless affirms the

Christian belief in the uniqueness of Christ. He believes that Hindus have less sense of sin than Christians. For them, the power of *karma* (the cumulative effects of deeds in past lives and the present one) is a chain that must be broken, but not a fall that defiles the inner nature and demands a saviour.[20] It may be more true to say that Hindus locate the origin and overcoming of evil and suffering in the transcendence of God, whereas Christians locate its defeat in the immanence of the incarnation, and Jesus's victory over sin and death on the cross. Is this an impasse or, as Hindus might believe, could it be two faces of the same ultimate reality?

Hindus, of course, have a very different view of reality than Christians. *Karma* and *dharma* (virtue, right, morality) are tied into a cyclical view of history, and avatars traditionally come when the cycle has brought about destruction and unrighteousness. All creatures, humans too, are bound up in a process of rebirth. Christians believe in a linear view of history, and in one life only, after which is judgement. In the face of such disparate fundamental understandings of existence, facile comparisons should falter. Yet it is just as foolish to maintain that no comparisons can be made. Any Christian with a Hindu friend knows how difficult, yet not impossible, comparisons are. And in a diverse yet increasingly interconnected world, good human relations cannot be built by refusing to consider the claims of others because they arise out of different historical or philosophical matrices.

HINDU APPROPRIATIONS OF JESUS

Intriguingly, it was Hindus, not Indian Christians, who first appropriated Jesus and reflected on his meaning within the Indian context. Early in the nineteenth century, the Brahmo Samaj (as it was called after 1843, though its origins date back to 1814 and it was reformed again in the 1860s), a Hindu reform movement based in Calcutta, pioneered Indian Christologies, through the works of Rajah Ram Mohun Roy (1774–1833), Keshub Chunder Sen (1838–84) and others. The Brahmo Samaj responded to Christian missionary activity, not by converting to Christianity, but by cleansing Hinduism from what its members believed were antiquated and outworn beliefs and customs. Jesus became an inspiration to them. Thus, for Ram Mohun Roy he was the Supreme Guide to human happiness, whereas Keshub Chunder Sen depicted him as true Yogi and Divine Humanity.

These and other Hindus incorporated Jesus into their world of philosophy, belief and action. Perhaps the two most famous Hindu exponents of Jesus have been Swami Vivekananda (1863–1902) and Mohandas Karamchand Gandhi. Vivekananda's speech at the World Parliament of Religions in Chicago in 1893 gave a strong impetus to a Vedantic, inclusive view of Hinduism, which is only now beginning to be challenged in India by other more exclusive views from its religious heritage. Gandhi's commitment to the Sermon on the Mount led him to believe in Jesus as the supreme *satyagrahi*, a struggler after the force of truth.[21] These Hindu appropriations of Jesus raise two questions about such 'borrowings' in our global village. The first is that, in the delicate balance between indigenization and conformity to another worldview, there are many snares for the unwary, a point to which we shall return in Chapter 6. The second is that others may appropriate not only the noble and the good from another tradition, but also the more contentious and undesirable. For example, Vivekananda accepted at face value the standard Christian interpretation that first-century Judaism was in a state of stagnation and suffering from which Jesus was to deliver it, and that the Pharisees and Sadducees might have been insincere and doing things they should not have done.[22] Thus discussions between two parties in modern dialogue can adversely affect impressions of another group or groups!

Not all Hindus have been persuaded that Jesus is an attractive figure. Dayananda Sarasvati (1824–83) founded a Hindu reform movement in 1875, whose aims were rather different than those of the Brahmo Samaj. His Arya Samaj set its face against idol worship and superstition, and placed morality and rationality at the centre of religion. Although he was influenced by Protestant Christianity, he inveighed against Christian faith as a foreign import and an agent of colonial oppression. Jesus therefore comes in for serious criticism and even ridicule. Sarasvati quotes Matthew's account of Jesus's words at the Last Supper ('Take, eat, this is my body. . . this is my blood'). He comments:

> Can a cultured man ever do such a thing? Only an ignorant savage would do it. No enlightened man would ever call the food of his disciples his flesh nor their drink his blood. This is called the Lord's Supper by the Christians of the present day. They eat and drink imagining all the time that their bread was the flesh of Christ and their drink his blood. Is not it an awful thing? How could those, who could not even keep aloof from

the idea that their food and drink were the flesh and blood of their saviour, abstain from the flesh and blood of others?

Moreover, with regard to the last discourse in John chapter 14, Sarasvati comments that:

> Had no one attained God before Christ? All this boasting about his Father's mansions and about his going to prepare a place for his followers and speaking with his own lips about his being the way, the truth and the life were nothing but a hoax and hence can never be true.[23]

To some extent, this verdict doubtless arises out of Sarasvati's anger with the imperial system and Christianity's connection to it. Yet the faces of Hindu India point in many directions. Not all interpretations of other ways are interpreted with generosity, not even by some Hindu interpretations that claim to draw their meaning from India's Vedic scriptures. Images of Jesus have been accepted and transformed by many Hindus, but rejected and ridiculed by others.

JESUS AND THE BUDDHA

One example of Hindu India's capacity to accept, marginalize and conform other ultimate visions to its own is in its treatment of Buddhism. Although it began in north India, and soon spread outwards into surrounding and then further areas of Asia, it became all but extinct in the land of its birth. Yet the Buddha became venerated by many Hindus as an incarnation of Lord Vishnu; ironically, since he was sceptical about the capacity of God or gods to deliver humans from their predicament.

Buddhism is growing in the Western world. One reason is that it offers a genuine alternative to Christianity. The way of the Buddha seems to these converts a more credible route for humans to follow than the way of Jesus. Over six centuries before Jesus, Gautama Siddhartha, the Buddha ('awakened one') tried many ways of meaning, without success. Then, under a Bodhi tree, he woke up to life's fullest meaning. He preached his first sermon at the Deer Park in Sarnath, near to Banaras, Hindu India's holiest city. It was on the four noble truths. The first is the truth of *dukkha*, often translated as 'suffering', but with connotations of impermanence and imperfection. The second is the cause of suffering, which is our clinging to or yearning after an ego, a permanent self that exists amid the wreckage of life. There is no such ego. The third noble truth is the end of suffering, *nirvana*, or enlightenment, when we concentrate on the present moment and experience the vastness of the enlightened mind. The fourth truth is the way that leads to the end of suffering and the achievement of *nirvana*, which is the noble eightfold path. Of the eight, the first two, right views and right resolve, indicate an understanding of the Buddhist way and an intention to follow it. Then come right speech, right action and right livelihood, which are concerned with correct living. Right effort, right mindfulness, and right concentration refer to higher levels of spiritual exertion and meditation.

Theravada Buddhism believes in only a few past Buddhas, and some to come, with one Buddha only for this present world age, Gautama. Mahayana Buddhists believe in numerous Buddhas and Bodhisattvas (beings destined for enlightenment). Some Christians and Buddhists have found fruitful grounds for assessing Jesus within this matrix of beliefs.

However, the philosophical bases of Buddhism and Christianity are quite different. Arising out of Hinduism, Buddhism accepts the idea of many births and a cyclical view of history. Indeed, it is crucial to an understanding of the Buddha's teaching. This can be illustrated from the night of Gautama Siddhartha's awakening. In the first watch of the night, he remembered his previous lives within *samsara*, the never-ceasing wheel of life. In the second watch, he understood that people's present experiences were caused by *karma*, their previous actions.

In the Buddhist view of things, God and the gods, too, are caught up on the wheel of *samsara*. They are not able to liberate people. Each individual has to work out her own *nirvana*. Some Protestant Christians have seen this as justification by works, but that is to miss the point of the different conceptual frameworks of the two religions of Christianity and Buddhism, and to misunderstand and trivialize the Buddha's teaching. Other Christian scholars have argued that Buddhism is nevertheless theistic, because it does not deny the existence of God or the gods. Yet many thoughtful Buddhists hold that their religion is practically, if not theoretically, atheistic. It may be that, from a Christian viewpoint, fruitful conversation can be had about God who cannot save even himself (Mark 15:31; Matthew 27:41f.; Luke 23:35). For most Buddhists, however, it is belief in God that condemns Christianity and even Jesus in their eyes. For example:

The nineteenth-century Japanese Buddhist scholar Enryo Inoue remarked once: 'It is neither because I favor Sakya-muni [Gautama the Buddha] nor because I am prejudiced against Jesus that I uphold Buddhism and reject Christianity. It is simply because I love truth and hate untruth.'[24]

Less provocatively but still challengingly, Lily de Silva has written:

One main reason that makes me appreciate Buddhism in preference to a theistic religion is its frank open-mindedness. The *Kalamasutta* exhorts the disciple not to accept a proposition as true just on the authority of the teacher, scriptures or tradition. Even logic is of limited value. One is advised to exercise one's judgement intelligently to see if a behaviour, when cultivated, is conducive to one's happiness or suffering. Verifiability is an important criterion of truth. Unverifiable propositions regarding the world and humans, such as whether the world is finite or infinite, eternal or not, and whether the world and humans were created by a God or not, for which proofs can never be found, are prudently left aside as useless speculative pursuits. That pragmatic attitude pleases me very much.[25]

Geoffrey Parrinder has suggested that every religion, whether it believes in a personal God or not, has saviour-type figures. There is something that needs such an exemplar, even in the most austere forms of faith. He believes that the Buddha functions like that for many Buddhists. He is effectively divine, having been deified by a kind of personality cult.[26] At the level of popular or folk religion, there may be something in this view. It could, of course, be extended beyond Buddhism, even to Islam in the way some of that religion's devotees celebrate and affirm the Prophet Muhammad.

It is one thing, however, to detect important, venerated figures in each religion, but quite a different matter as to whether they are 'salvation' models. The distinguished Buddhist scholar, Edward Conze (d. 1979) has shown how difficult it is to make meaningful comparisons between apparently similar terms in another religion's sacred language and one's own. When the Baptist William Carey and his missionary colleagues in Bengal translated the New Testament into Sanskrit in 1808, they used *trana* for 'salvation' and *tratur* for 'saviour', the root being *trai*, 'to protect'. Yet Buddhist terminology has no exact equivalent to the Christian conception of a saviour; certainly *tratur* is never used to translate any of Buddhism's 'saviour-type' figures. Conze contended that Buddhist beliefs about such figures are in many ways:

so similar to Christian views that missionaries have often seen them as a counterfeit gospel deliberately created by the Devil to deceive the faithful.

At the same time, when the exact words of the originals are faithfully rendered into English it becomes obvious that there are no precise equivalents to key terms; that the finer shades of meaning and the emotional flavours and overtones differ throughout, that much of this teaching must seem strange to Christians and that in fact the logic behind it is at variance with all the basic presuppositions of Christians.[27]

The force of Conze's argument is that when people of faith insist on exporting the words and terms by which they understand their own religion, they are liable seriously to misunderstand another's faith. Out of a natural desire to understand what they do not know solely on the basis of what they do, they may translate a word or concept in another's religious vocabulary by one that is in their own, which has certain superficial similarities but in fact scans a different universe of meaning.

Conze believed that it was not just doctrinal formulations which divided the religions, but even the ideal sort of person each strived after. He wrote:

> I once read through a collection of the lives of Roman Catholic saints, and there was not one of whom a Buddhist could fully approve. This does not mean that they were unworthy people, but that they were bad Buddhists, though good Christians.[28]

Indeed, Conze pointed out a number of apparently irreconcilable differences between Buddhists and Christians, two of which are particularly apposite in relation to Jesus. First, Buddhists desire to multiply saviours, not to restrict them. Secondly, Mahayana Buddhists assert that 'all saviours, Buddhas and Boddhisatvas alike, are mere fictions and images in a dream, that they have issued from the Void and are projections of man's inner consciousness',[29] whereas the lives of Christian saints are patterned after that of Jesus, a historical figure, or at least, after aspects of it. If Conze is right, then Christianity and Buddhism, Jesus and the Buddha, emphasize very different human qualities as particularly virtuous.

Yet there are some positive prospects. There are a growing number of marriages between Christians and Buddhists. This may lead to a more integrative assessment of the two religions and their human founders. Moreover, some younger Christian scholars, untainted by association with empire, have immersed themselves in Buddhism and are able to explain their own Christian beliefs as well as learn about those of others.

OUT IN THE WORLD

Jesus is out in the world. Naturally, he is conformed to the worldviews in which he becomes contextualized. Within Islam, he is a Muslim prophet, one who submits to the One God and points to the coming of a final messenger. Within Vedantic Hinduism, which is characteristically open-ended, he has been accepted as one expression among many appearances of the divine among humans. Within Buddhism, he has been accepted by some as a lower order teacher, compromised by his theism. The imperial context has led some people to condemn him as the agent of foreign government: rather ironic, given the original context of the man from Nazareth as subject to, and eventually slain by, an all-powerful, colonizing foreign power.

Other examples could be given of the influence of Jesus in many cultures and religions, yet of his transformation thereby into shapes unrecognizable to many Christians: for example, in the integration of Christian faith with African traditional religions. Many Christians would applaud his growth into a universal figure, but be puzzled at and even troubled by his conformity to others' perspectives, rather than their acquiescence and transformation to his.

The teachings of Gandhi illustrate a fruitful and creative interaction between two, if not three, religions in the modern world. His pacifist instincts were encouraged by reading portions of the teaching of Jesus, and by correspondence in 1910 with the famous Russian novelist Leo Tolstoy. They were also influenced by his own Hinduism, and a particular interpretation of the Bhagavad Gita (not, perhaps, the most obvious reading of it, since its context is a battlefield). Further, he grew up in an area of the Indian state of Gujerat which was deeply influenced by Jain beliefs in *ahimsa*, non-violence to all living beings. Later, many peace movements, not least the civil rights movement of Martin Luther King in the USA, were greatly inspired by Gandhi's vision. In this extraordinary interaction, the figure of Jesus has proved inspirational, either explicitly or implicitly, to religious people who have not been Christians, and to people of goodwill but no religious faith.

As the above vignette also illustrates, even when conformed to another world view, Jesus retains the capacity to challenge and inspire people to turn their lives towards transcendent reality, even if expressed in ways foreign to many Christians. Actually, the meaning of Jesus was developed within a Greek culture, away from the land of his birth. This was not as alien to the historical Jesus as some scholars portray. Greek civilization had been experienced within Palestine since the fourth century BCE, and Diaspora Judaism had long taken note of it, lived within it and been influenced by it. It is not necessary, nor particularly profitable, to maintain that the creeds of the fourth century CE misrepresent or distort the simple message of Jesus. Messages are rarely as simple as some people maintain or want. Those creeds were a remarkably sophisticated acculturation of Jesus to a new situation, and the convictions about him that they safeguard have proved capable of bringing many to faith, hope and love.

Yet it ill-behoves modern Western Christians, whose vision of God has been shaped within the matrix of that Graeco-Roman interpretation of Jesus, to forbid different cultures, and even other faiths, to seek his transplantation and, to some extent, accommodation to their contexts. Of course, this does not mean that Christians have to agree with the accounts others give of Jesus. It does mean that they ought not to forbid others to interpret him as they see fit; nor, indeed, can they reasonably hope to do so. It may be that Christians can learn from such variegated views about the human founder of their faith.

Even so, Christians will want to share their views about Jesus with others. In a post-imperial, postmodern world, how are they to do so? This will form the substance of the next and final chapter.

NOTES

1. See, for example Said 1978, *passim*.
2. Hussein 1994, 231.
3. Cragg 1984, 11; Cragg 1985, 212–14.
4. See further, Forward 1997, 66–72.
5. See, for example, N. Robinson 1991, 1f., 8–14.
6. Clarke 1990, 9.
7. A particularly good, or rather bad, example of this is William Phipps's recent (1996) work.
8. 'Ata ur-Rahim in his book, *Jesus, Prophet of Islam* (1991), quoted in Zebiri 1997, 59.
9. Arkoun 1994, 35–40; Forward 1997, 33–5, 110–16.
10. Borg 1997, 129.
11. See Martin Forward's contribution on 'Islam' in J. Holm with J. Bowker, *Themes in Religious Studies. Sacred Writings*, London, Pinter, 1994, 103–6.
12. Schimmel 1985, 256.
13. Ibid., 63.
14. Ibid., 64.

15. Forward 1998a, 131.
16. Forward 1998b, chapter 3.
17. His book was first written c. 1968, and a summary of his views on the Sermon on the Mount is given in Zebiri 1997, 66.
18. Parrinder 1987, 68f.; Parrinder 1997, 120–7.
19. See Julius Lipner's discussion in Scott and Selvanayagam 1996, 131.
20. Parrinder 1997, 238f.
21. For extracts from their own works, consult Griffiths 1990, 204–27.
22. Ibid., 207.
23. Ibid., 201.
24. DiNoia 1992, 109.
25. Forward 1995, 72.
26. Parrinder 1987, 13f.
27. Brandon 1963, 67f.
28. Ibid., 80.
29. Ibid., 79.

6

JESUS IN THE THIRD MILLENNIUM

In the year 1, Jesus was probably a small child, about four years old, and the Emperor Augustus's peace had descended, however superficially and resented by some, on much of the Mediterranean world. In the year 1000, the French Pope Sylvester II, a creature of the German Emperor Otto II, conferred the title of Apostolic Majesty on King Stephen of Hungary. Christianity reached Iceland and Greenland. Leif Ericson, son of Eric the Red, is supposed to have landed in what is now Nova Scotia, though Christianity was not to reach the Americas for some centuries thereafter. In England, Saxons settled at Bristol and Ethelred II ravaged Cumbria, then moved southwards into Wales to lay waste to Anglesey. In many places, there was widespread fear of the end of the world and of the Last Judgement.

In a curious way, the year 1 seems closer to many Christians than the year 1000. The story of Jesus has been pondered, internalized and emulated. He seems, therefore, to be a part of our world, as much as of his own. One thousand years nearer ours, a world of Viking invasions and popes who realistically yearned after widespread temporal as well as spiritual authority seems, in many respects, beyond our capacity to understand. The point is, of course, that Jesus's world is as puzzling, foreign and remote from our own as is the world of pagan Europe in the throes of becoming Christendom. How then can he speak to our world from his?

SUCH A WORLD AS THIS

Christians often think that Jesus has timeless truths to tell. This is not the case. Any truths he reveals about and to the human condition need to be contextualized. The last verse of a Christmas carol runs:

> Sacred Infant, all divine,
> What a tender love was thine,
> Thus to come from highest bliss
> Down to such a world as this!

What kind of world is this? The changes of the recent past have been unprecedented in their scale. The historian Geoffrey Barraclough contends that such things as the impact of technical and scientific advance, the dwarfing of Europe and the revolt against Western rule and values have resulted not only in structural change but also in qualitative difference from the past.[1] As a result, he argues for the provisional designation 'contemporary history' to replace that of 'modern history' for the period from the beginning of the twentieth century, or at least since 1945.

Political, social and economic transformations have been matched by widespread religious changes. Although traditional forms of religious observance or even beliefs may be declining in Western Europe, religions are undergoing development and even renewal in many parts of the world. Since 1945 a homeland has been established for Jews in Israel; Buddhist and Hindu traditions have undergone many transformations, both in their original lands and in those countries where devotees have migrated and settled; Islam has been rejuvenated by the end of empire; and new religious movements have flourished, especially in Africa and in Japan but also in the West.

What then are the prospects for Jesus in the new millennium? Many Christian theologians contend that a relevant Christian theology of religions, which takes the fact of religious pluralism seriously, is urgently needed in the contemporary world. They believe that we are living through a period when there has been a significant paradigm shift, a term borrowed from the philosopher of science, Thomas Kuhn.[2] He argued that there comes a point when new information about a scientific subject or area forces scientists to give up old models and find new ones to describe how things now look. As applied by theologians to the world of diverse faiths, the concept of a paradigm shift acknowledges that our knowledge of data about other faiths can no longer be contained within old theories. Rather, what is needed is a new theory which will cope more adequately with the facts of experience.

A PLURALIST WORLD: JESUS AT THE MARGINS?

In the last twenty years, there has been a remarkable consensus about the parameters of the debate about Jesus and the world's religions. It has been put forward with particular clarity in Alan Race's book, *Christians and Religious Pluralism*, first published in 1983. The subtitle draws attention to the book's concerns: 'Patterns in the Christian Theology of Religions'. There are three: exclusivism, inclusivism and pluralism. To put these patterns at their simplest: the exclusivist maintains that salvation is only given to those who make an explicit commitment to Jesus Christ; the inclusivist affirms that salvation is bestowed on more than just Christians, because of all that God has done through Jesus Christ; and the pluralist affirms that humans are saved within their own faith traditions, not (except for Christians) because of the person or works of Jesus.

It has been pluralists who have led this debate, and others who have responded to it. Naturally so, since pluralists are in the vanguard of those who wish for a paradigm shift, away from traditional notions about salvation and Christology, to more tolerant and open-ended attitudes towards the other.

One of the most influential pluralists has been John Hick (b. 1922). He dismisses the idea of a single world religion as unlikely to be achieved, and undesirable because some religions will always interpret ultimate reality as personal whereas others will define it as non-personal. He argues, from an astronomical analogy, that the old Ptolemaic paradigm placed Christ at the centre of the religious universe; though often, in practice, Christianity substituted for him:

> The traditional dogma has been that Christianity is the centre of the universe of faiths, with all other religions seen as revolving at various removes around the revelation in Christ and being graded according to their nearness to or distance from it. But during the last hundred years or so we have been making new observations and have realized that there is deep devotion to God, true sainthood, and deep spiritual life within these other religions.[3]

So what is needed is a Copernican revolution in Christian attitudes towards other faiths. The findings of Copernicus transformed the Ptolemaic map of the universe, so that people thereafter knew that the earth was not the centre of things, but that it and the other planets revolved around the sun. Now we need a paradigm shift to place transcendent reality, however named, whether personal or non-personal, at the centre. Christian faith, or even Jesus himself, is not at the centre of things. Along with other, equally true religions, Christianity is contingent upon and graced by that transcendent reality.

This has been a liberating view for many thoughtful Western Christians who have been aware of and shamed by Christianity's history of condescending and even destructive attitudes towards other religious groups: for example, towards Jews in medieval and modern Europe, or the first people of the Americas. They observe that many of their co-religionists are morally no better, and sometimes seem a great deal worse, than members of other faiths. Even so, such Christians might have a twinge of doubt about aspects of the pluralist approach. It is an ideological interpretation, moving beyond the simple, obviously true fact that there are many religions on earth, to a commitment to the conviction that such variety is a good and creative thing. Some aspects of it may not be so. Geoffrey Parrinder has observed:

> The Pluralist position is not satisfactory if it is taken to mean that religions will forever run parallel to each other without any mutual effect, for one great feature of today is that all religions may be affected by others. . . [It] is also unsatisfactory if it is taken to mean that all religions are the same, which they clearly are not, or that it does not matters what people believe. Questions of truth and goodness are important. The religion of the ancient Aztecs, who held up the beating hearts of their victims to the sun, was clearly not so good a faith as the peaceful way of the Buddha.[4]

Quite so. We could add that such judgements can be made within as well as between religions. The teachings of the peaceful Buddha have been sullied by some violent and exclusive attitudes, as shown by, for example, a few Buddhists in Sri Lanka towards Hindus and Christians who share their land. Some missionary methods in Christianity have not cohered with the teachings of Jesus about loving God and other people.

Pluralists tend to emphasize a history of Christian exclusivism. Hick's books often mention the Council of Florence (1438–45). It defined the axiom *extra ecclesiam nulla salus* (no salvation outside the church) to mean that all those outside the church are excluded from salvation. This was officially the Roman Catholic Church's teaching until the reforms initiated by the Second Vatican Council (1961–5). Yet pluralists do not always mention that the Council of Florence was directed at medieval fissures within Christendom more than at the wider world of other religions. Moreover, this exclusivist position was not the only tradition within the church. Justin Martyr (c.100–c.165) first articulated the doctrine of the *logos spermatikos* (seed-bearing word), which allowed him to affirm that God had prepared the way for Jesus, not just through the Hebrew Bible but also through Greek philosophy. His sentence, 'Whatever has been well said belongs to us' was developed, mainly within the Eastern Church. This can sound like crass inclusivism, but it need not be such. It could intend, at least to some extent, a generous attitude towards the wider world of beliefs. Moreover, an element of inclusivism is a necessary part of every attitude towards the 'other'; ironically, even pluralists are inclusivists at bottom, the more so for not recognizing, as all must do, that everyone views from her own perspective.

JESUS SAVES?

One example of Western cultural parochialism is its emphasis upon salvation. Joe DiNoia has noted that 'prevailing positions in the field of theology of religions for the most part focus their energies on allowing for the possibility of salvation outside the ambit of Christianity'.[5]

Hick believes that all religions are more or less equally valid paths to salvation or liberation. He does so by drawing on the philosopher Immanuel Kant's distinction between noumenal and phenomenal: the 'thing-in-itself' and its perception. That is: truth exists as it really is, but is also appropriated (to be sure, in fragmentary fashion) within cultural contexts, in ways that are appropriate to each context. We cannot know things (including transcendent reality, however expressed) directly, but only as we perceive them or apprehend their impact. This is an alluring but excessively rational reductionism: mystics in the various faiths may have a different tale to tell, which would emphasize a direct union with ultimate reality. It is also a very Western way of thinking, with its emphasis upon a sharp distinction between subject and object, leading to what others see as an extreme and sometimes fanatical individualism.

Hick counters criticisms of his views by broadening his definition of salvation:

> Suppose, then, we define salvation in a very concrete way, as an actual change in human beings, a change which can be identified – when it *can* be identified – by its moral fruits. We then find that we are talking about something that is of central concern to each of the great world faiths. Each in its different way calls us to transcend the ego point of view, which is the source of all selfishness, greed, exploitation, cruelty and injustice, and to become re-centred in that ultimate mystery for which we, in our Christian language, use the term God.[6]

This definition may, ironically, be the sort of explanatory addition to his basic thesis which Hick condemns in others' beliefs. (He condemns those who add epicycles to their exclusivist, Ptolemaic worldview.) Moreover, his Western, Kantian, subject–object perspective does not easily coalesce with transcending the ego. Further, this definition of salvation enables him to link it with liberation, so that he now prefers the hybrid term salvation/liberation.[7] Yet the two concepts are rather different. Beverley Clack has persuasively argued:

> At this juncture. . . a change from the language of salvation to the language of liberation is necessary. It seems to me that the challenge of feminist thinking lies in the way in which it has exposed the negative understanding of the natural world and the place of humanity within it assumed by much of the language of salvation. Moreover the language of salvation has been dependent upon the Genesis narrative of the Fall, a story which has been used against women who have been categorised by many of the leading theologians of the tradition as 'daughters of Eve', and thus responsible for the perilous state of fallen humanity.[8]

Certainly, salvation, as many theologians describe it, is an overused and inexact term. It is often summarized along the following lines. God's grace is over all, and every human discerns it in some measure. But evil haunts human hearts and structures, so God elects a people, Israel, and then a person, Jesus, to overcome it. The triumph of Jesus over death provides the hope that God will raise humans to eternal life. He does so through a chosen people, the church, which is the sign and first fruit of God's purpose to save all. In the end, all will be judged by God, and the results of his verdict will bring surprises. It is therefore very important for everyone to consider his or her own position and response, rather than those of others.[9]

Actually, this interpretation is based only upon a particular interpretation of part of the biblical material. For example, although salvation language is meaningful in the New Testament, it is not overwhelmingly important, and different writers interpret it in various ways. The word *soter*, meaning 'saviour', is used eight times of God (including six occurrences in the Pastoral Epistles). It is also used sixteen times of Jesus, mostly in the later books. In the Gospels, there is just one reference in John (4:42) and two in Luke (1:47, 2:11).

Most soteriological language of the New Testament does not point forward to the ideological interpretation outlined above. For example, that much examined verse, Acts chapter 4, verse 12, is not chiefly interesting for its verdict about the fate of all humankind. It is about the healing of a lame man by Peter, and could be translated: 'and there is healing (*soteria*) in no one else [than Jesus], for there is no other name under heaven given among people by which we must be healed (*sothenai*)'. Geoffrey Lampe has written that 'these words should be read in the proper context of Luke's reconstruction of the anti-Jewish polemic of the early church and not generalised beyond that context'.[10]

The Gospels are well aware that Jesus's dealings were overwhelmingly with his Jewish co-religionists, but they all indicate that his message had a universal validity. For example, although Matthew records Jesus saying, 'I was sent only to the lost sheep of the house of Israel' (15:24), this was within the context of a story about a Canaanite woman and her daughter in which he did in fact respond to the faith of a Gentile (as we shall shortly see). Moreover, his Gospel begins with the visit of astrologers or magicians from the East (2:1–12), and ends with Jesus telling the disciples to baptize all people everywhere in the name of the Father, the Son and the Holy Spirit (28:16–20). These are reminders that God's grace reaches beyond his chosen people, the Jews, to touch others through what he is doing in Jesus's life, death and resurrection.

What about Jesus's own attitude to members of other faiths? The question may be anachronistic, since an argument can be made that to define religions as bounded systems is a rather modern and Western bad habit.[11] Nevertheless, a little can be gleaned about Jesus's dealings with people of faith who were not Jews. Jesus was primarily interested in opening up for people trust in a creative, providential and parenting God. On the rare occasions he came into contact with Gentiles, the element of faith or trust remained of paramount importance to him. For example, when faced with the faith of the centurion who besought him to heal his servant, he was astonished and remarked that he had never before encountered such faith, not even in Israel (Matthew 8:5–13; Luke 7:1–10). This comment was not Jesus's contribution to the Christian history of anti-Jewishness (the primary emphasis in the story is on the man's faith, not the Jews' lack of it, though Matthew took the opportunity in his telling of the story to reflect his community's antagonism with Jewish groups half a century later). Rather, Jesus shared the negative and often ill-informed attitude of Jews of his day towards Gentile religion, and his words show his amazement that faith could be found in unexpected people.

His attitude towards the healing of the daughter of the Canaanite woman also illustrates this (Mark 7:24–30; Matthew 15:21–8). He first declined to heal, saying that it was not right to throw the children's bread to dogs, a brusque, even contemptuous comment. The woman replied that even the dogs under the table ate the children's crumbs. Such a witty and hopeful response so impressed and disarmed Jesus that he cured the daughter.

What does Jesus's emphasis upon faith in God in his meetings with Jews and others alike suggest to contemporary Christians? The chief impression is that the language of soteriology does not quite fit. Certainly, any narrow view that 'Jesus saves' seems a banal reflection upon what happens in these encounters. To be sure, Jesus enables faith in God, even in his own powers, to have its reward, but neither the destination of humankind as a whole, nor the acceptability of other religious traditions is of primary importance. Rather, what is at stake is God's faithfulness to those who, in their need, turn to him. Further, Jesus used many terms to refer to God: most notably 'Father', which, rather than 'Saviour', was his characteristic designation. The language of relationship, trust and love sits ill alongside beliefs that God's primary attitude towards people of faith who are not Christian is condemnation. In accepting the faith of the Roman centurion and the Canaanite woman, Jesus discovered that faith is not tied to or contained within a particular religious tradition.

This discovery by Jesus of faith as potentially a universal human quality, not tied to a particular group or groups, calls into question the apparently tolerant but actually rather dismissive attitude towards other faiths propounded by some Christians. They argue along the lines that only God knows who will accept the faith of those who do not locate it in Jesus's saving grace. This will not do. Christians are deeply interested in what sort of God God is, because Jesus is the human face of God. If love is at the heart of Christian faith, then it seems evasive to claim to be agnostic about the scope and generosity of God's attachment to and compassion for his human family.

Another argument for the limitation of the use of salvation language in relation to other faiths can be made by asking whether it makes sense to them. By and large, it does not. Characteristically, other religions do not ask whether they are saved by God. In Islam, for example, the Arabic word for salvation is found only once in the Quran (Q40:41). Sunni Muslims more characteristically want to obey the revealed will of God, by following the *sunna* (trodden path) of the Prophet Muhammad. Buddhists want to wake up from illusory egoism, into the freedom of the present moment and the hope of *nirvana*. Neither of these solutions to the woes of the world (nor the answers offered by many other faiths) is best, or even appropriately, framed in the language of salvation. This is a point to which we shall return.

A valiant attempt to preserve the centrality of a salvation model in a pluralistic milieu has been made by Mark Heim. He contends that salvation only makes sense in the plural: there are a number of 'salvations', each appropriate to particular aims and aspirations. Commenting on the widespread threefold model, he contends that:

> These three dimensions cohere in each tradition, and one does not exclude the other. If 'salvation' means the achievement of some desired religious aim, then we can — like pluralists – affirm that a number of paths lead to salvations: there is an 'any way' sign at many forks on the religious journey. If 'salvation' means a religious fulfillment of some determinate nature, then we may – like exclusivists – affirm that it is constituted by certain features to the exclusion of others: there is an 'only way' sign at many turnings. In either case we must – like the inclusivists – acknowledge that all these paths link with each other, that 'cross-traffic' is a real possibility. Many roads are also connecting routes and bear travellers over the same ground towards different destinations.[12]

This is a fruitful extension of the model, which helps to sharpen up genuine differences. My quibble with its whether it goes far enough. I have already argued that salvation, though a convenient category by which to understand other faiths, obfuscates more than it reveals, certainly of other faiths and to some extent even of Christianity. To be sure, it is true that each religion has a soteriological framework: each defines and prescribes for the human condition, though these frameworks vary considerably from one religion to the other, so that, as we have seen in chapter 5, Buddhism and Christianity are rather dissimilar phenomena. The concept of salvation tends to assume that a rather narrow view of the Christian aim or aims is appropriate for other religious quests. So this model needs to be abandoned rather than modified.

To sum up: salvation is not necessarily a centrally important Christian concept, not, at any rate, when it is narrowly defined as whether or not people of other faiths are acceptable to God.

JESUS AT THE CENTRE?

The model of exclusivism, inclusivism and pluralism has been controlled by the salvation question: are adherents of other religions than Christianity saved or not? Pluralists have assumed the centrality of that question but, eccentrically, have abandoned Christology, or at least subjected it to a radical reductionism. Hick's own Christian pilgrimage has seen him move from putting Christianity at the centre of things, to Jesus, to God, to the Kantian 'really real'.

The issue resolves around how we apprehend transcendent reality. From earliest times, Christians affirmed that Jesus revealed the invisible God. So Paul declares that 'it is the God who said "Let light shine out of darkness", who has shone in our hearts to give the light of the knowledge of the glory of God in the face of Jesus Christ' (2 Corinthians 4:6). The author of the letter to the Hebrews begins by declaring that 'Long years ago God spoke to our ancestors in many and various ways by the prophets, but in these last days he has spoken to us by a Son, whom he appointed heir of all things, through whom he also created the worlds' (1:1f.). Also, John's Gospel records that 'the word became flesh and lived among us' (1:14).

In a recent work, *The Metaphor of God Incarnate*, Hick develops Christological views appropriate for a pluralist position. He argues that although traditional Christian faith holds that Jesus of Nazareth was God incarnate, who became a man, died for the sins of the whole world and founded a church, Jesus did not in fact teach this. Further, the credal statements about the two natures of Christ, human and divine, are incoherent. The doctrine of the incarnation has been used to justify and perpetuate great evils, including anti-Semitism, the oppression of women by men and deep arrogance and hostility towards other faiths. For Hick, Jesus 'embodied a human love which is a reflection of the divine love'. He proposes a faith 'which takes Jesus as our supreme (but not necessarily only) spiritual guide . . . and sees Christianity as one authentic context of salvation/liberation amongst others . . . interacting in mutually creative ways with the other great paths'.[13]

There are problems with this from a historical point of view. We have seen that it is by no means certain that the Jesus of history merely pointed to God: 'Where did this man get all this?' (Mark 6:2) is still a question for Christians to ponder. Moreover, it is over-simplistic to blame the traditional view of the incarnation for great evils. That model has also inspired many people to do good.

Hick's definition of the incarnation as metaphor raises acutely the question of how far a religion can be reinterpreted before it evolves into something quite different. Certainly, developments happen. In Christianity, they happened very early indeed. In the Gospels, Jesus can be discerned as a man who fits no formula. Although titles soon came to be used of him, we have seen that he seems either never to have accepted them himself or else, more likely, to have reinterpreted them. The early church, however, soon came to use honorific titles about Jesus, drawn from the Jewish and pagan worlds. A title like 'Son of God', for example, would have modified its meaning as it moved from Palestinian Jewish to Hellenistic circles, and as it became a liturgical as well as a theological formula. By the fourth century, a Galilean Jew was described, in the words of the Nicene Creed, as the second person of the Trinity, 'the only-begotten Son of God'. Clearly, we are a long way here even from the language of the Gospels, let alone from how Jesus and his original followers described himself.

An important question is whether such language distorts the meaning of Jesus and his message, or whether, as C. F. D. Moule has suggested:

> All the various estimates of Jesus reflected in the New Testament [should be viewed] as, in essence, only attempts to describe what was already there from the beginning . . . They represent various stages in the development of perception, but they do not represent the accretion of any alien factors that were not inherent from the beginning.[14]

This may be overstated. As we saw in discussing the title 'Son of Man', different developments of a common passage can arguably be legitimate, or at least credible, elaborations of the original, yet draw out very different emphases and look very unlike each other.

Whether Professor Moule's thesis is convincing or not, it is surely a necessary enterprise for every generation to develop and contextualize a Christology, so as to preserve and transmit faithfully the gospel message of faith, hope and love. Moule's interpretation certainly draws attention to the fact that Jesus was so remarkable a figure as to draw to himself, shortly after his life and arguably during it, the most elevated of assessments by those who followed his way.

Incarnational theology remains, for good or ill, distinctive of Christian faith. Although aspects of the language of incarnation may be metaphorical, central Christian belief has, from early days, always rejected any attempt to reduce the mystery of Jesus, either to the idea that he was God walking the earth disguised as a human being, or to that of a man of outstanding spiritual integrity. There have often been attempts to emphasize one or other of these extreme positions, rather than the careful balance of traditional theology.

Nowadays, in the West, the tendency is to emphasize Jesus's humanity. For much of Christian history, the opposite has been true. There are dangers in this unbalanced view. The human Jesus portrayed in *The Metaphor of God Incarnate*, freed from the accretions of myth and philosophical terminology imposed by the world of late antiquity, has many resonances with Quranic and other developed Muslim views of Jesus. (Curiously, the possibilities of dialogue with Muslims on the basis of such a depiction of Jesus are not developed by Hick, or even mentioned.) In the world of Islam, too, Jesus is a spiritual and moral teacher of import, a very great human being. Yet there he does not seem a very Christian figure! The point is that Christians have always wanted to claim more for Jesus than that he is a superlatively good or spiritual person (as some Muslim mystics have interpreted him), or that he merely pointed to God (as the Quran affirms). From earliest times, such evaluations did not seem adequate assessments of his fundamental importance.

So the alluring call by pluralists for a theocentric rather than christocentric theology of religions could turn out to be a siren call to destruction. It espouses a simplistic, partial and reductionist view of Jesus – I would argue of the historical Jesus as well as the Jesus of early Christian theological reflection. It is an excessively rationalistic view, dominated by the spirit of the age and by a certain Western parochialism tied in to an arrogance that it knows best. Further, what Christians know of God is primarily shaped by Jesus, just as what Buddhists know of the way things really are is determined by the fact that Gautama Siddhartha woke up to an understanding of them. In that important sense, Jesus is the centre of faith for Christians as is the Buddha for Buddhists. When pluralists place transcendent reality, however named, at the centre of things, they fail to deal seriously with the issue of how people of faith apprehend that eternal mystery through particular foci.

It may be that the Eastern church's emphasis on icons points a more fruitful way forward for understanding the incarnation than the use of the word 'metaphor' such as Hick has espoused. Many Western Christians have misunderstood icons as idols. This is a very simplistic and misleading understanding. Rather:

> God took a material body, thereby proving that matter can be redeemed: 'The Word made flesh has deified the flesh,' said John of Damascus [c.675–c.749]. God has 'deified' matter, making it 'spirit-bearing'; and if flesh has become a vehicle of the Spirit, then so – though in a different way – can paint and wood. The Orthodox doctrine of icons is bound up with the Orthodox belief that the whole of God's creation, material as well as spiritual, is to be redeemed and glorified.[15]

Here is a deeply serious and Christian argument for the traditional Christian doctrine that Jesus was true God as well as true man. Jesus points to the possibility that all creation can become divinized, and grow into the image of God. For this to happen, he must be fully human and fully God. As St Athanasius (c.296—c373) put it, 'God became human that we humans might be made god.'[16] Only God can redeem humanity and make him a little lower than God (Psalm 8:5). Only a human being can help other humans participate in what God has done. So Jesus forms a bridge between God and humanity, heaven and earth, and makes humans become by grace what God is by nature. Jesus is, as it were, the ultimate icon.

It is significant that in his early life, John of Damascus was an official at the Muslim court in Damascus. His views contrasted deeply with those of Muslims about the nature of God, and to some extent were constructed in opposition to them. For example, his reflections on Genesis chapter 1, verse 26 led him to a very different view of monotheism than that of Islam. That verse reads: 'Then God said, "Let us make humankind in our image, according to our likeness. . .".' Like most of the Greek fathers of the Church, John did not think that image and likeness meant the same thing. He wrote that 'The expression *according to the image* indicates rationality and freedom, while the expression *according to the likeness* indicates assimilation to God through virtue.'[17] The image (icon would be the Greek term) signifies our human free will and all the moral and rational qualities which mark us out from the animal world and make each of us a person. It also means that we are God's offspring (Acts 17:28), so that between him and us is a point of contact and similiarity. And if we take advantage of this point of contact, we acquire the divine likeness; we become 'assimilated to God through virtue'.

The Eastern Christian view of *theosis*, or the deification of humans, contrasts strongly with Islamic and much modern Western Christian dualism, which posits an infinite, qualitative difference between humans and God. Sometimes, difference can focus what we truly believe, over against rather than in common with others. Divergence and disagreement are not an insuperable problem, but part of what it means to be human, though how they are handled may be extremely problematic.

A modern writer, after examining various Muslim commentaries on the Quran's teaching about Christianity, concludes that:

> In no way, then, does Biblical Christianity remain a fully valid 'way of salvation' after the advent of Muhammad. It is inconceivable under the Quranic definition of authentic Christianity, as interpreted by these ten commentaries, that a 'true' Christian who had been exposed to the Prophet's message would refuse to become a Muslim. Not to acknowledge the prophethood of Muhammad, which has been clearly foretold in the untainted version of the *injil*,[18] would itself constitute a betrayal of 'true' Christianity.[19]

This given-ness of the Quranic text has posed very great problems indeed for Christian and Muslim scholars in dialogue conferences. So it has for Christians like John Damascus, working for Muslim masters, and for Muslims who have worked with Christians. This points up an irony in the pluralist position. In fact, it does not cope well with difference but seeks to emphasize beliefs and practices held in common. Wiser are those who recognize the difficulties and struggle with them than are those who ignore or do not grasp them.

IS THERE A MISSION?

Since Jesus is central to a Christian understanding of God, in a way denied by Muslims and irrelevant to members of other faiths, this raises the question of mission. Christians have often regarded themselves as 'sent' by God to tell others of Jesus's interpretation of ultimate reality. They can base this on such a Gospel passage as 'the Great Commission' (Matthew 28:16–20). Geoffrey Parrinder has pondered whether the Christian missionary enterprise should be restricted:

> Certainly not addressed to Jews, probably not to Muslims, perhaps not to Buddhists and theistic Hindus, and efforts preserved for idolaters and illiterates. . . But it seems unlikely that any of the three great missionary religions, Buddhism, Christianity and Islam would publicly abandon their long-held international aims. . . The approval that is often given to medical missions, but withheld from propagandist work, indicates a deep feeling that the faith is to be expressed by service and that a little help is worth more than sterile debate.[20]

It is truly the case that many Christians have become impressed by the quality of faith demonstrated by their neighbours of another faith. It is also true that in India and elsewhere the gospel has struck deep chords where it has sought to improve the lot of others.

However, missionary zeal is far from abating in today's world, and is not just found in the traditional missionary religions. To introduce a personal note: in 1996, I visited many countries in Africa and also the USA to make a series of radio programmes called *The Missionaries* for the BBC World Service. My aim was not simply to describe the activities and aims of traditional Christian missionaries, but to look at the endeavours of members of many faiths to pass on their beliefs to a younger generation and also to outsiders. At the end of the twentieth century, when there has been mass migration of Hindus, Buddhists, Sikhs and others to parts of Europe and the Americas, there have been many new opportunities for members of these faiths to convince others of the truth of their faith. So, among other groups, I interviewed Swadhyayee Hindus, offering a socially active view of Vedic faith in many American cities; Muslim educational groups, intent on dispelling many Western caricatures of Islam, and gathering a number of converts; Jews for Jesus, and also Lubavitcher Jews working the streets of New York to persuade secular Jews to return to their religious roots; members of African Pentecostal groups, in full cry against the racism of Western churches, seeking to integrate a vision of a healing Jesus commensurate with beliefs they derive from African indigenous faiths; Christians broadcasting the message of the Christian as opposed to the Quranic Jesus into Muslim countries; Buddhists offering their faith as a solution to the activism of the West or to the political and human problems of the new South Africa.

Some of these interviewees were so convinced of the truth of their own convictions that they barely paused to think of the claims of others, or else simply dismissed them. Others had deeply pondered the truth-claims of others, and either rejected them, or felt they were committed to something as good or (usually) even better. Most were interesting, often charming and humorous, always dedicated people. Many were quite aware of the ethical dimensions of their work. For example, Christians broadcasting to Muslim lands knew that Muslims who converted could face rejection and even death, since apostasy merits the death sentence in some Muslim countries. They took steps to warn and help any individuals who contacted them, but also felt that faith in Christ is such a wondrous thing that it justifies risks. Other groups were just as committed to a vision of the truth, overriding all other problems and concerns.

This experience, perhaps strangely, did not make me cynical about the human quest for transcendent meaning. It was a privilege and an education to interview such vibrant, talented, committed people. I admired them, even when I profoundly disagreed with them, as I often did. It made me reflect that much contemporary Christian theological debate about Jesus is excessively concentrated on a history of ideas, into which people are fitted, however unsuitably.

Thus, mission seems an integral part of this diverse world, in which diversity might be a captivating, exciting, if combustible, reality, beyond the rather shallow, rationalistic and confining certainties of proponents of a pluralist theology of religions. In the divine supermarket of our modern or postmodern age, many visions of reality jostle for our attention. Differences are in fact crucial to how people construct their universes of meaning, and always have been. How then are differences to be handled in a world of divers faiths and ideologies?

JESUS AND A GLOBAL ETHIC

Hans Küng and some other thinkers from a variety of religions have argued that there will be no peace in the world until there is peace among the religions. They have formulated a Global Ethic upon which they hope all religions can agree. Küng and his colleagues have formulated 'four irrevocable directives' towards the creation of a Global Ethic:

commitment to a culture of non-violence and a respect for life; a culture of solidarity and a just economic order; a culture of tolerance and a life of truthfulness; a culture of equal rights and a partnership between men and women.[21] These are worthy aims. But it may be better to work towards an ethic that is corporately discussed than to impose directives, however worthy.

There are two other problems with this vision of a Global Ethic. The first is that it assumes, as does much pluralist thinking, convergence and agreement. To be sure, religions tend to applaud goodness, piety and the like. But there are ethical differences between them, and within each too, which need to be addressed. The second problem is more serious. The creation of a Global Ethic often seems to be driven by a secular agenda, as though the United Nations Charter for Human Rights is a more obvious basis for ethical endeavour and convergence than the moral teachings of the great world religions themselves. A number of Muslim leaders and countries, and others too, have expressed misgivings about the driving force behind the attempts, however well-meaning, to impose a common Global Ethic upon humans in today's world. Perhaps the creation of a religious United Nations would be more fruitful, where differences can be aired but in the context of a forum of discussion and mutual respect. That, however, is as yet an unfulfilled vision.

Meanwhile, the onus is on each religion to identify its own inner resources for living faithfully yet amicably in the contemporary world. It is true that religions are a significant factor in many of the world's troubled areas, and have often contributed to the troubles. To mention only Christianity: Northern Ireland, the Lebanon, Israel, Serbia are among the places where Christians live in actual or potential conflict either with other Christians or with members of other faiths. It may well be that they could identify common values with other groups and thereby transform their lives and those of other people. It is just as urgent for them to identify with Jesus's teaching about the kingdom, his Sermon on the Mount, and his reiteration of the commandment to love God and others, so that lives can be changed for the better, including their own. A contemporary Christian pluralist theologian who has particularly articulated this necessity is Paul Knitter. Of his five theses on the uniqueness of Jesus, the fourth urges that it 'can be found in his insistence that salvation must be realized in this world through human actions of love and justice'.[22]

THE FUTURE OF JESUS: A CHRISTIAN PERSPECTIVE

Theologians who have espoused the pluralist model of interpreting religious diversity have had many wise and pertinent things to say. Nevertheless, the model has, as we have seen, fundamental problems and needs to be replaced. What, then, lies beyond the pluralist model of understanding religious diversity from Christian perspectives? As yet, a captivating new model has not been fashioned.

Whenever it appears, it will need to reflect upon Jesus of Nazareth. If Hick's and other pluralists' interpretation of Jesus's importance to the world of the third millennium were to triumph in Christianity, Jesus would in practice become rather a marginal figure. This would be true not only outside but also within Christianity. He would be a metaphor only. Yet Jesus will not quite reveal his full potential within the constraints of metaphor, as a careful reading of the Gospels reveals.

In this section, I offer a personal vision of what he might offer towards the emerging world of the third millenium. There are two obvious limitations to this enterprise. The first is that Christianity cannot be simply interpreted as the works and words of Jesus. The great world religions are intricate, multi-varied phenomena. Jesus stands at the source of the great river of Christianity. Simple-minded and egocentric, indeed, would he be who mistook his own vision, or even that of Jesus himself, for the whole of a great world faith. Yet visions can change one's viewpoint on a great faith, and help to renew and refocus its meanings.

The second limitation is whether such an attempt to re-vision Jesus for the third millennium makes any sense. Can enough be known of the historical Jesus to undertake this enterprise? We have seen that successive waves of Western scholarship have affirmed, denied, then cautiously reaffirmed the possibility of locating a substantial person behind or within the evangelists' storytelling gifts. As with many nineteenth-century lives of Jesus, the articulation of such a vision may reveal as much about its articulator as about Jesus himself. Maybe that is not such a bad thing, so long as it is measured against other visions and scholarly standards. Furthermore, the history of two centuries of Western scholarship about Jesus has illustrated that austere views about the possibility of reaching and interpreting the historical Jesus cannot be sustained, for faith-full reasons. It seems that Christian faith depends, to some extent, upon locating and interpreting him. So what follows is a historically rather imprudent, though not, I think, indefensible interpretation.

Jesus pointed to and embodied God, who was located not only in a particular place, however holy and venerated, but was spirit, blowing where she will. This interpretation by John is illustrated in his account of Jesus's meeting with a Samaritan woman (4:24), a story that may well reflect a genuine historical encounter and conversation. God's kingdom is not boundaried by geographical areas but is the context within which the whole of life, personal and communal, can take place.

You enter the sphere of the kingdom by knowing your need of God. That need, more than whether you are good or worthy, is the major criterion of faith. Indeed, those who are well have no need of a physician, so it is the sinners rather than the righteous who turn to such a God as Jesus proclaimed (Mark 2:17). Accordingly, you must be like a child, confident and trustful (Mark 10:13–16). Or you are at the end of your tether, with nowhere else to go but back to your father, like the younger son in the parable of a dysfunctional family (Luke 15:11–32); or like the woman who has tried everyone else and everything else to be cured, without success, and so turns to Jesus (Mark 5:25–34).

That desperate yearning need is faith, or at least the beginning of faith. Such faith overrides all scruples and considerations. That woman did not stop to consider whether it was appropriate for her as a woman, especially since she was ritually unclean, to touch a man. Everyone is capable of exercising such faith, whether they be Jews or Gentiles, as Jesus discovered in his dealings with a Roman centurion (Luke 7:1–10) and a Canaanite woman (Matthew 15:21–8). Faith is a universal human quality. For this reason, perhaps among others, Jesus had a relaxed attitude towards purity laws, not because he was not interested in purity, but because he considered everyone and everything was potentially pure (Mark 7:1–23; Luke 11:37–41).

This, of course, was quite literally, the counsel of perfection. Everybody ought to be perfect, as is God himself (Matthew 5:48), but such is the quality of life in the fullness of the kingdom rather than the here and now. So there is a tension in Jesus's teaching between the kingdom that was present now to some extent, not least in his own words and deeds, and that which is one day to come in all its fullness. Jesus felt that his obedience in going to Jerusalem as a figure explicable, to some extent, in religious language as Messiah, the Son of Man and the Suffering Servant, would bring about the consummation of the kingdom. When that would come, and whether it would mean the transformation of the present world order or something more radical, is hard to

165

determine. At any rate, such a cosmic upheaval reminds us that transformation is not just personal, but communal, even global. Perhaps Jesus had no clear idea himself of how that upheaval would come about and what exactly it would constitute. It is in the nature of trust, of faith, to throw itself on God, in hope and obedience, without knowing all the answers. Moreover, Jesus was an extraordinarily prayerful and intuitive figure (Luke 11:1–12). He was not irrational, but (at the risk of phrasing this matter in an anachronistic way) he knew the limits of rationalism. Trust takes risks because it intuits that, in God's good time, he will bring all things to his gracious purpose.

Jesus was handed over to death. The resurrection came as a stunning answer, probably unseen even by Jesus himself. But this was not a vacuous happy ending. From the birth stories onwards, death and life are linked together in the story of Jesus. To encounter God is a transforming experience, so that one is not what one was but, as Paul would put it, a new creation, or at least in the process of becoming so (2 Corinthians 5:17).

Such a vision of Jesus could form the basis of a Christian theology appropriate for a diverse, interconnected world as it enters the third millennium since he lived, died and lives again.

NOTES

1. Barraclough 1967, 9-42.
2. It is the subject matter of his book, *The Structure of Scientific Revolutions*, 2nd edn, Chicago, Chicago University Press, 1970.
3. Hick 1983, 82.
4. Parrinder 1987, 224.
5. DiNoia 1992, ix.
6. Hick 1995, 217.
7. Ibid. 1995, 17, 21.
8. English 1994, 161.
9. See, for example, Lesslie Newbigin's summary in Wainwright 1989, 331–3.
10. Lampe 1997, 31.
11. Smith 1978, *passim*, esp. 1-79.
12. Heim 1995, 6.
13. Hick 1993, ix, 162f.
14. Moule 1977, 2f.
15. Ware 1993, 264.
16. Ibid., 21.
17. Ibid., 219.
18. The *injil* is a sort of proto-Gospel which Islam believes Jesus brought,

and which contained data agreeing with that of the Quran. The present Gospels are at best a corruption of that proto-Gospel.

19. McAuliffe 1991, 290.
20. Parrinder 1987, 205.
21. Küng 1996, 17-26.
22. Swidler and Mojzes 1997, 11.

BIBLIOGRAPHY

Addas, C. 1993. *Quest for the Red Sulphur.* Cambridge, Islamic Texts Society

Altizer, T. J. J. 1998. *The Contemporary Jesus.* London, SCM

Appleton, G. 1961. *On the Eightfold Path: Christian Presence Amid Buddhism.* London, SCM

Arkoun, M. 1994. *Rethinking Islam: Common Questions, Uncommon Answers.* Boulder and Oxford, Westview

Bammel, E. and Moule, C. F. D., eds. 1984. *Jesus and the Politics of his Day.* Cambridge, CUP

Barraclough, G. 1967. *An Introduction to Contemporary History.* Harmondsworth, Penguin

Borg, M., ed. 1997. *Jesus at 2000.* Colorado and Oxford, Westview

Bornkamm, G. 1960. *Jesus of Nazareth.* London, Hodder & Stoughton

Bowker, J. 1970. *Problems of Suffering in Religions of the World.* Cambridge, CUP

— 1978. *The Religious Imagination and the Sense of God.* Oxford, Clarendon Press

Brandon, S.G.F. ed. 1963. *The Saviour God.* Manchester, Manchester University Press,

— 1971. *The Trial of Jesus of Nazareth,* London, Paladin

Braybrooke, M. 1990. *Time to Meet. Towards a deeper relationship between Jews and Christians.* London, SCM

Brown, J.M. 1972. *Gandhi's Rise to Power. Indian Politics 1915-1922.* Cambridge, CUP

Brown, R.E. 1977. *The Birth of the Messiah.* London, Geoffrey Chapman
— 1994a. *An Introduction to New Testament Christology.* London, Geoffrey Chapman
— 1994b. *The Death of the Messiah.* Vols. 1 and 2. London, Geoffrey Chapman
— 1997. *An Introduction to the New Testament.* New York, Doubleday
Buber, M. 1951. *Two Types of Faith.* London, Routledge & Kegan Paul
Clarke, P. ed. 1990. *The World's Religions. Islam.* London, Routledge
Cohn-Sherbok, D. 1993. *The Crucified Jew. Twenty Centuries of Christian Anti-Semitism.* London, Fount
— 1994. *Judaism and Other Faiths.* Houndmills, St. Martin's Press
Cohn-Sherbok, D. ed. 1991. *Islam in a World of Diverse Faiths.* Houndmills, Macmillan
Coughlin, C. 1997. *A Golden Basin Full of Scorpions. The Quest for Modern Jerusalem.* London, Little, Brown and Company
Cracknell, K. 1986. *Towards a New Relationship. Christians and People of Other Faith.* London, Epworth
— 1995. *Justice, Courtesy and Love. Theologians and Missionaries Encountering World Religions 1846-1914.* London, Epworth
Cragg, K. 1984. *Muhammad and the Christian.* London, DLT
— 1985. *Jesus and the Muslim.* London, George Allen & Unwin
Crossan, J.D. 1991. *The Historical Jesus. The Life of a Mediterranean Jewish Peasant.* Edinburgh, T & T Clark
— 1995. *Who Killed Jesus? Exposing the Roots of Anti-Semitism in the Gospel Story of the Death of Jesus.* London, HarperCollins
Daniel, N. 1993. *Islam and the West. The Making of an Image.* Oxford, Oneworld
Davies, S. 1983. *The Gospel of Thomas and Christian Wisdom.* New York, Seabury Press
D'Costa, G. ed. 1996. *Resurrection Reconsidered.* Oxford, Oneworld
Dillistone, F.W. 1984. *The Christian Understanding of Atonement.* London, SCM
DiNoia, J. 1992. *The Diversity of Religions.* Washington D.C., Catholic University of America
Dodd, C.H. 1961. *The Parables of the Kingdom.* London, Collins, revised edition
— 1973. *The Founder of Christianity.* London, Fontana
Drury, J. 1985. *The Parables in the Gospels. History and Allegory.*

169

London, SPCK

Eck, D. 1993. *Encountering God. A Spiritual Journey from Bozeman to Banaras.* Boston, Beacon

Eliot, T.S. 1954. *Selected Poems.* London, Faber & Faber

English, D. ed. 1994.*Windows on Salvation.* London, DLT

Fackenheim, E.L. 1994 edn. *To Mend the World. Foundations of Post-Holocaust Jewish Thought.* Bloomington and Indianapolis, Indiana University Press

Forward, M. 1997. *Muhammad: A Short Biography.* Oxford, Oneworld

— 1998a. *A Bag of Needments. Geoffrey Parrinder's Contribution to the Study of Religion.* Bern, Peter Lang

— 1998b. *The Failure of Islamic Modernism? Syed Ameer Ali's Interpretation of Islam as a Religion.* Bern, Peter Lang

— 1998c. *Gods, Guides and Gurus: Theological Reflections on Travels with my Aunt.* Swansea, Tŷ John Penri

Forward, M. ed. 1995. *Ultimate Visions.* Oxford, Oneworld

Funk, R.W., Hoover, R.W., and the Jesus Seminar 1993. *The Five Gospels. What Did Jesus Really Say?* New York, Macmillan

Grant, M. 1994. *Saint Peter.* London, Weidenfeld and Nicolson

Grant, R.M., 1963. *A Historical Introduction to the New Testament.* London, Collins & Harper

— 1971. *Augustus to Constantine.* London, Collins

Grayston, K. 1990. *The Gospel of John.* London, Epworth

Griffiths, P.J. ed. 1990. *Christianity Through Non-Christian Eyes.* Maryknoll, Orbis

Heim, S.M., 1995. *Salvations. Truth and Difference in Religion.* Maryknoll, Orbis

Heim, S.M. ed. 1998. *Grounds for Understanding. Ecumenical Resources for Responses to Religious Pluralism.* Cambridge, Eerdmans

Hellwig, M. 1983. *Jesus the Compassion of God.* Wilmington, Michael Glazier

Hengel, M. 1986. *The Cross of the Son of God.* London, SCM

Hick, J. 1983. *The Second Christianity.* London, SCM

— 1993. *The Metaphor of God Incarnate.* London, SCM

— 1995. *The Rainbow of Faiths.* London, SCM

Hick, J. and Knitter, P. eds. 1987. *The Myth of Christian Uniqueness.* London, SCM

Hilberg, R. 1985. *The Destruction of European Jews. vol. 1.* New York and London, Holmes & Meier

Hilton, M. 1994. *The Christian Effect on Jewish Life*. London, SCM

Hilton, M., with Marshall, G. 1988. *The Gospels and Rabbinic Judaism. A Study Guide*. London, SCM

Hooker, M.D. 1991. *The Gospel According to St Mark*. London, A & C Black

Hussein, M.K. 1994. *City of Wrong. A Friday in Jerusalem*. Oxford, Oneworld

Isaac, J. 1964. *The Teaching of Contempt*. New York, Holt, Rinehart and Winston

Jacobs, L. 1995. *The Jewish Religion. A Companion*. Oxford, OUP

Jeremias, J. 1972 third revised edition. *The Parables of Jesus*. London, SCM

— 1964 revised edition. *Unknown Sayings of Jesus*. London, SPCK

— 1966. *The Eucharistic Words of Jesus*. London, SCM

— 1971. *New Testament Theology, volume 1. The Proclamation of Jesus*. London, SCM

Jones, I.H. 1994. *The Gospel of Matthew*. London, Epworth

Josephus, F., trans. Feldman, L.H. 1965. *Jewish Antiquities Books XVIII-XX*. London, William Heinemann Ltd

Kee, H.C. 1990. *What Can We Know About Jesus?*. Cambridge, CUP

Kelly, J.N.D. 1995. *Golden Mouth. The Story of John Chrysostom, Ascetic, Preacher, Bishop*. London, Gerald Duckworth & Co.

Keenan, J.P. 1989. *The Meaning of Christ. A Mahayana Theology*. Maryknoll, Orbis

Klausner, J. 1928. *Jesus of Nazareth*. London, George Allen & Unwin

Klein, C. 1978. *Anti-Judaism in Christian Theology*. London, SPCK

Knitter, P.F. 1996. *Jesus and the Other Names*. Oxford, Oneworld

Koester, H. 1990. *Ancient Christian Gospels*. London, SCM

Küng, H. ed. 1996. *Yes to a Global Ethic*. London, SCM

Lampe, G. 1977. *God as Spirit*. Oxford, OUP

Lapide, P. 1984. *The Resurrection of Jesus*. London, SPCK

Lieu, J. 1997. *The Gospel of Luke*. London, Epworth

Lott, E.J. 1988. *Vision, Tradition, Interpretation. Theology, Religion and the Study of Religion*. Berlin, Mouton de Gruyter

Lott, E. 1998. *Healing Wings. Acts of Jesus for Human Wholeness*. Bangalore, Asian Trading Corporation

Lüdemann, G. with Özen, A. 1997. *What Really Happened to Jesus. A historical approach to the resurrection*. London, SCM

Maccoby, H. 1992. *Judas Iscariot and the Myth of Jewish Evil*. New York, The Free Press

Martin, R.C. and Woodward, M.R. with Atmaja, D.S. 1997. *Defenders of Reason in Islam*. Oxford, Oneworld

Martin, R.P. 1975. *New Testament Foundations. Vol.1: The Four Gospels*. Exeter: The Paternoster Press

McAuliffe, J.D., 1991. *Qur'ânic Christians. An Analysis of Classical and Modern Exegesis*. Cambridge, CUP

Meier, J.P. 1987. *A Marginal Jew. vol. 1*. Doubleday, London

Miller, J.M. 1997. *Jesus at Thirty. A Psychological and Historical Portrait*. Minneapolis, Fortress Press

Moule, C.F.D. 1966 revised edition. *The Birth of the New Testament*. London, A & C Black

— 1977. *The Origin of Christology*. Cambridge, CUP

O'Hare, P. 1997. *The Enduring Covenant. The Education of Christians and the End of Antisemitism*. Valley Forge, Trinity Press International

Parrinder, G. 1987. *Encountering World Religions*. Edinburgh, T & T Clark

— 1995. *Jesus in the Qur'ân*. Oxford, Oneworld

— 1997. *Avatar and Incarnation. The Divine in Human Form in the World's Religions*. Oxford, Oneworld

Pawlikowski, J.T. 1982. *Christ in the Light of the Christian-Jewish Dialogue*. Ramsey, Paulist Press

Perrin, N. 1974. *The New Testament: an Introduction*. New York, Chicago, San Francisco, Atlanta, Harcourt Brace Javanovitch Inc.

Phipps, W.E. 1996. *Muhammad and Jesus. A Comparison of the Prophets and their Teaching*. London, SCM

Race, A. 1983. *Christians and Religious Pluralism*. London, SCM

Rahman, F. 1989. *Major Themes of the Qur'ân*. Minneapolis, Bibliotheca Islamica

Räisänen, H. 1997. *Marcion, Muhammad and the Mahatma*. London, SCM

Remus, H. 1997. *Jesus as Healer*. Cambridge, CUP

Riches, J. 1990. *The World of Jesus. First-Century Judaism in Crisis*. Cambridge, CUP

Robinson, N., 1991. *Christ in Islam and Christianity*. Houndmills, Macmillan

Robinson, J.M. 1959. *A New Quest of the Historical Jesus*. London, SCM

Rowland, C. 1982. *The Open Heaven*. London, SPCK

Ruthven, M. 1989. *The Divine Supermarket. Travels in Search of the Soul of America*. London, Chatto & Windus

Said, E.W. 1987. *Orientalism*. London, Routledge & Kegan Paul

Sanders, E.P. 1985. *Jesus and Judaism*, London, SCM

— 1990. *Jewish Law from Jesus to the Mishnah*. London, SCM

— 1992. *Judaism Practice and Belief 63BCE – 66CE*. London, SCM

— 1993. *The Historical Figure of Jesus*. London, Penguin Press

Sanders, E.P. and Davies, M. 1989. *Studying the Synoptic Gospels*. London, SCM

Sanders, J.T. 1987. *The Jews in Luke-Acts*. London, SCM

Saperstein, M. 1989. *Moments of Crisis in Jewish-Christian Relations*. London, SCM

Schimmel, A. 1985. *And Muhammad is his Messenger. The Veneration of the Prophet in Islamic Society*. Chapel Hill, University of North Carolina Press

Scott, D.C. and Selvanayagam, I. 1996. *Re-Visioning India's Religious Traditions*. Delhi, ISPCK

Schottroff, L. 1995. *Lydia's Impatient Sisters. A Feminist Social History of Early Christianity*. London, SCM

Schweitzer, A. 1954 edition. *The Quest of the Historical Jesus*. London, A & C Black

Schweizer, E. 1971. *Jesus*. London, SCM

Shillington, V.G. ed. 1997. *Jesus and His Parables*. Edinburgh, T & T Clark

Shorto, R. 1997. *Gospel Truth. The New Picture of Jesus Emerging from Science and History and Why it Matters*. London, Hodder & Stoughton

Smith, M. 1973. *The Secret Gospel. The Discovery and Interpretation of the Secret Gospel According to Mark*. London, Harper & Row

— 1978. *Jesus the Magician*. New York, Harper & Row

Smith, W.C. 1978. *The Meaning and End of Religion*. London, SPCK

Sparks, H.F.D. 1964. *A Synopsis of the Gospels*. London, A & C Black

Spong, J.S. 1996. *Liberating the Gospels*. San Francisco, Harper

Stauffer, E. 1960. *Jesus and His Story*. London, SCM

Stemberger, G. 1995. *Jewish Contemporaries of Jesus. Pharisees, Sadducees, Essenes*. Minneapolis, Fortress

Stuart, E. 1997. et al. *Religion is a Queer Thing. A Guide to the Christian Faith for Lesbian, Gay, Bisexual and Transgendered People*. London,

Cassell

Suetonius, G.S., trans. Graves, R., 1957. *The Twelve Caesars*. Harmondsworth, Penguin Classics

Sugirtharajah, R.S. ed. 1993. *Asian Faces of Jesus*. London, SCM

Swidler, L. 1993. *Yeshua. A Model for Moderns*. Kansas City, Sheed & Ward

Swidler, L. and Mojzes, P. 1997. *The Uniqueness of Jesus. A Dialogue with Paul Knitter*. Maryknoll, Orbis

Tacitus. P.C., trans. Grant, M. 1971 revised edition. *The Annals of Imperial Rome*. Harmondsworth, Penguin Classics

Theissen, G. 1987. *The Shadow of the Galilean*. London, SCM

Theissen, G. and Merz, A. 1998. *The Historical Jesus. A Comprehensive Guide*. London, SCM

Thomas, M.M. 1969. *The Acknowledged Christ of the Indian Renaissance*. London, SCM

Trocmé, E., 1997. *The Childhood of Christianity*. London, SCM

Vermes, G. 1973. *Jesus the Jew*. London, Collins

— 1993. *The Religion of Jesus the Jew*. London, SCM

— 1998. *Providential Accidents. An Autobiography*. London, SCM

Wainwright, G. ed. 1989. *Keeping the Faith*. London, SPCK

Ware, T. 1993. *The Orthodox Church*. Harmondsworth, Penguin

Whittaker, M. 1984. *Jews & Christians: Graeco-Roman Views*. Cambridge, CUP

Wilson, S.G. ed. 1986. *Anti-Judaism in Early Christianity. Volume 2 Separation and Polemic*. Ontario, Wilfrid Laurier University Press

Wright, N.T. 1996. *Jesus and the Victory of God*. London, SPCK

Zebiri, K. 1997. *Muslims and Christians Face to Face*. Oxford, Oneworld

Zeitlin, I.M. 1988. *Jesus and the Judaism of his Time*. Oxford, Blackwell

INDEX